Conversations with Ernest Gaines

Literary Conversations Series

Peggy Whitman Prenshaw
General Editor

Conversations
with Ernest Gaines

Edited by John Lowe

University Press of Mississippi
Jackson

Books by Ernest Gaines

NOVELS
Catherine Carmier. New York: Atheneum, 1964; North Point Press, 1981.
Of Love and Dust. New York: The Dial Press, 1967; Bantam Books, 1969; Norton, 1979; Vintage, 1994.
The Autobiography of Miss Jane Pittman. New York: The Dial Press, 1971; Bantam Books, 1972.
In My Father's House. New York: Knopf, 1978; Norton, 1983; Vintage, 1992.
A Gathering of Old Men. New York: Knopf, 1983; Thorndike, 1984; Vintage, 1984.
A Lesson Before Dying. New York: Knopf, 1993; Vintage, 1994.

SHORT STORIES
Bloodline. New York: The Dial Press, 1968; Bantam Books, 1970; Norton, 1976.

CHILDREN'S BOOKS
A Long Day in November. New York: The Dial Press, 1971.

Copyright © 1995 by the University Press of Mississippi
All rights reserved
Manufactured in the United States of America

98 97 96 95   4 3 2 1

The paper in this book meets the guidelines for permanence and durability of the Committee on Production Guidelines for Book Longevity of the Council on Library Resources.

Library of Congress Cataloging-in-Publication Data

Gaines, Ernest J., 1933–
    Conversations with Ernest Gaines / edited by John Lowe.
        p.   cm. — (Literary conversations series)
    Includes index.
    ISBN 0-87805-782-X (cloth : alk. paper). — ISBN 0-87805-783-8
(paper : alk. paper)
    1. Gaines, Ernest J., 1933–   —Interviews.   2. Novelists,
American—20th century—Interviews.   3. Southern States—
Intellectual life—20th century.   4. Afro-Americans in literature.
5. Southern States—In literature.   I. Title.   II. Series
PS3557.A355Z464   1995
813'.54—dc20   95-13838
                                                                                CIP

British Library Cataloging-in-Publication data available

Contents

Introduction

In a recent article, *The Chronicle of Higher Education* trumpeted
the ascent of a "new star" on the literary horizon, Louisiana's Ernest
Gaines. Those of us who have been teaching his works for years
were pleased, but also somewhat amused; after all, this "star"
has been in the American literary galaxy since *The Autobiography
of Miss Jane Pittman* (1974). That early novel, which placed
Gaines on the literary map, was nominated for the Pulitzer Prize,
and was made into a memorable film that led to an Emmy Award
for Cicely Tyson. To be fair, the *Chronicle* was actually paying
tribute to the man who had recently published yet another masterwork, *A Lesson Before Dying*, which won the National Book Critics
Circle Award, and was also nominated for the Pulitzer Prize. This
came on the heels of Gaines's being awarded the prestigious MacArthur "genius" award. Herman Beavers's important new study of
Gaines's work (and that of James Alan McPherson's) is about to
appear, and *Critical Reflections on the Fiction of Ernest J. Gaines*,
edited by David Estes, has just been published. The fourteen
scholars who contributed to the collection provide telling readings
of every one of Gaines's novels, his stories, and the films that have
been made from his work. Other ambitious studies are in progress;
we seem to be on the verge of a veritable Gaines goldrush.

   Yes, the literary life has been good lately for Ernest Gaines, but
it has always engaged his devotion and energy, even in the worst
of times, when his books weren't being read, when his money was
running low, when he lost beloved friends and relatives, and then
his trusted agent, Dorothea Oppenheimer. One of the reasons the
Chronicle could use such a headline, frankly, is that Ernest Gaines
has been shockingly underrated until recently. In America, literary
fashions wax and wane for good and bad reasons, but several of the
more recent tendencies in both popular and academic assessments
have obscured Gaines's gifts. First, he writes about a largely rural
community, isolated by both its southernness and its special Louisi-

ana qualities, which it is true make it exotic, but at the same time
somewhat inaccessible, even for many African Americans. Gaines,
however, clearly finds the state's unique qualities fascinating: "I
think that Louisiana's probably the most romantic and interesting
of all southern states; the land, the language, the colors, the
bayous, the fields, all these things together, the combination of all
these things, I think, make it an extremely interesting place. If I
were to come from any southern state, I think Louisiana is the one
that I would choose." This stance has been constant during
Gaines's career. During the early years of his career, his interests
and topics changed somewhat, but his basic style and choice of
setting have remained constant, and this preference for localized
chronicle, in which racial struggle may or may not take a central
role, has not always positioned him well with critical fashions. His
fictional world of Bayonne and St. Raphael Parish has yielded a
remarkably detailed and rich imaginative realm, one simultaneously
brimming with all the terrors and beauties of rural Louisiana.
Many times he remarks on his inability to write about other subjects,
even those as close to him as his experiences in California or in the
army. Only Louisiana elicits his imaginative gift, and he understands this as part of his southern heritage, a gift, he feels, that
crosses racial, gender, and class lines alike. Gaines also asserts that
local or regional fiction, because of its roots in basic humanity,
can transcend the many barriers that divide the peoples of this
world, and reach out to those who on the surface inhabit very
different realms.

One reason for Gaines's neglect is his refusal to cater to stereotypes. Unfortunately, most popular images of Louisiana lead
readers to expect scenes set in New Orleans, replete with wrought
iron balconies, Bourbon Street jazz, and quirky urban characters who
live lives of abandon. Gaines has never written about New Orleans,
and, until lately, hasn't spent much time there. Moreover, he
more often than not has set his stories in the past, which has meant
that his African American characters have been presented on his
canvas in apparently subservient positions, rather than in the often
violent, revolutionary poses favored by some of Gaines's contemporaries such as James Baldwin, Ishmael Reed, John O. Killens,
John Wideman, or David Bradley. Another problem for Gaines's

reputation has been that his lucid, descriptive style, so largely
shaped by European masters such as Tolstoy and Turgenev, has
produced a mode of writing that seemingly lacks "flash," in its
meditative, careful constructions, its meticulous attention to and
privileging of dialogue, and its restraint. In a critical age that dotes
on the pyrotechnical stylistic experimentation of Reed, Baraka,
Coover, DeLillo, and Morrison, Gaines was bound to be somewhat
ignored.

Those who accuse Gaines of inattentiveness to recent racial
conflict too often forget the importance of recognizing the ante-
cedents of contemporary struggles. Gaines reminds us that "much
of our history has not been told; our problems have been told, as
if we have no history." Writing that history matters to Gaines.
Moreover, its upheavals have registered powerfully in his own
life, which began on a rural plantation and now continues in San
Francisco, Miami, and points in between. His own struggle for an
education, a literary voice, and critical and popular recognition as a
writer has echoed many of the themes his characters have embod-
ied, albeit in less dramatic fashion. His writing career began during
the sixties in San Francisco, and continued onward in a stream of
words that parallelled those of other African American voices, such
as Martin Luther King, Malcolm X, James Baldwin, Amiri Baraka,
and Gaines's friends James Alan McPherson, Alice Walker, Ishmael
Reed, and Al Young. His narratives provide a useful and instruc-
tive foreground to the more contemporary stories these other writers have told.

The fact that Gaines has sometimes been seen as operating
outside "the protest tradition" isn't surprising. All African American writers must struggle with the situation of being or not being
"representative" of a people and their continuing struggle for
racial justice. Since Gaines began writing during the turbulent
sixties, when many writers were espousing a kind of radical activism
through art, he has always been subject to questions about the
degree of his involvement in racial struggle, particularly since his
characters and settings were seemingly often far removed from the
central arenas of contestation. Consequently, Gaines speaks out
again and again against putting a kind of artistic straitjacket around
African American writers; for him, *any* writer should write

"truly" about what he or she knows best. He believes that African
American writers who always focus on what he calls "the problems" for largely white audiences often miss opportunities to present aspects of African American culture that all people—
including African Americans—can enjoy. Gaines has said that
conflict with whites constitutes only one aspect of African American
life: "We also carry on a full life: we love, women have children,
men gamble, shoot at people, have fights, everything. . . . I read
something in the papers just yesterday where Baldwin said that he
should not despair because he has no right to despair. His job is
to go on and work, to do some more work."

Gaines's dedication to his ideals has paid off. Now, partly on the
strength and popularity of his last two works, and renewed
interest on the part of numerous critics, his books are all back
before us. The best result of all this new attention has been to
remind everyone how steadily valuable the work of Ernest Gaines
has been over the years; how accurately his novels have depicted
the lives of a certain group of people, the amazing cultures they
have created and influenced over the past hundred years; and the
poignant and powerful manner in which these lives have spoken to
the ongoing problems of being "different," southern, gendered,
and American.

This should emerge clearly now that readers may explore all of
Gaines's work consecutively. Those who only know *Miss Jane*, or
perhaps *A Gathering of Old Men*, will be in for a revelation, now
that the other books are back in print. Going through his entire
oeuvre, one sees how masterfully his narratives develop and build,
often to an almost unbearable momentum, finally erupting with
violence, beauty, and revelation. With the full canvas of St. Raphael
Parish unfurled again, it seems time to examine the views of this
important but neglected writer on the many subjects and issues that
inform his fiction, which speaks more forcefully now than ever before.

Doing so enables us to take a backward glance at our national
history, in microcosm. These interviews begin at the end of the
sixties, and continue up to the present day. As such, they reflect
not only the events in Gaines's life, but the events in the world
around him that influenced that life. His remarks here suggest a
profound interest in the vectors of history and happenstance, as

he explains why most of his work has been set in the past. His
accounts of researching actual events, from Huey Long's death
to the movement of slaves after Emancipation, demonstrate his
determination to fill in the blanks of history in his sustaining
fictions. He continually reads the present against the record of the
past as well: as he has observed, conditions haven't really
changed all that much for African Americans; "A lynch mob is a
lynch mob . . . you can live in New York, you can be in police blues,
or you can be a gang of kids and have someone accidentally go into
the wrong neighborhood . . . anything can happen at almost
any time."

The force of these remarks finds ample illustration in Gaines's
fiction. Few short story collections in our literature can match the
power and subtle, understated intricacy of the tales in *Bloodline*,
which though discrete, speak so clearly to each other as they limn
the continuities and conflicts of an interracial society in the throes
of change. The sheer dramatic momentum found in *Of Love and
Dust* will compel new readers as well, and draw them into disturbing
new considerations of economies based in racial oppression, as
well as forbidden love that knows no racial boundary.

As these interviews disclose, there were many sources for these
and Gaines's other narratives, originating nodes which converged
in dramatic fashion to prod Gaines's imagination into action. As he
reveals in the first interview included here, *Of Love and Dust* became
a possibility as a novel when Gaines saw a knife fight in a rural bar
and put it together with some perceptions he had had a few years
earlier when listening to Lightnin' Hopkins's song, "Mr. Tim
Moore's Farm." The inner turmoil and the indentured condition
of Marcus, the central character in the novel, suddenly emerged in
Gaines's mind.

Despite the repeated eruption of violence, confusion, and racial
struggle in his work, Gaines's personal life has tended toward the
obverse, in its relatively steady, albeit often difficult path. Accord-
ingly, readers seeking sensational revelations about Gaines the man
will find little of that here. Yes, interviews reveal at least a portion
of the complexities and profound meditations of the person who
inspired them, especially when the subject is prone to plain statement of fact and abhors pretense. Yet such writers, and Gaines is

clearly one of them, often jealously guard their privacy as well; although he talks frankly, if generally, about his youthful drinking and bohemian lifestyle, Gaines has always deflected personal questions, particularly about members of his immediate family, and his interviewers over the years have respected this. In light of the fact that Gaines has no intention of composing an autobiography and has thus far mostly discouraged a biography, these conversations offer an invaluable means for understanding the motivations, philosophy, and aesthetics of a complicated, profound writer, who can sometimes mask his darker sentiments with humor or indirect discourse. Conversely, his obvious enjoyment in discussing the gradual unfolding of his remarkable talent, the events of his career, and his loving tribute to those who "helped him to stand," especially his Aunt Augusteen, somewhat offsets his reticence about other matters. We also find here, not bitterness but a bemused consideration of the "bad press" he got during the sixties and seventies (and occasionally receives even today) for supposedly being nonpolitical, or at least nonactivist. Instead of anger, we find a sense of determined opposition to injustice, coupled with a warmth and sympathy toward all people; more specifically, we also find a man obviously proud of who he is and of the culture that both produced him and inspired his insight.

These latter facets often find expression in his writing as well, and in his remarks on that body of work and its production. Gaines teaches creative writing and obviously enjoys discussing the intricacies of a writer's situation and craft. He pays tribute here to the various editors and literary friends who personally offered constructive criticism, especially his agent Dorothea Oppenheimer and his editors Bill Decker and Ed Doctorow, and shows how they helped him in particular situations. More frequently, he extols the literary masters who shaped his work early on— Turgenev, Tolstoy, Faulkner, Hemingway, Welty; he also asserts that it doesn't really matter if the writer in question holds views antithetical to his own: "I don't care what a man is. I mean, a great artist is like a great doctor. I don't care how racist he is. If he can show me how to operate on a heart so that I can cure a brother, or cure someone else, I don't give a damn what the man thinks; he has taught me something. And that is valuable to me. And that is valuable to others and man as a whole.''

Surprisingly, we find few African American writers on Gaines's list of literary influences, partly because he simply didn't encounter them until rather late in his career. But he professes an admiration for the works of Jean Toomer, Zora Neale Hurston, and those of his California friend, Alice Walker. Like these three writers, Gaines has always used the everyday material of African American folk culture, particularly music; as he reveals in the earliest interview included here, he has avidly collected records of blues, spirituals, and jazz. A blues aesthetic has permeated virtually all of his works. The jook, for instance, in *Of Love and Dust* vibrates to the rhythms of the region, but the stories themselves constitute the true blues ethos of the novel. Marcus Payne, the novel's protagonist, was partially inspired by the heroic stances of Muhammad Ali. Gaines clearly understands that history itself has been woven into the record of popular culture; Ma Rainey, B.B. King, and Muddy Waters, he notes, sang about the great flood of 1927.

As these interviews indicate, Gaines attends to written records as well. He thoroughly researched actual events that appear in *Miss Jane*, for instance, such as the assassination of Huey Long. He also consulted records of the oral memoirs of ex-slaves. But like Zora Neale Hurston, it was all that talk he heard and continues to hear in the community that has had the most profound influence on his remarkably oral narratives, and much of actual history becomes translated into the conversations of his characters.

Although one could argue that this marks him as being most profoundly shaped by specifically African American cultural modes, all these influences speak to each other in his imagination, where artistic tools have no other priority than function; as he says here, ''the understatement in Hemingway is as profound as the understatement in the music of Basie.'' He listened to both the blues and to Moussorgsky's *Pictures at an Exhibition* while writing *Miss Jane*.

Navigating between apparently distant cultural poles has much in common with Gaines's larger program of finding solutions to seemingly insoluble problems. In perhaps one of the most significant pronouncements in these conversations, Gaines indicates his interest in those who try to effect change. "In many cases, those who are controlled by the past can be just as human and sometimes more human than those who try to change things. Yet, there must always be those who try to change conditions; there must always be those who try to break out of the trap the world keeps going in . . . to break away from the past, from one philosophy to another, is a burden that one person cannot endure alone. Someone else must pick up from there and go on."

With few exceptions, the interviews in this book appear just as they did originally. They are arranged in the order that they occurred, rather than by their publication date. Many of them inevitably touch on recurring issues, as each interviewer of course wants to discuss key aspects of Gaines's work. Interviewers tend to ask the same kinds of questions, even if they know their predecessors have already asked them, no doubt because they believe, along with Gaines (who cites Goethe as his authority), that "everything's been said, but it needs saying again." This rings particularly true in this case because Gaines must be re-presented and re-interpreted for each new wave of students and readers. His comments have more resonance when they are produced by the contemporary moment, and by the work he has most recently done, which will always affect, retrospectively, views of the work *already* done.

Although Gaines often repeats himself, there are significant, often startling variations (more rarely, contradictions) that foster sudden insights into both Gaines and his work. Obviously, some interviewers drew him out more, and he proved more expansive, more meditative on some occasions than on others. Well into this collection, for instance, talking about his 1948 migration to California, Gaines suddenly tells his interviewer that if he had gone, say, to New York rather than the West, he probably would have become a playwright, a good one, in fact a better playwright than he is a novelist! On another occasion, in responding to yet another question about writers who have influenced him, he talks poignantly of how he just the day before learned something by watching a lady sweep her yard.

On the other hand, many of these conversations differ in scope and tone, partly because the interviewers come from so many differ-

ent realms and represent a variety of journals, magazines, newspapers, and various types of institutions. Some conversations take
place in Louisiana; others in California, including one that occurred
in Gaines's apartment. While some interviewers choose to engage
Gaines in rather general discussions of his works, others hone in to
provide an intense analysis of a particular text, often just after
the work in question came out. My interview with Gaines, the most
recent here, has not been previously published, nor has the one
the author did with Michael Sartisky, which took place before a
live audience.

The tape of that evening, like many of these conversations, offers
abundant proof of Gaines's vibrant sense of humor, even of
mischief, as he sometimes plays with his interviewers, or confesses
some of the wicked literary "tricks" he's learned to play in his
craft. Although he claims to be unable to tell a joke, he makes us
laugh time and again.

We will always have studies of Gaines's use of place; new trends
in literary theory, however, suggest that yet another aspect of his
work may be explored through these conversations. Gaines has
come to the fore in many critical studies lately because of his
searching appraisal of the masculine search for identity, particularly
that of African American men. His parables of manhood lie at the
heart of virtually every novel and story he has written, including
The Autobiography of Miss Jane Pittman, and one could argue that
the cumulative force of this thematic has found its most powerful
expression in his recent masterwork, *A Lesson Before Dying*. The
interviews here, especially the 1988 conversation with Gaudet and
Wooten, offer great insights into a set of issues that are increasingly
coming to the fore in social *and* artistic discourse, particularly as
we continue to experience the tragic condition of having more young
African American men in prison than in college. But as Gaines
himself notes, this search for masculine identity is metaphoric of
a larger human need, what he calls "the importance of standing,"
which his crippled Aunt Augusteen taught him, even though she
never walked a step in her life.

Whatever the issues at hand, Gaines's great work has been to find
fitting artistic expression for them, and it seems to me that
Gaines, during the last decade of interviews, has become more

relaxed, more expansive, almost eager to explain and explicate his works' aesthetics. Perhaps this has resulted from his obviously growing pleasure over the years in teaching creative writing at the University of Southwestern Louisiana, in itself a rich subject in the later interviews. In any case, the reticence of the early interviews seems banished. Compare, for example, the wealth of information he provides for *A Lesson*; we not only have a master writing at the peak of his powers, but one who *knows* it and can thus speak positively and helpfully about his gift and his achievement. Perhaps even richer conversations, and one fervently hopes, novels, lie ahead.

This book has been made possible by the involvement of many people, especially Seetha Srinivasan, and including Peggy Prenshaw, Reggie Young, David Estes, Marcia Gaudet, Ruth Laney, Tanya Bickley, Herman Beavers, and of course, Ernest Gaines. I thank them all.

JL
October 1994

Chronology

1933–40 Ernest James Gaines is born 15 January 1933, on River
Lake Plantation in Oscar, a hamlet in Pointe Coupee
Parish, Louisiana, to Manuel and Adrienne Gaines. Ernest is the first of twelve children Adrienne would bear,
seven of them by Manuel Gaines, five by her second
husband. Gaines's father leaves the family while Gaines
is still a small boy; his mother moves to New Orleans to
find work, leaving Ernest and the other children on the
plantation in the care of their great aunt, Miss Augusteen
Jefferson, a sister of Gaines's maternal grandfather.
Adrienne Gaines eventually marries Ralph Norbert Colar,
Sr., a merchant seaman once employed on nearby
Parlange Plantation.

1941 While attending rural schools, Gaines begins work in the
fields, earning 50 cents a day.

1945 Gaines is sent to work in the swamp, as Cajun workers
supplant African Americans as sharecroppers. He begins to write and stage plays for the local church; begins
three years of attendance at St. Augustine Middle
School for Catholic African American children, in nearby
New Roads, Louisiana.

1947 Adrienne and Ralph Colar move to Vallejo, California,
where she finds work in a factory.

1948 Gaines leaves Louisiana to join his mother and stepfather
in the Vallejo area. Initially lives in a multicultural
government housing project; after family moves to downtown Vallejo, begins to spend time at the public library,
reading.

1949 Writes a novel (an early version of *Catherine Carmier*)
and mails it to a New York publisher, who rejects it. Gaines
burns the manuscript.

1951–57   Graduates from high school; attends Vallejo Junior College, graduating in 1953; serves two years in the United States Army, 1953–55 (stationed in Guam); enrolls at San Francisco State College; graduates in 1957. Publishes "The Boy in the Double-Breasted Suit" and "The Turtles" in *Transfer*, the school's literary journal, in 1956.

1958–59   Wins Wallace Stegner award and studies at Stanford University in the Creative Writing Program. "A Long Day in November" is published. Begins his association with editor Dorothea Oppenheimer which continues until her death in 1987. Wins the Joseph Henry Jackson Award for Best Novel-in-Progress.

1962   Publishes "Just Like a Tree"

1963   Publishes "The Sky Is Gray" (eventually made into a film for television), inspired by James Meredith's integration of the University of Mississippi; returns to Louisiana for six months and claims the visit saves his writing and possibly his life.

1964   Publishes his first novel, *Catherine Carmier*

1967   A second novel, *Of Love and Dust*, is published; Gaines wins National Endowment for the Arts Study Award.

1968   *Bloodline*, a collection of short stories, published

1970   Receives Rockefeller Grant-in-Aid

1971   *The Autobiography of Miss Jane Pittman*, Gaines's third novel, receives great acclaim, becomes a best-seller, is nominated for the Pulitzer Prize, and is eventually made into a television movie starring Cicely Tyson. *A Long Day in November* is published as a children's book.

1972–74   Gaines begins a novel, "The House and the Field," but abandons it to begin *In My Father's House*. Chapter One of "The House and the Field" is published in the *Iowa Review* Winter 1972 edition. Gaines awarded a Guggenheim Fellowship; wins the California Gold Medal, the Louisiana Library Association Award, and the Black Academy of Arts and Letters Award for *Miss Jane*.

1978   Gaines's fourth novel, *In My Father's House*, published

1981   Begins teaching each fall term at the University of South-
         western Louisiana in Lafayette; receives permanent
         appointment as Writer-in-Residence in 1983.

1983   Publishes *A Gathering of Old Men*, which is made into a
         television film

1993   Gaines's sixth novel, *A Lesson Before Dying* is published,
         wins the National Book Critics Circle Award, and is
         nominated for the Pulitzer Prize. Plans are made to make
         a major motion picture of the book. Gaines marries
         Dianne Saulney, a Miami attorney originally from Louisi-
         ana; begins to spend part of each year in Miami. Gaines
         awarded a MacArthur Fellowship totalling $375,000.

Conversations with Ernest Gaines

An Interview: Ernest J. Gaines

Gregory Fitzgerald and Peter Marchant / 1969

From *New Orleans Review* 1 (1969): 331–35. Used by permission.

Ernest J. Gaines, child of a Louisiana plantation, won a Wallace Stegner Creative Writing Fellowship to Stanford in 1958 and the following year received the Joseph Henry Jackson Literary Award. Atheneum published *Catherine Carmier,* his first novel, in 1964; his second, *Of Love and Dust,* was published in 1967 by Dial Press, who brought out in 1968 to considerable acclaim his collection of stories, *Bloodline.* Mr. Gaines now lives in San Francisco, where he is at work on his third novel, once more utilizing the Louisiana plantation setting he knows so well.

The present conversation results from Mr. Gaines' appearance in February, 1969, on the Writers Forum program at the State University of New York, College at Brockport. With Mr. Gaines are Gregory Fitzgerald, Director of the Forum, and Peter Marchant, author of *Give Me Your Answer Do.*

This is one of a series of interviews to be published in book form, edited by Robert Gemmett and Philip Gerber.

The editors are both of the Brockport English Department. Mr. Gerber has recently published critical volumes on Robert Frost and Theodore Dreiser; Mr. Gemmett's edition of William Beckford's *Biographical Memoirs of Extraordinary Painters* has just been published by Fairleigh Dickinson University Press.

Fitzgerald: I have been reading your remarkable novel *Of Love and Dust.* Can you tell us what inspires a book such as this?

Gaines: I don't know when the idea of *Of Love and Dust* came into my mind; I really don't know. But here are a couple of things which led up to my writing it: my hobby is collecting records—when I have the money to do so; I collect jazz records, the spiritual, folk music, and blues, especially the rural blues of the Negro. I was listening to one of Lightnin' Hopkins' records one day entitled

"Mr. Tim Moore's Farm." Lightnin' Hopkins is one of the great
blues singers of this country and someone I consider a worthwhile
poet. As I was listening to his "Mr. Tim Moore's Farm," one of the
verses of the song struck me. It went something like this: "The worst
thing this black man ever done, when I moved my wife and family
to Mr. Tim Moore's Farm. Mr. Tim Moore's man never stand
and grin, say if you keep out the graveyard, nigger, I'll keep you
out the pen." Now, a period of about ten years passed between the
time I first heard that record and the time I started writing my novel
Of Love and Dust, but I remember that verse.

Fitzgerald: You said there were "a couple of things" that led to
the novel?

Gaines: Yes. Hearing "Mr. Tim Moore's Farm" was one. The
other was something that happened to me a couple of years later. I
was visiting some of my people in Baton Rouge, Louisiana, in 1958,
and a friend of mine and I went to a bar out in the country. This
is the same parish in Louisiana that Rap Brown comes from; this is
the same parish in Louisiana from which James Farmer in 1963
escaped a lynch mob by riding the back of a hearse disguised as a
dead man. My friend and I went to this bar, and in this bar I saw a
fight between two young men. This bar is surrounded by fields—
cane, corn, cotton—and most of the people who come here are
from the country or from small towns not very far away. They come
to drink; they come to dance; they come to gamble; they come to
fight; they come to steal your woman; they come to steal your man;
they come knowing they might end up in jail that night, but still
they come. They come to forget the hard work in the fields all week;
they come to forget, to forget, and to forget, and they're ready to
accept whatever fate is awaiting them. If nothing terrible happens,
then the night has been somewhat of a success; if something bad
does happen, then these things are expected in a bar such as this
one. So it was here that I saw the knife-fight between the two
young men. Fortunately for both, the fight was stopped before
either was fatally wounded. Now, when I saw this fight, just as
when I heard the record by Lightnin' Hopkins, I had no idea that
either event would eventually lead into writing *Of Love and Dust*,
or writing anything else. There was a period of eight or ten years
between those events and the time I wrote one word of the book.

Marchant: So it took this long for your first novel to get under way?

Gaines: It took that time—but it was not my first novel. Hardly. During that time I wrote at least four other novels. Only one, *Catherine Carmier*, was published. I wrote at least two dozen short stories, of which only six were published. I had been writing all the time. But now it was early spring of '66. I had very little money; I had practically no money at all; I had been sponging off my friends and my brothers for drinks, and I had not bought one drink for them in over a year. I had not given my poor mother a birthday present, a Christmas present, or a Mother's Day present in over two years. My girl had dropped me quite a while ago—a normal thing, I feel, when a man is unable to buy a hamburger in a place like McDonald's. I needed the money; I needed money badly. But I didn't want to go out on an eight-hour-day job that would take me from my writing.

I wanted the money, but I wanted to earn it by my writing and by writing only. Now, if that was the case, I had to get something done. There had to be another novel in me somewhere that a publisher would accept. I don't know how the tune "Mr. Tim Moore's Farm" got back into my mind; maybe I heard it played again; I really don't know. Or maybe when I went back to Baton Rouge in 1965 and visited that same bar in the country that I had visited in '58, I saw something there that began to stir my imagination. Anyhow, in early spring of 1966 I got started on the novel. I started with these two ideas: "Mr. Tim Moore's man never stand and grin, say if you keep out the graveyard, nigger, I'll keep you out the pen"—that, and with the fight between the two young men in the bar. So all right, I had two ideas, but where did I go from there?

Fitzgerald: To construct your plot? Did that come quickly?

Gaines: The plot—the story anyway. I kept asking myself, where do I go? Where, where, where; I kept asking myself. Then things began to fall into place. I was born on a Louisiana plantation in 1933, and I left from there in 1948. The novel takes place in the summer of '48. But during those fifteen years, I had learned a lot about plantation life and about the people who lived in that part of Louisiana. I knew that Mr. Tim Moore's man, whom Lightnin'

Hopkins sang about, didn't necessarily have to be an overseer on a farm in Texas; he could be a Cajun overseer on a plantation in Louisiana. I knew that my young man in the bar could have landed on that plantation if he had killed that other boy in the knife-fight. So I had him kill the boy, and I had the owner of the plantation bond him out of jail.

In this way I brought my young killer to the plantation. But where would things go from there? I had a good starting point, but was that enough? What am I going to do with my young killer? He's no plantation worker; he's not even a country boy; he's from the city, Baton Rouge. He's a playboy. He's a lover. And he hates authority, especially when this authority is given out by a Cajun whom he considers white trash. So what am I going to do with these two people? I have two people on my hands who will never—can't ever—get along with each other. What am I going to do with them? Let me see now. Let me see. My young killer is going to be here five, seven, maybe ten years of his life. He will need a woman. Yes, yes, he will need a woman, and she will be my third character. Now he must start looking for that woman, but he doesn't want just any woman, no, not a lover as himself; he wants the most beautiful woman on that plantation. But when he finds her, he finds that he can't have her. And why not? Because she is the overseer's mistress.

My imagination really starts moving when I start writing!

Marchant: May I ask you a question? Your material dealing with the brutal white overseer and the black man is very hot political stuff. At the same time, you're writing about blacks and whites who are people first, who only happen to be black and white. One feels sorry for them and at the same time one laughs at them. Do you possibly get this from the Russians?

Gaines: Maybe I do. My first heroes, I suppose, were the Russian writers. I think they have influenced many writers.

Fitzgerald: What attracts you to the Russian writers? Is it their sense of the soil, of being close to the earth, to the people?

Gaines: I think so. I think the thing I recognize in Russian writers, especially when they're writing about the peasant, is some of the same sort of thing that I've experienced in the southern part of the United States. I've gotten this from Tolstoy, Chekhov, and Turgenev much more than I've gotten it out of the white American writers who deal with the same sort of thing. When the white writers are writing about the blacks of the fields, they seem to make them caricatures rather than real people, but the Russian writers made their peasants real. I felt that they did. I suppose this is why I've studied them and loved them so much.

Marchant: I'd like to know how you happened to discover the Russians.

Gaines: Once I started reading, I used to read everything, and I suppose I just stumbled on them. Turgenev's *Fathers and Children* was first. This was in the library at Vallejo, California (when I first came to California I was living in Vallejo) and I read it. What I read I liked, and from then on I went for the Russians.

Fitzgerald: You mentioned Vallejo, and also the fact that you were born in Louisiana. What about those early years? Were you a plantation worker?

Gaines: I went into the fields when I was about the age of eight, or maybe nine. I think my first job was picking up potatoes—white potatoes—we called them Irish potatoes. I worked for about 50¢ a day, and stayed there until I was fifteen. So, by the time I left for California, I knew a lot about the work and life on a plantation. For instance, in the novel, I mentioned having the plantation owner bond my young killer out of jail and putting him to work in his field. This was a normal thing in the forties. Some of our best southern gentlemen did it; this was still going on in the fifties. And as late as 1963, when I was in Louisiana, a friend of mine pointed out a black youth who had killed another black youth and had been bonded out and put to work only a few days later. The only catch here—when the prisoner, the convict, found himself bonded out of jail—was that he usually spent twice as much time on the plantation than he would have spent in the penitentiary. Many times he found himself working just as hard, and maybe even harder, and there was nothing he could do about it, because the day he decided to run, the white man was going to put the sheriff on his trail again. So when I brought my young killer to the plantation, I knew the kind of house he would have to live in; I had lived there fifteen years myself. I knew the kind of food he would eat; the same kind that I had eaten. I knew the kind of clothes he would wear, because I

had worn the khaki and denim clothes myself. I knew the work he
would have to do. I knew the people he would come into contact
with day in and day out.

I had many other experiences, of course, I went to the one-room
schoolhouse. . . .

Fitzgerald: That's the background, isn't it, for much of your
fiction? Is it not the same schoolhouse that we see in your story
"A Long Day in November?"

Gaines: Yes, it's the same school I went to, yes.

Fitzgerald: Well, how did you make the transition from plantation
worker to fiction writer? When did you begin to write?

Gaines: When I went to California—I hadn't tried to write until
then. But I was terribly lonely for my friends and relatives. And as I
said, I went into the libraries to read. And I read and read, but I did
not see myself and my friends and family and relatives in the stuff
that I did read. I didn't see us in the Southern writers. I didn't even
see myself in the Russian writers, although the Russians came
close. So I began to try to do it myself and, of course, I went back
to my childhood to write about. I suppose that most writers,
when they first start out, try to write about their childhood, and this
is what I did. And I'm still sticking to it. On and off, it's been
about twenty years, I suppose, that I've been trying to write now.
Professionally, I think that I've been writing since about '57. By
"professionally" I mean writing every day—four or five hours a
day. Every day, since '57.

Fitzgerald: Do you see yourself as a humorist at all?

Gaines: I don't tell jokes. Whenever I do tell a joke, no one
laughs. So I'm not a joke-teller. My brother is, but not myself. I
think I am more of a listener, really. I listen. I like to listen to the
way that people talk, and I like to listen to their stories. Then
when I get into a little room some place, I try to write them down.
Just like a man hearing a song some place, and he's afraid to sing out
on the street or some place else, but when he gets into a bathroom,
he starts singing, and he thinks that he's the greatest in the world. But
this is what I do in writing. I go to a little room; I go to my little
desk, and try to write something down. But I'm no storyteller,
I'm only a listener.

Marchant: But your work is not without humor. It seems very difficult now for a black writer to write about whites and blacks in a way that's funny, provoking an easy laughter. Yet you manage to do it.

Gaines: No, I don't think it is so difficult. As I said, my brother tells jokes about whites and blacks all the time, and he can make them very funny. A story can be tragic, and he can make it very funny. You see, where I came from, my people were sharecroppers. After the land was turned over from the plantation system, it was turned into a sharecropping system, so my uncles and my father were sharecroppers. Their competitors were the Cajuns, the white people there. The people you make fun of more are the people who are closer to you. So when my people had to make fun of something, when they had to laugh, they made fun of the whites. You always make fun of your competitors. They are the people very close to you. And we had this relationship all the time. I saw these people, the Cajuns, every day; we went to the same store, but we could not drink in the same room. They didn't allow that. But we bought our food at the same place, and we talked to each other going to and from the fields. All this was going on. And the Cajuns have this distinct way of speaking, with this French accent, it's a broken accent. Of course, we could not speak English any better than they could speak French, but we thought they sounded very funny. And I suppose when my own people would speak French using the Creole accent, we sounded as foolish and funny to the Cajuns as they did to us. But still we laughed, and I'm sure they laughed at us also.

Marchant: Mr. Gaines, do you feel alienated in any way from your people in Louisiana—the people you grew up with—now that you are living in San Francisco?

Gaines: No, I don't. I keep going back to Louisiana to see the people all the time. Some I cannot communicate with, others I can. In a bar over a drink, you can talk to almost anybody. We could talk about old times.

Fitzgerald: These are the people who appear in your fiction. I recognize them. What strikes me as being rather remarkable about them is that in an age when contemporary characters in fiction are so anti-heroic, your characters are sympathetic or empathetic. How do you account for your mode of writing outside the vein of what seems to be so popular with many contemporary writers?

Gaines: Well, as I've said before, I've never read about my people in fiction, and before I can make them anti-heroes, I have to try to give them some good qualities. I don't read too much contemporary fiction. So I don't follow these writers' ideas too much, I suppose.

Fitzgerald: Then you feel that contemporary fiction has had relatively little effect on your own work?

Gaines: Oh, yes, I suppose. I haven't stopped reading contemporary fiction altogether, but I don't read it daily, or weekly, or anything like that. I still read Hemingway. I'll pick up a Hemingway book any time to read a story or a novel. I'll pick up Faulkner, too. Someone like this I'll read all the time.

Fitzgerald: I'm wondering about another element of your background. You have suggested that you're interested in jazz music. Do you think that it has been an influence on the development of your work?

Gaines: I think jazz is basically folk music. Originally it was, though I'm not sure what they're doing with it now. And folk music is a very simple thing. All folk music is very, very simple. Listening to jazz, I find simple rhythms, simple repetitions. In order to communicate jazz to the layman it has to be simple and, of course, these musicians were playing to people just like themselves, uneducated people. I wish to reach the same sort of thing in my fiction, to use the simplest terms in the world, you know, terms like *Jesus wept*; I think that's the most simple statement you can make. It's probably the most beautiful two-word sentence that has ever been written. It has all the meanings in the world in it. Another thing about jazz is that to be impressive it has to be repetitive. You get hooked upon a phrase and you stay with that phrase until you have really convinced the people.

Fitzgerald: In some of the stories in your new collection, *Bloodline*, I notice that you tell the story not only in the first person, but from the point-of-view of a child. This poses, of course, certain problems for the writer. Could you tell us how you came to write so convincingly from the point-of-view of a five-year-old in "A Long

Day in November," and from that of an eight-year-old in "The Sky is Gray"?

Gaines: I suppose we have all been children once, and the knowledge of the child's viewpoint is perhaps something that was buried down in my subconscious since that time. In each story I've myself gone through much of the same experience as these kids have, not all but much of it. This was in me all the time, but I had to find a way to bring it out. Both Joyce and Faulkner helped me to do it. In the first part of Faulkner's *The Sound and the Fury*, the Benjy part, Benjy uses the simplest terms to express his feelings: "the gate is cold," "the fire is good," "I stamped my shoes on," all this sort of thing. This childlike section is so convincing that I really fell in love with it. I really did. At the same time that I was reading Faulkner I was also reading Joyce. I had, personally, the experience of the little school the child goes to in my story, the house he lived in, the quarters he walked in, the heater in the little school, the bench that he had to sit on because he had no desk. I had all this experience. So I got Faulkner's rhythm and I got Joyce's "day" thing; you know, as in *Ulysses*, the "Let's do it all in one day" sort of thing. So I had this kid to start with and I said, "O.K., I'm going to take Mr. Faulkner's rhythm and Mr. Joyce's idea of day, and go kid." And I did that. This is how I did it. But I don't know if it's anything so different—I suppose we've all done it. Twain did it late in life when he wrote the *Huck Finn* and *Tom Sawyer* books. Hemingway did it. They all have done it; Steinbeck, Chekhov, they all have done it. The child stuff, yes. They were much older than I when they did it, too.

Marchant: A few minutes back, you talked of watching a fight between two boys in the same parish which begat Rap Brown. But yet you manage to avoid being politically didactic. You obviously resist being a political writer, but do you hope to do something in that vein with your writing?

Gaines: Oh yes, definitely so. To me, literature expresses man's feelings and relationships much better than politics ever can. I think there are many Rap Browns who can tell you in a political way what's going on. What Rap Brown would say is: look what the whites are doing here! What Ernie Gaines is trying to say is: I see and I agree with you; but we also laugh and we laugh as much or more than other Americans, we dance as much, and sometimes better, and we sing as much, and we have dishes like gumbo and jambalaya and southern fried chicken and shrimp and all this sort of thing. And we love these things also. Besides the conflict between the white and black, we also carry on a full life: we love, women have children, men gamble, shoot at people, have fights, everything.

Fitzgerald: Well, one of the interesting things to me is that your book is really the first one I've ever read that really revealed the innate gentility and nobility of your people. This struck me as an outstanding quality of it.

Gaines: I just try to capture what I see of people and what I hear.

Fitzgerald: I'm thinking specifically of the characters in "The Sky is Gray." Here's a mother with such a really wonderful strength, a strength that comes from the earth, a strength that goes beyond the strength of Faulkner's Dilsey to a kind of independent, proud spirit. She is rearing a son in the same tradition, and she succeeds very well indeed. That toothache that the little boy, James, has—it sounds as if it has to be one of your own personal experiences.

Gaines: Yes, I had a toothache when I was a child at that age, and I had to ride the bus, just as he rides. At that time, on a bus in the South, you had a little sign hanging over the aisle and it said "White" on one side and it said "Colored" on the other side, and you had to sit behind that little sign. I also went to a Catholic school in this little town, which I call Bayonne in the story. I also could not eat uptown. There was no place for me to eat; whether it was cold or sleet or rain; and there was no place to eat. There was no place to warm a child eight years old. To do it, a mother had to take him back of town, which was about a mile, ¾ of a mile, something like that, and there was no transportation unless someone picked you up when they saw you walking by. You have that in the story. I also knew about the dentist's waiting room, the cluttered little place that might be full of people waiting to have dental help. Of course, there were all black people in here; the whites were sitting someplace else. So I had gone through all that. This is why I knew what a child would experience. As a writer, I was interpreting the feeling of this child at the time I myself was 30 years old, but

I did know the experiences that he would have gone through. I knew the things that he was going through, yes.

Fitzgerald: While Mr. Marchant was talking about the political aspects of your writing. I couldn't help but think that the scene in the dentist's office in "The Sky is Gray" could easily be seen as a marvelous presentation of black militancy, on the one hand, and tradition, on the other. The people gathered in that room seem to be from all walks of life, as if you were deliberately creating a kind of microcosm of the South. Would you agree with this reading?

Gaines: I would hate to say yes because no matter what I do, no matter how much I write, I feel I will never fully represent the South, really. Just little bitty pieces. I would hate to say that any story or book is "really" representative. You can catch a little touch of it maybe, sometimes.

Fitzgerald: To what extent do you feel that you have come under the influence of contemporary writers? Do you feel that Mr. Ellison's work has influenced you in any way or that of other black writers?

Gaines: No, it hasn't. I didn't read anything at all by Ralph Ellison until I had formed my own style of writing. My early influences were Faulkner, Hemingway, the Russian writers such as Tolstoy, Turgenev and Chekhov. I think I've also been influenced by Greek tragedy, but not by Ellison or any black writers. I knew very early what it was I wanted to write about. I just had to find out a way to do it, and the white writers whom I've mentioned showed me this way better. I looked at Hemingway as a man who can really construct paragraphs; when I want to construct a good paragraph, I read a little Hemingway. You can look at Turgenev's structure of his *Fathers and Children* for a perfectly constructed little novel, or at F. Scott Fitzgerald's construction of *The Great Gatsby*. You look at everything in Tolstoy, who I think is the greatest of them all, the greatest man to write a novel. So you learn from all these people; I've learned from all of them. I learned how to get what was in me onto the paper. As I said about the story "A Long Day in November," I had to get it from Faulkner and from Joyce, but not from Richard Wright or Ellison or Baldwin or anybody like that. They showed me how to get it much better than the black writers had done because so many of them really dealt with style, whereas I think the black writers are much more interested in content—you know, putting it down like it is—and the style is sort of secondary.

Marchant: Do you find that it helps you to live in San Francisco and write about Louisiana from that distance?

Gaines: Well, in San Francisco if someone's against you, they know how to vote you out of an area. If someone's against you in Louisiana, or if I wrote a book and they did not like it or me in Louisiana, they might shoot me anytime. So it's much safer to live in San Francisco than it is in Louisiana. I think I could write in Louisiana just as well, but I know that, saying some of the things I say, I cannot live in Louisiana and say these things; I mean I can't say them daily and still go through my life every day. And I don't feel that I want to write about something and not have guts enough to live it. What I mean is that, if I were to live in Louisiana and write about an interracial love affair, I should be brave enough, myself, to love; and brave enough to stand beside anyone else who tried. In San Francisco, I could do these things. In Louisiana it might be a little problem to do the same things. So, as you know, I live in San Francisco.

Marchant: Are the old social patterns breaking up in Louisiana? Are they changing?

Gaines: Yes—in some cases. In the cities they're changing much more. In the countryside you have much of the same sort of thing as years ago. The physical makeup of the country is changing. People are chopping down more trees and plowing up more land, but the people themselves are pretty much the same. In the cities, I noticed this last time that more people are eating at the same counters, blacks and whites together. There are more black people working as clerks. I went to one of the biggest, newest buildings in Baton Rouge, the Louisiana National Bank, only a week or so ago, and I saw two black clerks working as tellers in the bank. This was unheard of two years ago. But things have changed. Now take this little drugstore on the corner of Third Street and North Blvd. in Baton Rouge; in here all the people are eating together, blacks and whites eating at the same counter, a black boy behind the counter is serving and ringing up the cash register. Once this black boy could come in and clean the dishes off the place, but he could never serve anybody. At a later time he could serve and he could collect the money, but he could not ring up the cash register; he had to pass the money from the customer to the white clerk. Now he can do both. But just across the street—well, that's another story.

Marchant: How long will it take those across the street to catch up?

Gaines: Only God knows.

A Conversation with
Ernest J. Gaines
Fred Beauford / 1972

From *Black Creation* 4 (1972): 16–18.

The author's picture on the back cover of Ernest J. Gaines' book, *The Autobiography of Miss Jane Pittman*, shows an extremely sad face set in passive melancholy, seemingly pondering all of the unfortunate incidents of an unfortunate world.

But the Ernest Gaines who was speaking to me—his dark eyes shining, his smile large and warm, his hands opening outward in broad expansive movements as we sat in his modest San Francisco apartment—discussed eagerly his main passion in life: writing fiction.

I had asked him about a character, a wise old woman who sees all and knows all, that appears and reappears in most of his works.

"Well," he was saying, "I was raised by an older person in the South until I was fifteen years old—I came to California when I was fifteen—it was my aunt and she never walked a day in her life. And she used to look after us children: myself and my other brothers and sisters. We didn't have electricity so we had to bring wood for the stove. She could patch clothes and when she got tired of that she would go out into the garden like that garden by that old house over there."

Gaines pointed to a photograph hanging on his wall of a large, worn grey house, a photograph which he had taken on one of his frequent trips back home.

"There is a vegetable garden there," he said, referring to the picture, "but that isn't our house."

He turned and pointed again, only this time to another part of his wall, and to another photograph, and to another large worn timeless grey structure. "That is our house over there," he said.

"But we had a garden just like that. All of these old plantation houses had a little garden next to them. And my aunt could even come down the steps. She used to slide down the steps and come

16

into the garden. And she was very strong physically because she had to crawl across the floor with her hands. And very intelligent.

"And although my older characters in my books are not based on my aunt literally—and I don't know if they are at all—I mean her moral strength yes—and any kind of defect that they may have that they do not let get in their way, or let it keep them from doing their work and feeling sorry for themselves—I read something in the papers just yesterday where Baldwin said that he should not despair because he has no right to despair. His job is to go on and work, to do some more work."

I mentioned to Gaines that Baldwin had also said recently that he (Gaines) was one of the best young Black writers around today. We both laughed but not because we did not believe Baldwin meant well, but because surely Baldwin should have known that Gaines has been writing since 1952 and could hardly be called a "young writer."

Ernest Gaines was born January 15, 1933 on a Louisiana plantation and can remember working in the fields for fifty cents a day as a child of nine. Later he became a graduate of San Francisco State College and a recipient of a Wallace Stegner Creative Writing Fellowship to Stanford University. His first novel, *Catherine Carmier* (1964), was awarded the Joseph Henry Jackson Literary Prize. His other works include a novel, *Of Love and Dust* (1967), and a collection of short stories, *Bloodline* (1968).

In addition, Gaines' stories have appeared in *Negro Digest, Southern Writing of the Sixties, The Best Short Stories By Negro Writers* and *American Negro Short Stories*.

But getting back to the interview, Gaines is one of the few Black writers who deals with the Black "peasantry" of the South, and he does this despite that fact that he has lived in a big city since the age of fifteen. I asked him why.

"It's really my background," he answered, "and if the Black man is not the peasantry of this country, then there is no peasantry. And no matter what you do and no matter who the writer is, sooner or later he deals with the peasantry of a country. The greatest writers of every country have dealt with the peasantry of that country. Tolstoy was perhaps one of the greatest writers of the world and without the peasantry I don't know if Tolstoy. . . ."

He let the point trail off but I picked it up and reminded him that it was *Count* Tolstoy who lived in the big house and that Ernest Gaines worked in the fields and that it could not be suggested, as with Tolstoy, that Gaines overly romanticized his peasants.

He only partially agreed but pointed out that for his example he could have used Faulkner, who he said, "probably romanticized the peasantry." And since he mentioned Faulkner, I asked him about the statement that I have heard on many occasions that Faulkner was one of the few American writers, Black or white, who created a bonafide Black hero.

"I wouldn't consider all of his characters great," he answered, "but I would say that in certain scenes Faulkner did capture great Black characters . . . but I think that more than the creation of characters, Faulkner created great language and that impressed me very very much. I have learned as much from Faulkner's language—handling of the language of both Blacks and the Southern whites—as from anyone else. Faulkner has been an influence on my writing."

One also detects a trace of Hemingway, especially in Gaines' earlier works. Was Hemingway also a factor?

"Hemingway? Definitely yes. And this is one of my criticisms of so many of these younger Black writers in that they say that a white man can't teach them anything. Hemingway can't teach you how to write about Black people. Nobody can do that. But one of his major themes was grace under pressure and there is nobody in this fucking world that has been under more pressure than the Black man. And I can't think of anybody who has come through more gracefully."

Of course Gaines was right on all counts. But Black writers, including himself, get little recognition from the white world. So to a large extent the anti-whitism on the part of Black writers is mainly a case of not wanting to promote one's enemy, mainly a case of reaction to. . . .

"Listen," he said, stopping my thoughts midway, "I don't care what a man is. I mean, a great artist is like a great doctor. I don't care how racist he is. If he can show me how to operate on a heart so that I can cure a brother, or cure someone else, I don't give a damn what the man thinks; he has taught me something. And that

is valuable to me. And that is valuable to others and man as
a whole."

So we are talking about learning skills: style, structure and things
like that, as opposed to ideas, impressions and feelings?

Gaines now appeared as the concerned professor, sternly lectur-
ing a bright but wayward student, the face not quite as serious as
the one on the back of *Miss Jane*, but the broad warm smile gone
nevertheless.

"I am speaking of several things," he answered. "I am speaking
of transition. I am talking about how to go from room to room."

Mechanical things.

"Mechanical things? Yes! Yes! Of course. Faulkner showed me a
lot about things like that and I have no interest in Faulkner's
philosophy. I could no more agree with his philosophy no more
than I could agree with Wallace's. But this man taught me how to
listen to dialogue; he taught me how to leave out. You can say one
word and if you say it right and build up to it and follow through,
it can carry as much meaning as if you had used an entire sentence.
And the understatement in Hemingway is as profound as the
understatement in the music of Basie. Of course not their philosophies.

"But I do respect men under pressure. You said something before
about the younger men in my works. That they go through hell
but come through some kind of way. That they beat them down
physically but that they rise up. This is the kind of thing that I learned
from Hemingway more than from anyone else. Some critics have
said that this is one of the things that Malcolm could have taught
us: that you go through hell but come out a whole man. I think that
I was trying to get some of that into my literature before I had
read Malcolm."

What about this strong young man who appears in your works?
Is he based on any of your personal experiences? Is this someone
you knew?

"No! No!" Gaines answered. "I think that he is all of us. I mean,
I couldn't say that all of us have come through gracefully under
pressure. We haven't. But there are many of us who have come
through under pressure, pressure against the race."

And in spite of all the personal pressures that Gaines himself has undoubtedly experienced, if only because he was born Black with a keenly aware mind, most of his characters, as attested to by the overwhelmingly critical acclaim he has received, are well-rounded folk who love, cry, fight, kill, eat gumbo and go to church. And one of the major criticisms of Black writers, both young and old, is that they fight their political battles, and their need to avenge the still continuing pressures out in the pages of their works, rendering their characters, Black and white, meaningless caricatures.

I asked Gaines how had he avoided using his pen so heavy-handedly?

The stern professor "disappeared" and the warmly smiling author reappeared as he heard mention once again of the people he had created.

"I think that I like all of my characters," the author said, the smile a little bashful now, a little boyish, "no matter what they turn out to be. If I create them, I love them. I never create a white character that I don't like. Neither do I create a Black character that I don't like. I may not like all of his weak points or his mean points or his brutal points, but he always has something I like.

"After all, I am God over my characters; and God made a lot of bastards running around down here and I guess he likes them."

"And," he added, "this is where art comes in." But apparently Gaines had been through this before and knew the question that someone, if not me, would raise.

"And if I say something about art," he said, answering the unasked question, "someone will say 'art for art's sake' and there goes Gaines again. But I don't mean that kind of bullshit. But the artist—novelist, short story writer—must always study form. Form is very important. If there is no form in a book or a story, I am not even going to be bothered reading the damn thing.

"I think that someone who is crying and sobbing and weeping all over the damn paper has forgotten one thing and that is control over what it is that he is doing. So when I am creating characters, I can hate them and maybe I might cry out all kinds of four letters words and maybe my throat will get all tight but I will cut it all out of the novel the next day."

But with the racial memory at work don't you *really* want to do it sometimes to that bastard you have created?

"But I think that I do it sometimes. Take the massacre scene in *Miss Jane Pittman*. The artist must be like a heart surgeon. He must approach something with sympathy, but with a sort of coldness and work and work until he finds some kind of perfection in his work. You can't have blood splashing all over the place. Things must be done very cleanly."

Gaines is presently at work on a new novel in which he will continue to explore a theme which runs throughout his other works: the search of the young man for the missing father.

"I sort of made a joke about it," he said, "in 'A Long Day in November,' the first story in *Bloodline*. I made a comedy that the father gets involved in mechanical things. Or gets involved in anything else but the education of the son. The true education of the son. But it means much more than that. It was a symbol. It symbolizes this crazy mechanized world. And when the father loses his wife and his child then he starts going through all kinds of changes to try and get them back. But in the following story, 'The Sky is Gray,' when the mother and the child go to a little Southern town, it becomes sort of a search for the father. If the father were there things would be much better. Although he is just going to have a tooth pulled the son finally has to become a man himself. That is the last line in the story."

Where are all the fathers?

Gaines uttered a little laugh as if he was slightly embarrassed by the question.

"Well, I was raised by a stepfather. My mother and father split up very early—and it is a theme that enters everything—and I don't know where the fathers are. If you take a lot of the younger writers, they say that they were revolutionaries and were thrown in jail . . ."

But isn't that true to a certain extent?

"Well I don't agree that all the fathers were thrown in jail. I agree that they might have left for good reason but I don't think that they were thrown in jail because they were revolutionaries. I am working on that theme in the book that I am working on now. And not that the father was thrown in jail, but because of the situation in which he lived he became irresponsible and couldn't hold the family together. I am talking about the condition in which he lived. We can take so many angles on this, which I am trying to do in the book, and see just why did he leave.''

In spite of Gaines' answer it still seemed to me that the young men in Gaines' books were revolutionaries, and they were killed, and if they were not in fact fathers, then they were at least potential fathers, and didn't it amount to the same thing that the younger writers are saying?

"Yes," he partly agreed, "the son becomes the father. The son becomes the father, yes. But I don't think that it is a revolutionary thing. The son was separated from the father on the auction block and they have been looking for each other since. So it is not a revolutionary thing. I think that it is just that they have never been close together.''

What about son and mother?

"Son and mother have always sort of been there. Because let us take for example the white father who rapes the Black woman. No matter what happens, the child was the product of the mother. The father never had to look after the child. The mother had to look after that child. So that the child would always be with the mother. That is why the boy and the mother are always together in my books.''

Gaines indicated that since he was working on the subject in his next novel it would perhaps be better if we dropped it. So we shifted our conversation to the question that all Black novelists are sooner or later asked, and the question that probably excites them least. I asked him if there were any new writers on the scene that excited him?

"Well I am kind of down on most of them," he answered with the little self-conscious laugh.

Why? But then the question was unnecessary because he had said earlier that young writers today think that they cannot learn anything from anyone and that they think that they create everything.

"Their use of language—misspellings, broken sentences and the connection of words—is as original as the 20th century. I mean Stein, Joyce, cummings—I could name probably a dozen people who have done the same thing. I mean, these young writers have definitely learned from these people. And to say that they have not is to tell a damn lie," he added, however.

Then what is the reason for this? The lack of a literary tradition
that does not teach us what went before?

"It is not so much a lack of tradition. But no matter what we do,
we are impressed by what has happened before us and things that
are around us. These things have an influence on us no matter how
you feel about it."

What about the notion that has been advanced by a number of
Black writers that the Black writer has been put into a straight
jacket by white publishers because books about the despairing,
violent-prone, pathological big city Black sells better?

"I wouldn't disagree totally with that statement," he answered.
"The average Black novel about the ghetto of New York or
Chicago or Watts would sell better than any book that I could write.

"Since Wright's *Native Son* came out the books about the cities,
the big city ghettoes, have sold. I would say that most of your
publishers are interested in that kind of a book by a Black more
than he is interested in a book by a Black about any other subject.
Wright established almost a blueprint and it has been the most
popular seller to a white audience."

What about those who are talking about a new "Black Aesthetic"? Have they also been ignoring those books that deal with
Black life?

"You can get ignored by Blacks . . . the subject is just not a
popular one without the propaganda," he said.

Gaines said that it took him ten years to become the writer that
he is today. During that time he worked in the Post Office, set type in
a printing shop and held a variety of jobs, but all the time he was
writing at least five hours a day. And recognition must have
seemed slow.

But with *Miss Jane Pittman*, it now looks as if Ernest Gaines will
get what he deserves. For example, colleges and universities
around the country are beginning to teach his books. In addition,
this year he was given the Louisiana Library Award, the first time
in 22 years that the prize has been given for a work of fiction. He
was also awarded the California Gold Medal for the best book by
a Californian for the year.

But more important, he is no longer being ignored by Blacks. In

New York this year the *Black Academy of Arts and Letters* presented him with its top award for fiction.

Astrology buffs will no doubt point out that for Capricorns, the climb is always slow, but that they will ultimately reach the heights.

Ernest Gaines may not have reached all of his goals, but he has come a long way. And with grace.

Ernest J. Gaines
John O'Brien / 1972

From *Interviews with Black Writers*. Ed. John O' Brien. New York: Liveright, 1973. Used by permission.

The fiction of Ernest J. Gaines is often compared to that of William Faulkner. The initial similarities are apparent: Gaines' mythical creation of a locale in Louisiana in which all of his stories originate or take place, his oral narrative, his preoccupation with themes of change, stasis, and time. But unlike many other writers who demonstrate the influence of Faulkner, Gaines has taken these Southern literary materials and made them his own. Although Gaines is careful not to dwell too long in conversation on how he relates to other writers or how others have influenced him, and even hesitates to make daring statements about what departures he has made from his predecessors, he has learned from them.

But unlike Faulkner, who was enamored of the past because its strict social order at least offered man stability, Gaines in his fiction labors to escape the immobile past and to view change as necessary in sustaining life. This effort has been long and arduous. Many of his earlier characters broke from the past at the expense of alienation and death. So, although Marcus in *Of Love and Dust* resists the racist and unjust plantation system into which he was born, he also becomes its victim. It was perhaps not until the concluding story in *Bloodline* that Gaines was able to create a character, Aunt Fe, who is in tune with an order of nature which demands a respect for the past as well as a realization of the need for growth. At the same time that she is ready to accept her impending death, she also assents to the social upheavals that are about to occur.

It is in his much praised recent novel, *The Autobiography of Miss Jane Pittman*, that Gaines discovers and convincingly portrays a character who works harmoniously with time. Miss Jane Pittman learns that time itself is change and that it is only by accepting it as such that man can order the present. Otherwise he becomes a

25

slave to history and a stifling social order that blindly repeats the evils of the past. Whereas in Faulkner the characters are usually trying to upset the natural order of things by stopping time or making it move backwards, Gaines, with some remorse about the loveliness of certain qualities of the past, reaches toward a future that can potentially shape the world in a more humane way. Death is not the ultimate enemy that man submits to out of despair and frustration, but is part of a natural process which in itself is good and in which man must take his place.

Gaines' first novel, *Catherine Carmier* (1964), concerns the return home of a young man who has left the South and, by so doing, left behind the cultural values of the plantation life. He is unable to understand and reconcile the old and the new, and fails to persuade Catherine Carmier to leave with him for the North. The second novel, *Of Love and Dust* (1967), continues many of the same themes, as Marcus attempts to usurp the plantation system by revolting against the landowner. Although his attempt assures him of personal honor, he is killed. *Bloodline* (1968) consists of five long stories which are very closely related. The first is about a small boy who experiences his first painful encounter with the real world when his parents separate. He goes to bed that evening, only partially educated by the events of the day. The last story in the book treats a young man who has traveled away from the South and has now returned to change it. Gaines' most recent novel *Miss Jane Pittman*, is narrated by a centenarian who tells her version of "history" to a young naïve history teacher. Because of Miss Jane Pittman's age and vast experience, Gaines is able to portray someone who undergoes and transcends the dilemmas that faced the characters of his earlier stories. Despite the imminent danger involved, she, at the end, is preparing to attend a protest march in the South and thus help initiate the social and political reforms that took place in America in the 1960s.

The interview was conducted in November, 1972. I sent Gaines tapes and a sheet of questions. He continues to live and work in San Francisco where he is now completing his fifth book.

Interviewer: I wonder to what extent you have felt the influence of Hemingway and Faulkner? Jerry H. Bryant in his critical article

on your work argues that there are both stylistic and thematic
similarities between your work and theirs. For instance, he points
to the stoicism of Hemingway's characters, found also in characters
like Proctor Lewis in "Three Men" or Marcus in *Of Love and
Dust*.

Gaines: Of course I was influenced by both Hemingway and
Faulkner. I think all of us who were trying to write during the
fifties have been influenced by them. But I was not conscious of
Hemingway as I was writing the story "Three Men" or the novel
Of Love and Dust. I should point out that Proctor Lewis and
Marcus Payne are the same character; I wanted to show what
would have happened to Proctor Lewis had he gotten out of prison,
the chances he would have taken to attain his freedom. The
stoicism in these two characters was not because of Hemingway's
influence on me. I was writing these stories during the time when
young blacks were standing up against the establishment. They
were no longer doing what everyone thought they ought to do,
whether it was the white man, or the law, or their own black people.
So that was an influence. Then I also knew a guy on whom I
based Proctor Lewis. This guy had been involved in a killing; three
men had jumped him and he had killed one with a knife. He had
been working as a mechanic for a white man and when he was
thrown into jail his boss came to get him out. But he told him that
he would serve his time. So these characters were not necessarily
influenced by Hemingway at all.

Interviewer: Bryant goes on to suggest that when your own
distinct style emerged in *The Autobiography of Miss Jane Pittman*,
so did your own vision, which no longer shared Faulkner's sense of
the past or Hemingway's sense of defeat.

Gaines: I don't know whether my characters have ever accepted
defeat. Proctor Lewis does not accept defeat; I think he rises above
defeatism. When he asks himself where is his own father now that
he needs him and the father is not there, he then turns to the boy
and he becomes the father of the boy. That to me is not defeatism.
As far as sharing Faulkner's sense of the past goes, I don't know
whether my sense of the past is exactly that of Faulkner because I
don't know how to interpret Faulkner. I don't think that *Miss
Jane Pittman* marks a departure from my other work. I just think

that I was doing something different from what I had done in
other books. I could not have possibly written *Miss Jane Pittman*
the way I had written *Of Love and Dust* or the *Bloodline* stories. Miss
Jane's interpretation of life is quite different from the way Jim Kelly
saw life in *Of Love and Dust* or the way the characters see life in
Bloodline, especially the characters in "Three Men." I don't know
whether I have actually broken away from the Hemingway and
Faulkner influence. I don't know whether that's possible to do, just
as I don't think it's possible for me to break away from the
influences of jazz or blues or Negro spirituals or Greek tragedy or
James Joyce or Tolstoy. Perhaps what is happening now is that
I've been writing longer and I have developed my own style,
whatever in the world that may be. But I don't think that I've
broken away from anybody's influence, because I don't think I tried
to imitate anybody in the beginning.

Interviewer: In another interview you mentioned that the Russian
writers, especially Tolstoy, Chekhov, and Turgenev, as well as
Greek tragedy, had strongly influenced you. Could you say what
exactly those influences have been, how they appear in your
work?

Gaines: Well, when I first started reading I wanted to read about
my people in the South, and the white writers whom I had read
did not put my people into books the way that I knew them. When
I did not find my people in the Southern writers, I started reading
books about the peasantry in other places. I read the John Steinbeck
people of the Salinas Valley, the Chicanos as well as the poor
whites. This led me to reading the writers of other countries. Then
in some way I went into the Russians and I liked what they were doing
with their stories on the peasantry; the peasants were real human
beings, whereas in the fiction of American writers, especially Southern writers, they were caricatures of human beings, they were
clowns. So, initially I read the Russians because of their interest
in peasant life. Then I began reading everything that they wrote
because of their styles. I read Chekhov's stories, plays, and
letters; from there I went to Tolstoy, Pushkin, and Gogol. I think
that the Russians are the greatest writers of the nineteenth-
century. No other country produced names like Gogol, Tolstoy,

Turgenev, Dostoevsky, and Chekhov. And when you think of it,
these men were all living at about the same time.

Interviewer: And what about Greek tragedy?

Gaines: The Greek tragedies were always limited in space and
time. Most of my work, at least before *Miss Jane Pittman*, if it
did not take place within a few hours it took place within a few
days. But I must also go back to Hemingway and Joyce to explain
this, because I think they were doing the same thing. Their stories
did not go over a long period of time, they were usually confined to a
few hours. So I was not only influenced directly by the Greeks, but
also by the influence they had upon other writers whom I was
reading.

Interviewer: One of the recurring themes in your fiction is the
conflict between the past and the present, between change and stasis.
Many of your characters are victims of the past—Tee Bob in *Miss
Jane Pittman*, who, despite his own willingness to change, cannot
overcome his racial and cultural past, and Jackson in *Catherine
Carmier*. Other characters seem quite content to have the past
control them, even though it may be a past which is corrupt. Do
you see your work as involving this great struggle to discover how or
when man can escape the past which tries to hold him captive?

Gaines: There will always be men struggling to change, and there
will always be those who are controlled by the past. In many
cases, those who are controlled by the past can be just as human
and sometimes more human than those who try to change things.
Yet, there must always be those who try to change conditions; there
must always be those who try to break out of the trap the world
keeps going in. Man must keep moving. In the case of Tee Bob and
Jackson, they were victims of the past. They tried their best to
escape the influence of the past, and I think their attempt to do this
can lead to someone else picking up where they left off. This is
the kind of thing I am doing in all of my work. These characters
make an attempt toward change, and some other character might
continue where they left off. But to break away from the past, from
one philosophy to another, is a burden that one person cannot
endure alone. Someone else must pick up from there and go on.

Interviewer: Has there been a change in your own views, as

they're expressed in your novels, about how this conflict will
be resolved?

Gaines: I don't know how this conflict between the past and the
present will be resolved. I don't think I am talented enough to
explain that kind of thing in my writing, I'm not philosophical
enough. There will be someone else, later, who can do this much
better than I.

Interviewer: Well, as Bryant's article convincingly argues, I think
that your philosophical concerns are more than you may admit.
But I wanted to ask you about the concept of manhood in your
fiction. All your male heroes are possessed of a need to prove
that they are men, and their attempts—which seem to be lifelong
ones—always end in death. For Ned and Jimmy Aaron in *Miss Jane
Pittman* that testing involves declaring their freedom in the face of
those whites who have other plans for them; for Joe Pittman it
means trying to break in a horse. Raoul Carmier must prove his
manhood by exercising complete control over his land and his
daughter. When Miss Jane visits the hoodoo she suggests that men
test their manhood in the most "foolish" of ways. I wonder
whether you think that Jimmy and Ned have found the proper basis
on which to prove themselves?

Gaines: You must understand that in this country the black man
has been pushed into the position where he is not supposed to be
a man. This is one of the things that the white man has tried to deny
the black ever since he brought him here in chains. As Joe Pittman
says in *Miss Jane Pittman*, a man must do something, no matter
what it is, he must do something and he must do that something
well. My heroes just try to be men; but because the white man has
tried everything from the time of slavery to deny the black this
chance, his attempts to be a man will lead toward danger. The
hoodoo lady and Joe Pittman both say that man has come here to
die. So whenever my men decide that they will be men regardless
of how anyone else feels, they know that they will eventually die. But
it's impossible for them to turn around. This is the sense of Greek
tragedy that keeps coming back in my writing, that men are destined
to do things and they cannot do anything but that one thing.
Whatever that one thing is, it is to be done as well as the man can
do it.

Interviewer: Jackson in *Catherine Carmier* is one character who is trying to establish his manhood, but the ending is somewhat ambiguous as to whether he has been successful. Do you think that Jackson has been successful in his usurpation of Raoul but that he himself will not reap the benefits of his action? Should this ending be seen more in mythical terms?

Gaines: I think that you have already answered the question. This is what I meant before, when I said that Tee Bob or Jackson might be victims, but that someone else will pick up where they left off and will continue the effort to escape from darkness to light, or from the past to the present. Perhaps, however, some people do not find the present much better than the past, even though they know how bad the past was.

Interviewer: Do you think the ending of that novel suggests that there is no solution for Catherine? She seems unable to separate her love for Jackson from her loyalty to her father. Is she fated to a situation from which there is no escape?

Gaines: People who have truly deep feelings are always tragic. They just cannot change the way that so many of us can. Definitely, she is a tragic figure, and she has no control over her condition. We go right back to Greek tragedy again. People like Catherine Carmier cannot determine their way of living, it is fated that they must live a certain way. But without those kind of people I am sure that this world would be a much more unpleasant place to live in.

Interviewer: Jackson also seems to be trapped. By leaving the plantation when he did, he is not able to adjust now that he has returned. This theme of the black becoming alienated from his own culture is a common theme in many black novels and short stories. Were you aware of Du Bois' treatment of this theme in *The Souls of Black Folk* or of Toomer's, in *Cane*?

Gaines: No, I was not aware of this theme running through black literature. I've never really read all of Du Bois' *The Souls of Black Folk* and I did not read Toomer's *Cane* until long after I had written *Catherine Carmier*. But just as in any race of people, when a young man leaves an area to go to a more enlightened area it is hard for him to come back to his home. Thomas Wolfe said it, and it's been said since the beginning of time. Once I left the South, which

I did when I was fifteen years old, it was hard for me to go back and act the same way with my friends and people. Oh, I could drink and talk with them, but when it came down to accepting certain things as they did, it was just about impossible for me to do.

Interviewer: Is Jackson the last hope that Catherine has of escaping the past?

Gaines: I may hit myself later for saying this and other people may not like it, but I don't think that Catherine could exist outside of the South, I think that she would die like a fish out of water. As long as there is one other person left, she would want to be there. I know many women like Catherine who wanted to leave and did leave, but many of them went back. Many of them have left and stayed away, but I don't think they were happier once they did.

Interviewer: Is there an implicit condemnation of Jackson for lacking compassion toward the old tradition? Should he, like Catherine, be willing to sacrifice his life for this dying culture?

Gaines: Jackson cannot be like Catherine again. Jackson had gone North and had received an education that was quite different from the way he was brought up. It's impossible for him to go back. I've had men in other situations, like Ned in *Miss Jane Pittman*, who did go back, but of course he went back as a grown man. He went back after he had seen the world and felt that he should go back in order to teach others. Jackson does not have that kind of feeling about others at that time in his life. He was still searching for himself. And though he did not find himself in California, he knew that he could not do it back home even with someone as beautiful and who loved him as much as Catherine Carmier.

Interviewer: Why was the book named after Catherine Carmier when Jackson is really the central character?

Gaines: The answer is really almost a joke. I had been writing this book for a very long time and I had no title for it until the day I sent it off to the publishing house. I had called it several things, including some titles I don't think should be put on paper (laughing). I had been trying to write this novel for about five years. I didn't know anything about writing a novel when I first started, so it had given me a lot of trouble. So I simply ended up calling it *Catherine*. When I sent it to my editor, Hiram Haydn, he told me that I should give it a second name; so I simply called it *Catherine Carmier*. The book

was much longer in earlier versions and it had much more to do
with Catherine and her family than it did with Jackson. Though
Jackson was the central character, much more of the action
concerned Catherine, her background, and her family.

Interviewer: Do you think that Catherine's decision to stay with
her defeated father is noble or cowardly?

Gaines: I don't know whether it's one or the other. It was fated
that she stay there; I don't think she could decide her fate. Even
if she had gone with Jackson, which she really wanted to do, she
probably would have turned around and come back. It's almost
impossible for Catherine to have left the South, especially at that
time. Perhaps, as Della says, twenty years hence Catherine may
have been able to do so, but not that night. I've been back to the
South several times and I have seen girls much like Catherine
who wanted to leave their family's tradition but who could not. Of
course, there are others who could leave, but Catherine had to
stay there.

Interviewer: In *Of Love and Dust* Jim Kelley acts as a kind of
moral guide to the action, much like Nick in *The Great Gatsby*.
But as with Nick, it is suggested that Kelley's worldly wisdom is
short-sighted and may actually help in producing evil. Isn't this the
realization that Kelley himself comes to at the end, when he decided
that he and Aunt Margaret are very much alike? Each helps to
sustain an evil social system, though each in his own life tries to
avoid doing evil.

Gaines: I don't know whether I agree with you that Jim is helping
to sustain an evil system. I don't think that Jim knew he could
change anything at that time. What he found out at the end was that
there had to be people like Marcus, that people like Marcus existed
and that they had as much right to do what Marcus did as did people
like himself. But he himself was not in any position to change the
system. When he said that he and Aunt Margaret were alike he was
just saying that he was not like Marcus. But I don't think that he
or Aunt Margaret could have done anything else. After being
influenced by Marcus, all Jim could do was what he did in the
end—pack up and leave.

Interviewer: Do you think that Marcus's rebellious action pro-
duces any real change? He succeeds in displacing Bonbon, but won't

Bonbon simply move on to doing something similar somewhere
else?

Gaines: If there's any change it is the influence that Marcus has
had on Jim. Jim leaves the plantation, and perhaps after thinking
about Marcus some more he will be a different person. I really don't
know. As far as I am concerned, he is a great person here at the
plantation where the action of the novel takes place. As far as
Bonbon goes, I don't know. I think I state in the story that
Bonbon was determined by society and his environment. I suppose
that the idea that man is determined by society runs through most of
my work. Whenever my heroes decide to rebel against this condition, physical death usually results. In the case of Marcus,
though, something else takes place too. Marcus is very noble at the
end when he refuses to run because running would destroy his
manhood. Jim's awakening is due as much to Marcus's death as to
his life. But all this is after the fact. After I end a novel I am no
longer concerned with what my characters do. That's another story.

Interviewer: Especially in this novel you do not seem to share
Faulkner's nostalgia for the past. The past in this novel, though
ordered, is usually evil and is the single greatest obstacle to change.

Gaines: I don't know that the past is usually evil. There are some
very beautiful things in the past. The people are beautiful; Aunt
Margaret is as beautiful as anyone in the present. Though I don't
long for the past, I don't see the past as basically evil, any more than
I see the present or future as necessarily good. What we experience
now or in the future can be just as terrible or worse than what we
experienced in the past. But I find the differences between the
three, dramatic, and something that I like working with. I find
good and evil in all of them. The young to me are not necessarily
good, any more than the old or the past is necessarily evil.

Interviewer: With the exception of Marcus and Louise, all of the
characters in the novel are controlled by their conceptions of the
past. In fact, they insure that the past will be repeated because they
refuse to recognize the possibility of change.

Gaines: You have got to understand that Marcus and Louise are
in love, and with them anything is possible. It's the same story you
find in *Romeo and Juliet*. They feel that they can get away with it
and that there's nothing to harm them. Whereas the people who

have lived longer cannot conceive of any other life than the one
they have been living. But after the lovers have died, then—and
only then—can the others see a future that permits change. There
has to be this kind of tragic action before they can see things
differently. This is why all the characters except Marcus and Louise
feel that whatever is will continue to be.

Interviewer: Why was Kelley unable to keep his wife? Here is a
man who was always so wise and practical, who always knew
how to stay out of trouble. Does this suggest a flaw in his
"wisdom"?

Gaines: Kelley couldn't keep his wife simply because his wife
wanted things that he couldn't afford to give her. She wanted a
good time, she wanted—what is it he calls it—"silk drawers." So
Kelley just has the problem that any husband might have.

Interviewer: Can you recall how the image of "dust" evolved in
Of Love and Dust? The image seems to oppose what is suggested
by "love."

Gaines: You're absolutely right that dust is the opposite of love. I
think that the dust is death. When a man dies he returns to dust.
If you lived on a plantation you would find that there's no value to
dust at all; it's just there. Dust is the first thing Jim sees when he's
sitting out on the porch at the beginning of the novel. When the dust
finally settles, Marcus is walking toward the house. So the dust brings
Marcus to the plantation. The dust is always there. Whenever
Marcus goes by Louise's place the dust rises, or whenever
Marshall Hebert moves around in his car, the dust starts flying.
Louise realizes at the end that it is the opposite of love. It is a symbol
of death.

Interviewer: What went into arranging the five stories in *Bloodline*? I know that they do not appear in the order in which they
were written, so I wonder whether you intended a thematic development. Do you think that there is a sense of growth and maturation
in the characters of the later stories that is not present in the
earlier ones?

Gaines: The first story is told by a six-year-old child. The second
story is told by an eight-year-old child. The third story is by a
nineteen-year-old. The fourth story is by someone in his earlier
twenties. The final story is told by many characters. I definitely

arranged these stories in this order because there is growth. In the
first story, "A Long Day in November," a six-year-old child can
only see a certain amount of things, he can only interpret a certain
amount of things. That's why his story is limited physically to the
plantation. By the time he's eight years old in "The Sky Is Gray"
it's time for him to get out of the quarters. He ends up in a small
Southern town where he sees a little bit more. Though he does not
understand everything that is going on, he can understand much more
than the six-year-old. In "Three Men" the boy is nineteen and has
committed murder. Of course, his experiences are much broader
than the first two boys'. From there you go to "Bloodline" where
Copper Laurent has traveled much more than Proctor Lewis in
"Three Men." He has not seen just the brutality that the young
black can suffer in the South, but he has seen what the world has
done to men everywhere. By the time you come to the last story
there is much more experience to interpret. You have both older
women and older men. You have the point of view of the white
woman. There are many different experiences coming into the
story. So there is a constant growth from the first to the last story.

Interviewer: I saw the child's returning to bed at the end of "A
Long Day in November" as a refusal to change, an acceptance
of defeat.

Gaines: I don't think it is the most significant thing about the
story. The most important thing is his waking up in the morning
and going outside because, you might recall, he didn't want to get
up. He had a hard time getting up. When he finally goes back to
bed that night he feels quite good. He feels good being under the
covers and he feels good that his mother and father are back
together again. And he feels that tomorrow will be a better day
for him.

Interviewer: Christianity and "the Christian" are often satirized
in your fiction because they are often hypocritical and seem to
represent one more institution that does not permit change, especially social change.

Gaines: Yes, I suppose I agree with you that Christianity is an
institution that does not want to recognize or permit change. But
you must remember that most of my work has been written in the
last eight or nine years. Most of the things I write about happened

before the Civil Rights demonstrations. At that time the Church was only concerned with sending someone to heaven rather than with creating social changes. It was not until Martin Luther King came along that the Church really became involved in social and civil injustices. The people whom I felt actually lived the Christian life were not necessarily Christians, as is the case in "The Sky Is Gray," where the old couple takes the mother and boy out of the cold. That particular incident was based upon people I actually knew.

Interviewer: Why did you choose to have an "Introduction" to *The Autobiography of Miss Jane Pittman*? Would the novel have been greatly different without this note that the book is the editorialized reminiscences of Miss Jane?

Gaines: I think that the Introduction was very important. It was the first thing I wrote. I couldn't see the novel any other way except with such an Introduction. I put it there because I could not see how a person who is a hundred-and-ten years old could actually tell the story, and I wanted to use the whole community to help Miss Jane tell her story. When I first started writing the novel it was a short biography of Miss Jane Pittman. Then there were many people after her death who talked about her. After I had gone so far trying to tell it from that point of view, I changed it because I didn't think the other characters could get to those intimate thoughts that I wanted. Once I started to tell it from this personal point of view, I wanted this Introduction to show how these other people helped her tell the story. I've seen this kind of storytelling many times before. One person may be the main narrator but there were these other people around to help her along if she could not remember or if she got tired talking. I also used the Introduction because I wanted to explain some things about my writing. I said that Miss Jane used the simplest terms and that she believed in repetition. These are characteristics of my own writing. Another reason for the Introduction is that the book covers a hundred years and I wanted the reader to know exactly how all this came to pass. I wanted it there as an explanation for when Miss Jane started rambling from one episode to the next. I suppose I also put it there to make the story seem credible. It is hard for people to believe somebody like Miss Jane actually exists.

Interviewer: Do you think that this fictive editor of yours is naive? He says that he teaches history and hopes that Jane's narratives will help him to explain history to his students. Yet there is the suggestion that he may be missing the most important and subtle things about what Miss Jane tells him. For instance, he complains about the episodic form of her stories which appear to him to be going in ridiculous directions. He wants her to tell him about facts and events; she succeeds in explaining "how" history works.

Gaines: Yes, I think he's naive in a way, just as we all are naive about the true history of blacks in this country. We have Du Bois, Douglass, and Booker T. Washington, but we don't have the story of the average black who has lived to be that age. After Miss Jane starts to ramble he does see that she is not going in any definite direction. I suppose that until we started editing the tape we would have felt the same way. But Miss Jane has not read all these books on what a narrative should be and she could only narrate history the way she saw it.

On the Verge: An Interview with Ernest J. Gaines

Forrest Ingram and Barbara Steinberg / 1973

From *New Orleans Review* 3 (1973): 339–44. Used by permission.

Ernest Gaines was born on a Louisiana plantation not far from Baton Rouge. His novels include *Catherine Carmier* (1964), *Of Love and Dust* (1967), and *The Autobiography of Miss Jane Pittman* (1971), the last of which won wide critical acclaim, as did his short story cycle, *Bloodline* (1968). Presently, he lives in San Francisco and is at work on another novel, *In My Father's House*. The interview was conducted by Forrest Ingram and Barbara Steinberg in Baton Rouge, where Mr. Gaines comes occasionally to visit his family and friends.
[New Orleans Review]

NOR: In *The Autobiography of Miss Jane Pittman*, you place a lot of emphasis, as Faulkner and other Southern writers do, on the river. Why is that?

Gaines: Well, I think there's something about the river that connects Southern writing, just like there's something about the land. I grew up on False River in Pointe Coupee Parish and, of course, the river played a very big part in the lives of people at that time. We got about as much food from the river as we got from the earth.

NOR: How long did it take you to write *Miss Jane*?

Gaines: About two and a half years.

NOR: Are you working on another novel?

Gaines: Yes, and I might get caught up in other things too. Some people want me to work on television scripts and such things. I don't really want to do it, but if it's my own stuff, I might look into it. One of the reasons I'm down here (Baton Rouge) right now is because we are in the process of selling *Miss Jane* to the movies. The people from Hollywood are supposed to join me next week

and we're supposed to look over some possible shooting locations
in this area.

NOR: It's not going to be easy to catch the flavor of *Miss Jane*.

Gaines: No, it won't be easy. Everybody is asking me if I am
going to work on the script, and I say no, because it'll be too
much of a problem. I know it's going to be hard to catch this mood
in a two-hour movie—hard to put a hundred years on tape. So I
would rather not be directly involved as a technical advisor. I think
what they want to do here is use two or three actresses with alike
bone structure: one for the little girl caught in the swamps, I think,
and another one with Mr. Pittman, and one that ages sort of
gracefully, I suppose, for the last parts.

NOR: You really achieved a sense of felt life in the scene where
Mr. Pittman is killed by the horse.

Gaines: I was thinking of Moby Dick when I did the horse. I was
thinking that nobody should break him, but then I thought, well, I
don't want to play with that Moby Dick thing. Moby Dick gets
away, and the horse should be broken somehow.

NOR: Why did you make a woman the central character?

Gaines: Well, it would have been pretty bad to name a man Miss
Jane! (laughter) But that's not it . . . I'm just kidding.

NOR: It seems to me that in all of your work you bring your male
characters to the verge of manhood and then leave their future
unknown but hopeful. You give them strength of character, but the
future is not on their side. Your women act more, they go further.
Do you take that from what you see as the real historical context,
the context of black people's history? Black women have had
more opportunity to act (as the dominant member of the family, the
mother, for instance). The woman can act, whereas the man is
kept from acting. Is that what you see for the future, or where we
are now—that the black man is still on the verge?

Gaines: Yes, right. You've answered it. You've answered your
own question. I think that at the moment, right now, the black
man is on the verge, like they say Rap Brown is, because these guys
aren't going to do what they talk about doing. In the title story of
Bloodline, Copper comes home and he's mad; he's seen a lot of
things and he's gone mad . . . or rather, he's on the verge of

madness. And he will not free people, but somebody else might do it. Someone else will pick it up and carry it a little bit farther.

NOR: Doesn't Emmanuel in the last story pass beyond the verge?

Gaines: No, even he's on the verge of things. He doesn't do it, you know. I don't know of anybody who ends up doing it.

NOR: Do you have any idea where the black man in America is going?

Gaines: (Laughter) I don't know where anything is going. That's my feeling: I just don't know where things are going.

NOR: Do you have a vision that you'd like to see come true? Would you, in the future, like to write about a black man in a different kind of role?

Gaines: I suppose so, but I don't know whether I'll ever see that actually happen. I don't know whether I'll live that long. I'm neither pessimistic nor optimistic about that sort of thing. I mean you hope for the best, but . . . .

NOR: What do you think about Ralph Ellison?

Gaines: I like Ellison very very much. And someone in reviewing *Miss Jane* said I was closer to Ellison than I was to other black writers.

NOR: But Ellison doesn't really have a Southern sense of the land being important. He concentrates on the internal struggle always. But, of course, we don't have much to go by. We have *Invisible Man*, and *Shadow and Act*, but that's it.

Gaines: I met Ralph, well I saw him last Saturday night at a party in New York. I came from San Francisco to New York and then here. I think at the moment that his new book is supposed to be shaping up.

NOR: Oh, that's been a rumor for five years.

Gaines: Well, his wife is supposedly typing it right now . . . that's a good omen.

NOR: Why do you choose the autobiographical form so often, the first person narrative?

Gaines: The number one reason I choose it is because I can't really write from the third person omniscient point of view. Oh, I can, I do it, but it's harder to do. Hemingway once said that anybody can write a book in the first person. I don't know whether I'd agree with that, but I feel that in most of my work it's easier to write from the first person point of view. Much easier

for me. It took me about five years to write *Catherine Carmier*
which is a little bitty book, simply because, well, I didn't know how
to write a book, and because from the omniscient point of view, I
had to get the grammar and everything so well. Another reason is that
I'm very very proud of my Louisiana background, the people I
come from—my uncle and the people we drink with, the people I
talk with, and the people I grew up around, and their friends. I
always try to use the dialects that they use. If I was writing from
the omniscient point of view, I would use that language only when
I'm doing dialogue. I come from people who told stories. I came from
a plantation. I wish someday we could go down there. I'll show you
the plantation where I come from. The old houses are being torn
down; the cemetery is still there. All the things are being torn down.
There are one or two houses still there though. They are just as
they were . . . an old man who lives there now says they were built
during slavery. So these things are over a hundred years old, and
they're there still. I like to catch the feeling of that place; I can
catch it through that language.

NOR: Do you think you'll continue writing about Louisiana and
the South?

Gaines: Till I get it all out of me, yes. I hope I never do. I don't
think there's anything more important.

NOR: You're not thinking, say, of taking up California as a setting
for your books?

Gaines: I have tried to. I think I've written four novels about
California, but they've all been very very bad, because my heart
may have been in it, but my soul was not.

NOR: Yes, you can choose the subject you want to write about,
but you can't choose what things you can make live.

Gaines: Yes, absolutely. And this is one reason why the novel I'm
working on right now is set in Louisiana.

NOR: What are you going to call it?

Gaines: I'm calling it *In My Father's House.*

NOR: What's the subject?

Gaines: Well, I really don't talk about anything when I'm working
on it, but it's generally about the old fight between father and son
type of thing. I think in this particular instance, the father is looking
for the son, whereas in most of my other stories the theme has

been son looking for father. Well I did have father looking for son in "A Long Day in November." And "The Sky is Gray" is sort of like son looking for father. I mean if the father was there maybe it wouldn't be so cold. In "Three Men" you get the same sort of thing. When Proctor is laying on the couch he screams for his father, and when the father does not show up a little boy is thrown in the cell. The man cannot find father, so he must become father. The same thing in "Bloodline." Copper says: "This is my father's place, and it belongs to me. This is it. This is my place." It's a continual theme of mine.

NOR: Frank Laurent in "Bloodline" is really very well drawn. I caught overtones in him of Creon from *Antigone*. You mentioned one time that you liked Greek Tragedy a lot. And in "Bloodline" as well as in *Antigone* there's the idea that the law is there, and even the leader can't change the law.

Gaines: I think that is another theme in all my things—you don't change the law.

NOR: Those who make the law become victims of it.

Gaines: Of course, Laurent is a victim of it. He didn't make the law, but he's a descendant of those who did make the law so he's the one caught in it.

NOR: Which of the characters do you like the most in "Bloodline?"

Gaines: I think the two of them, Frank Laurent and Copper. I like someone who has to touch his chest every now and then to keep living. But I don't really think Frank Laurent touched his chest all the time. I think what he's doing is sorta like making the sign of the cross, and I think at times he didn't have to touch it for God to keep his heart beating. But these things are the subtleties, you know. This is the kind of thing you lose out on in first person. From the omniscient point of view, the author can catch all these subtleties. He can indicate that Frank does not touch his chest all the time, and of course the author can reenter the mind and say exactly what is going on, whereas Felix [the narrator] cannot. He just sorta stands there and sees the physical things that are going on. And he thinks he can imagine what is happening, like when the guy is coming in from the field and tells him how Copper has been treating everybody, so Felix thinks he can imagine what's going on in this guy's mind, because he knows what would be going on in his mind if he was sitting there. But he doesn't know exactly what is going on. These are the kind of things you lose when you tell it from the first person point of view. You lose so much but you gain so much too.

NOR: You expand your technique, I think, in the last story in *Bloodline* when you put together in one story many people's points of view and then you finally get, I think, the advantages of both the first person and the omniscient narrative.

Gaines: Yes, I think that is absolutely so. But even there you lose a little bit. You don't get it all.

NOR: But you're really choosing for intimacy with the reader.

Gaines: Intimacy with my characters, yes, and then they can share it with the readers.

NOR: Is the structure of "Just Like a Tree" derived primarily from Faulkner's *As I Lay Dying*?

Gaines: Oh, absolutely. Well, I read Chaucer's *The Canterbury Tales* and that has something to do with it. But I think Faulkner has influenced me more than any other writer and, of course, *As I Lay Dying* has influenced me. Definitely. Just as Eudora Welty's "Worn Path" has had definite influence on "The Sky Is Gray." There's no plagiarism or anything involved. But since you can't write out of a void, you need some crutch somewhere; you need somebody to say ok this is one route you can take.

NOR: You talk about all the things that you're fond of. What are you bitter about?

Gaines: Bitter about? I'm concerned with humanity rather than being bitter. Oh I don't like racism; I don't like bigotry; I don't like many things. But when it comes to my work, the important thing to me is to get out a piece of work that I feel is art . . . and art that is as perfectly round as you can get it. I can't let anything get in the way of that. But, well, I'm bitter toward racism, bitter toward war, but everything I write shows what man is. Although my characters might be black it doesn't mean that they represent only black people. But for anybody to make it, he might have to become an individual, and not depend on anyone else to do it for him. So a white kid growing up in a completely racist family or society, maybe he has to come out there and become that individual and face it. I think we're always on the verge of things . . . I don't think we've ever done anything really. I mean we've built skyscrapers and bridges, but we haven't solved anything really.

NOR: You're talking not in terms of technological things but in terms of art. History of painting, history of music, history of writing?

Gaines: Well, I don't know how to answer that. What I mean is that mankind is always on the verge, on the verge of going a little bit farther. People ought to stop wars. They ought not to go out there and bomb everybody. Maybe I don't feel that I've done anything really either. I've worked and I don't think that I'll ever finish. I hope I never finish. I hope that when I die, I'm in the midst of writing the best story I've ever written. And I hope I never finish, because once you finish, as Faulkner says, you cut your neck or something—there's nothing else to do. Like people who climb mountains; if they climb the biggest one, then what do they do next?

NOR: Well, besides making a living, having enough to eat, having a roof over your head and so forth, you're reaching a public and you must have some kind of feeling for people's reaction. Don't you hope at least that you evoke a greater understanding among your readers? That people one passes on a dusty road and never gives a thought to become more real to the people who have read your books? Wouldn't you like a greater understanding of the people of Louisiana, especially the black people, or the black people of the South, to reach the American reading public, the ones who read your books? Or do you think that's too much to hope for?

Gaines: I don't know how to answer that. Of course I hope that my books can do something, but I don't know that they ever will. I don't know why one writes. I suppose you write because you must write.

NOR: Certainly in the last couple of years you've gotten a great deal of recognition. *Miss Jane Pittman* was a tremendous success. Very few people have that kind of success. Does that feel good?

Gaines: Of course! It feels very good. I liked going to Southern University and LSUNO. Blacks and whites would come up and say "oh, I liked your book." If Louisianians say that to me that's more important to me than anything else in the world. Of course

the money; I need to eat, and I need a little Jack Daniels every now
and then (laughter).

NOR: Do you think Louisianians would understand more than
anybody else?

Gaines: No, no, no, not necessarily that. But they would appreciate something that I did. You know, "We appreciate it because
it's you, and you're a part of us, and we are important too." There
are so many now that don't feel that they're important enough that
you should write books about their lives. And then there are the
writers who want to express themselves, but when you see some
of the things they write . . . they are writing in the style of Henry
James! They feel their own language is not important enough even to
express their lives. And then they find you do it in their simple language.

NOR: Could I ask some specific questions about *Bloodline*? Some
people call it an episodic novel. Did you conceive it that way?

Gaines: No, I did not. I wrote "The Sky Is Gray" after I wrote
"Just Like a Tree." That would have been in '63, because I wrote
"Just Like a Tree" in '62, four years after I wrote "A Long Day in
November." I thought the three stories were good enough to be
published as a small book. Malcolm Cowley was one of the guys
who thought so. Then Cowley himself took "A Long Day in Novem-
ber" to New York, and through that story and through him was how
I got the people in New York to begin to get interested.

NOR: Cowley has done a lot to get young writers started.

Gaines: Well, he was at Stanford at the time I was there. He used
to come down there every year to teach at least one or two
quarters. He liked my stuff and I used to sit around and talk
with him.

NOR: What about the other two stories? Did you write them
specifically for *Bloodline*?

Gaines: The other two, yes, I definitely wrote them for the book.
When I was working on them, suddenly I wanted them to fit in with
what was going on here. I think the next one was "Three Men" and
the last one was "Bloodline" itself, the title story. But once I realized
that I was writing a group of stories that had some similarities, I
wanted them to have relationship with the other ones.

NOR: What kind of relationship?

Gaines: Well, I mean the progression. My definition is that "A Long Day in November" is like planting a grain, and it's sprouting. The kid is six and you can see he's very limited in seeing things, you know, and all the action takes place on the plantation quarters.

NOR: So, you had three stories and then you wrote two others to try and fit them in. Did you do any revising of the first three stories, in order to make them fit more harmoniously with the others?

Gaines: Yes, I cut the first one down.

NOR: Why did you place the stories in their present order?

Gaines: Because of age, that's one thing. Age and experiences. Number one: a six year old, then you progress to an eight year old, and an eight year old kid will be able to observe more than a six year old child. The six year old child went up and down the plantation quarters with his father and mother—you know: little schools, kitchen, bath, a toilet out in the backyard and all that sort of thing. Now the eight year old child must leave the quarters, that womb-like thing, and he must go someplace else. So he gets on the bus, and he goes to a Southern town . . . .

NOR: Where he's not certain he can eat, or rest, or anything. It's a microcosm of the small fears that are out in the world.

Gaines: Yes, well, you see, the six year old child could have had the same experiences as the eight; he could have had the same thing at six but he could not have seen it with the perspective of an eight year old child.

NOR: There is a kind of stoicism in the boy that comes out—as also in the next story "Three Men." The boy seems willing to place himself in the midst of pain, in order to become a man.

Gaines: He wants his father first, and when the father does not show up, what else is there?

NOR: He's got to be it.

Gaines: He's got to be a father! He's got to stand for something else . . . at least you're supposed to. A friend of mine in San Francisco who's an ex-cop gave this story ("Three Men") to some of the guys in the prison, some old cons, and he said "What do you think of this story," and the guy says "I don't know what jail

he went to, because not too many of us around here would give that
kind of advice.''

NOR: The main character in "Three Men" is a father substitute
in a sense—he says "Do better than I have done."

Gaines: Yes. But the old convicts did not feel that too many of
them would have given that advice.

NOR: Can we go back briefly to why your stories in *Bloodline* are
put together the way they are?

Gaines: Well, as I said, there's the progression in ages as well as
experiences. A six year old would not experience what Proctor,
the eighteen or nineteen year old would experience. The six year
old child—all his action is in the quarters; the eight year old child
moves out of the quarters, and he goes into a small Southern town,
which gives him a feeling of much of what a small Southern town
would be like. He meets whites, he finds there are certain areas
where you cannot go. In the plantation, in the quarters, he could
go almost anywhere; everybody knows him, so he can move
around; that's his home, that's everything. Then he moves out of that,
just like the six year old boy, who doesn't want to come out from
under the covers when the mother's trying to get him out because
he knows it's cold out there. The eight year old kid begins to feel
all these things when he moves out and stands on the road to catch
the bus going to Bayonne Institute. He has to walk to the back of
the bus and all that sort of thing—there's a little sign. So he sees
so much more than the six year old child can see. And in "Three
Men," there's a murder; one has committed a murder. So that
gets you into different experiences. When one takes a life, he's
different from any man who's never taken a life.

NOR: You leave Proctor with a difficult choice at the end. You
leave it ambiguous, whether or not he's able to do what he hopes
he will do.

Gaines: My men are always standing like they're waiting to go
through a door.

NOR: In a way, Proctor is facing the worst there is to face.
There's a sense of enormous pain that's going to come to him. At
the end of the story you're left with the fact that he's going to have
to go through so much that's brutal, and so alone, with only his own
integrity to maintain him. It's going to be total loneliness every day.

I feel that he really has the hardest road to hoe of all the characters in the book. Is that why that's the central story in the book, or is the book really assymetrical? Do you place a greater emphasis on "Bloodline" itself?

Gaines: Well I think in "Bloodline" you go beyond that. In all the other stories you're centered around my little area of Bayonne, you're on the False River, of the Pointe Coupee Parish area. In "Bloodline" you go beyond, you go farther. For example, Copper in "Bloodline" finds a long string of brown hair on the electric chair. So he knows damn well that not only my people are being brutalized; somebody else is being brutalized too. And this is the kind of thing that might have really snapped his mind. He could have fought the rest of his life, or maybe he could have been like Proctor, but then when they started putting white boys with brown hair in the goddamn chair, something else is happening in this world.

NOR: I thought that he was the kind of person that had just been touched by the casualties in Vietnam and that sort of thing. Everybody's death and pain bothered him; it's no longer racial.

Gaines: Yes, that's what he's going through, that's the point where Copper had reached.

NOR: When you get to the last story, "Just Like a Tree," do you try to draw a connective line with the other stories?

Gaines: Yes, I think that everything sort of came together at the end. All the characters' experiences, and the many points of view, and many side points, you know, like the little boy Chuckie would come in on the scene, and Emmanuel will come in, and the white gal from the big house comes in on the scene, the dude from up North moves in. And you progress in time.

NOR: There's really a great similarity between Aunt Fe and Jane Pittman, isn't there? I mean *Miss Jane Pittman*, in a sense, is the story of Aunt Fe's life.

Gaines: Why do you say things like that? You're much too sharp! The first version of *Miss Jane Pittman* was entitled "A Short Biography of Miss Jane Pittman." I had a group of people from a multiple point of view telling the story. And then I said, "Oh goddamn, this is too much like 'Just Like a Tree';" I've got the same characters telling the same thing. All I've done with Aunt Fe is that instead of her dying, I tell everything that happened before she

died. *Time* magazine picked up the same thing. They said it
seemed like a continuation of "Just Like a Tree."

NOR: And at the end, of course you run into the greatest
adventure of all, as Peter Pan says, death. Aunt Fe welcomes
death because she's not going to be pushed out of the way. In death,
in the last act, she has the final control over her own destiny and
her life. She's not going to be pushed around.

Gaines: My maternal grandmother died just two years ago last
April. She used to work at this plantation where I come from.
She was the cook at this place (unlike Dilsey, quite unlike Dilsey)
for about twenty, twenty-five years, she cooked at this plantation
house. My paternal grandfather was the yardman. He would be like
Felix, the guy who kept all the tools, did cleaning, and all this sort of
thing. And my grandmother died—all she talked about was the
South—and she was the greatest cook probably that ever lived. She
had mastered French Creole cooking. And she kept up her insurance, because she wanted to be buried here. When she died, there
were no arguments as far as I was concerned that Momma was
coming back to the place where we grew up. And there were
other people in the family who said "Well she's dead now, does it
matter?" But to me it mattered and to her it mattered. She never
did say "Send my body back home" or anything like that. We never
did talk about death like that, but we know. She'd say "I'd like to be
buried there" you know, but she never said "Send my body there."
She'd just say "I'd like to be buried home."

NOR: Did you get a lot of characteristics of Jane Pittman from
her?

Gaines: I've never really thought about it. She was very very
strong and about 80% white. She was sturdy. Maybe I got
something from her. No job was too hard, you know. And I think
that's a characteristic of Miss Jane, too.

NOR: Well, Miss Jane also has a lot in common with Aunt Fe.
You don't get it so much from Aunt Fe herself, but from the other
people that come and talk with her and sit with her on the porch.

Gaines: I'll tell you about that. I left the South when I was fifteen.
Until I was fifteen years old, a lady raised me who never walked
a day in her life. She crawled over the floor as a six month old child
might do. She had the strongest pair of arms. She could whip
hard. I had to go out and break the switch, bring it to her, kneel

down, and get my whipping. She cooked for us. In winter, she sat on a little bench beside the wood stove, where they cut the wood. "Bring the wood there, light the fire," she would say. And she would lean over her little bench and put the wood into this little stove. She could wash. She'd sit on this bench and lean over. We had these old wash boards—you know those old wash boards?—and she'd just wash, wash, wash, with an old bar of soap. There was no washing powder then. And our clothes: she also patched our clothes, sewed our clothes, she baked cakes and this sort of thing. But that was not even enough for her. She would, in the evening, when work was over, when she'd cook food and all that sort of thing, she'd crawl over the floor, over the porch out into the garden to work. It's that kind of spirit Miss Jane has. It's like Aunt Fe's strength.

NOR: I have another question. Throughout the first four stories of *Bloodline* at least there's a religious element. There's the preacher in the first story who is completely ineffectual in helping the man get his wife back. And then there's the priest in the second story who says "You've got to say Catholic prayers before God will hear you," and that's ineffectual also. And then in the third story . . .

Gaines: Oh yes, and in "Bloodline" it's the same thing that I'm doing in the new book now. Copper says something like "God only serves those people who created him," or something like that.

NOR: That's right, "God serves the people who made him." But also in that second story, there's a fight between the atheist and the preacher, where the preacher of Christian love gets up and strikes the boy in the face. Anyway, I'm wondering what your personal religious beliefs are.

Gaines: I was indoctrinated into the Baptist religion when I was quite young, and at the same time I was going to a Catholic school. I went to Catholic school for about three years while I was in Louisiana, and by the time I started writing I figured that any religion or none at all were equal to just about the same thing. Not any of them are gonna really cure things, or solve all the problems.

NOR: So, in your stories, are you saying that religions do not change the human situation? Is that what each of these scenes seems to say?

Gaines: Well I don't think religions solve anything. It's good to

believe, because I think people must believe in religion. For you
to survive you must have something greater than what you are,
whether it's religion or communism, or capitalism or something
else, but it must be something above what you are. But as of right
now, I don't think orthodox religion has solved anybody's problems. Even in *Miss Jane Pittman*, you know, Miss Jane would
prefer listening to the Dodgers play the Giants on Sunday. She's
religious, but she can catch up with that next Sunday.

NOR: She's not awed by religion.

Gaines: No. She's comfortable and she can do without it one
Sunday for a baseball game.

NOR: You went through creative writing courses. How valuable
do you think college creative writing programs are to beginning
writers?

Gaines: Well, I found it helpful that there were other kids there
writing. I had just come out of the army and I enrolled in San
Francisco State College. I had finished two years of Junior College
in Vallejo, California, and I found others who had the same kind
of problems I had. They teach you to read other writers, published
writers, like Hemingway, Faulkner, O'Connor, Joyce. And then
they would read our work and they would show us exactly where
we were lacking or where we could be helped. It was good to talk
to others about writing, but I found that I did not follow them too
much. When I first started out writing—taking writing courses—the
hippie thing was going strong in San Francisco—I had nothing to do
with that crowd. I didn't run to the North Beach, drink wine, sit
on the floor and talk about writing. I didn't do that sort of thing.
The thing that I found helped my writing was that people took an
interest in me very early. They singled me out and gave me a lot of
help. I was the only black in the class. There must have been
about twenty to twenty-five people, and I was the only black. They
were very encouraging. And then when I went to Stanford I had
money and time to work, and I think after a writer has started out,
the most important thing is that he has time to work, and someone to
pick up a piece of work and say I think you should do something
here or something there. Another important thing is reading.
Instead of reading Mickey Spillane, read Hemingway, instead of
reading Jacqueline Susann's *Love Machine*, read *Gatsby*, instead of

reading a short story by somebody else, read Chekhov, or de Maupassant. Things like this they tell you to do. They say, "read this" and it may be something you haven't heard of. If someone outside told the same thing, you wouldn't need to go to the classroom.

NOR: So the things you found most helpful were the reading of some good writers and careful comments on your work.

Gaines: Yes, direction in good writing, the reading of good writers, the time to work, and someone to encourage you. A prof would come by and tell you, hey, that was a good story! Now, that's the greatest thing in the world that can happen. Of course, nobody generally does that until you begin to publish and get some recognition. After I'd gotten some recognition, I got several monetary awards: Guggenheim, Rockefeller, and others. But the teacher, if he's sensitive, if he cares, can be extremely valuable to the student.

NOR: Would you agree with Ring Lardner that there's no way to turn a born druggist into a writer?

Gaines: I would agree that there's no way to teach a writing class to someone who's not interested in writing. To help him at all, I think it would be necessary that he's been writing.

NOR: Did you publish anything that you wrote during the time you were in writing classes?

Gaines: Oh, yes. I wrote two short stories at San Francisco State and they were published in a little magazine called *Transfer* or something. In fact, I had my first story published in *Transfer*. They were just organized in 1956 and I had the first story published in the magazine. I think I still have a copy at home; I don't have a copy of my second story.

NOR: What is your first story called?

Gaines: It's the introduction to manhood sort of thing. It's called "The Turtles." My prof at the time thought "The Voice of the Turtles" would be good.

NOR: When did you start writing?

Gaines: I probably started writing about 1950, maybe a little earlier. My stepfather told me to get off the streets, so I ended up in the libraries. I started writing probably around '49.

NOR: You were only about 16?

Gaines: Sixteen years, yes. But I started writing daily in 1957.
That's when I graduated from college.

NOR: Do you remember having a dream about being a writer?
Had you always wanted to be a writer?

Gaines: Well, I can go back to when I was 13 or 14, and remember
that I put on little plays and all. I put them on in this church, and
I had to rewrite everything. Not only did I have to rewrite, but I
had to be the director. I had something like a little mock-wedding
going on. My back was toward the audience and the people who
were getting married—and the best man and all—faced the audience. I had my script over the Bible, and I would read my part,
because I never learned the damned part. So that's the way I
started trying to write from the time I was about 13 years old.

NOR: You have written "an autobiography" of Jane Pittman;
have you ever thought of writing an autobiography of yourself?

Gaines: Oh no, no. I'll never do that. I hope I never do that.

NOR: Are you political at all?

Gaines: No. I don't think I am. Oh I vote, I think I'm going to
vote for McGovern. There's no point in not voting.

NOR: When you get together with other writers, do you talk
about writing?

Gaines: I don't really get together with writers too much. I have
some good friends, I have one good friend, Jim McPherson who
wrote *Hue and Cry*, a collection of stories. He's in Berkeley. I used
to see Jim about once a month, and we'd talk about writing.

NOR: Do you know Al Young?

Gaines: I know Al, yes. He's over at Stanford. I think I've seen
Al twice since he's been at Stanford.

NOR: We haven't talked about *Catherine Carmier* yet.

Gaines: Well, that's a romantic thing. A guy from the north comes
back and he sees this beautiful girl. They used to be childhood
sweethearts, well, not sweethearts, but they knew each other, they
probably loved each other secretly, and then all of a sudden they see
each other again; and it's like . . .

NOR: *Romeo and Juliet*?

Gaines: Yes. As a matter of fact it was published in England and
they called it a black Romeo and Juliet.

NOR: Do you read many magazines and books?

Gaines: I read very few magazines. I read the classics; I read Faulkner, I read Hemingway, I read maybe a little bit of the Bible, I was reading Gorki just recently, Tolstoy, Chekhov.

NOR: You barely mentioned Henry James. You do not like him at all?

Gaines: Oh, yes. What I was saying earlier was that a lot of the black kids whom I've been around feel that this is the kind of language they must write in, and I think when I started writing I tried to write like James.

NOR: Is there anything else that you would like to say to your audience?

Gaines: (Laughter) No.

A Conversation with
Ernest Gaines

Ruth Laney / 1973

From the *Southern Review* 10.1 (1974): 1–14. Used by permission.

I interviewed Ernest Gaines when he was in Baton Rouge to help scout locations for the filming of *The Autobiography of Miss Jane Pittman*, which will be seen on CBS television early in 1974. He seems to be that rarity, a genuinely modest man who wonders why people would want to read about him. Gaines was born on a plantation near New Roads, Louisiana; at sixteen he boarded a Trailways bus bound for San Francisco, where he still lives. He has published three novels: *Catherine Carmier* (1964), the first draft of which he wrote at fifteen; *Of Love and Dust* (1967), which James Baldwin called "a really fine and truthful study of the black-white madness"; and *The Autobiography of Miss Jane Pittman* (1971), which describes a 110-year-old woman's journey from slavery to the black militancy of the sixties. *Bloodline*, a much acclaimed collection of short stories, appeared in 1968. Gaines is now completing his fourth novel, *In My Father's House*.

In conversation, Ernest Gaines's simplicity and humanity shine steadily; he considers his words carefully, and beside him more facile talkers sound shallow. It is this quality—his essential human-ness—which I hope is conveyed here.

Laney: Your moving introduction to *The Autobiography of Miss Jane Pittman* reads in part, "to the memory of my beloved aunt, Miss Augusteen Jefferson, who did not walk a day in her life but who taught me the importance of standing." Could you tell me something about her?

Gaines: She was my great-aunt, and she never walked a day in her life. She'd crawl over the floor as a child six or seven months might crawl over the floor. But her arms were very strong. She'd cook for us—we'd bring the things to the stove for her and set it on a little table in front of her, and she'd mix the things up. She could make bread, bake our bread—we had the old wood stoves then.

She could wash our clothes: she sat on a bench and leaned over the tub and used the washboard, you know those old tin things. She could sew our clothes. She used to use the sewing machine. She could not use her feet, but she could use her hands—how she ever did this I really don't know. You know those old things with the pedal down here—she would reach down and do this with her hands, because there was no other way to run it. It was one of these old machines, probably one of the oldest ones. I wish I knew where it was today—if I could find it, I'd keep it forever. Besides that, she used to go into the little garden to work among her vegetables. She'd crawl over the floor, out of the house, down the steps into the yard, into the garden. Other times, she would crawl into our back yard to pick up pecans.

Laney: She must have been a courageous woman.

Gaines: Well, this is the kind of courage that I tried to give Miss Jane in the book. Many of my characters have tremendous courage and I think it is basically because of her. She never felt sorry for herself a day in her life. I never heard her complaining about her problems. And as a result nobody felt sorry for her.

Laney: When you were growing up in Louisiana did you ever think about writing?

Gaines: Oh, yes. When I was about twelve or thirteen, I put on a little play in church, and I'd act as writer and director and make-up man and everything else. It was really a lot of fun doing. Miss Jane talks about Jimmy doing that once, he puts on this play and everybody laughs. She talks about that just after he gets religion. They want him to be a minister or something, and he doesn't want to, but he puts on this play and entertains everybody for one night. That happened, I did that.

Laney: Did you go through the experience of "getting religion" as Jimmy does in *Miss Jane Pittman*?

Gaines: Yes, I went through all that. You've seen these baptisms, haven't you, where you have to go through all of that before you get dumped in the water? It was in False River, I was baptized in False River. I think now they might use a lake or something; some of them are such high-class they have the things in churches now, you know. But mine was in the river. I was about twelve.

Laney: Were you reading many books at this time in your life?

Gaines: No, I was not reading. I doubt that I read two novels before I went to California. But I come from a long line of storytellers. I come from a plantation, where people told stories by the fireplace at night, people told stories on the ditch bank— especially this time of year, when you have the sugar cane shuck that you can burn, mix it with some firewood. People sat around telling stories. I think in my immediate family there were tremendous storytellers or liars or whatever you want to call them. My aunt was not a storyteller, she was more of a recorder; she could tell about what happened in the past. She remembered quite well. Since Auntie could not go to their place, the old people used to come to ours. They would talk and talk and talk, and I listened to them. *Miss Jane Pittman*, before it became an autobiography of Miss Jane Pittman, was a short biography of Miss Jane Pittman— that is, a group of people telling about her. Because originally she had just died and they'd come together at someone's house, much like my aunt's. They would do the same thing now. Say there was a funeral today, or a wedding, the old people would sort of gather in a little room and they would talk about things, you know. They might start with the wedding, or they might start with that particular funeral, but by the time they end up, they've talked about everything that happened the last twenty years.

Laney: You moved to California when you were fifteen. How did that come about?

Gaines: My stepfather was in the Merchant Marine, and my mother followed him to California. I had finished the little eighth grade school, and I did not have any high school that they wanted to send me to nearby. I did not have close enough relatives in the town with whom I could stay. So I went to California. I flagged down a Trailways bus. You know, you take out your handkerchief and stand on the river and wave it down and get on it. I went as far as New Orleans by bus and caught a train out of New Orleans and went on to a place called Crockett, California, just across the Bay from Vallejo. That's where we were living at the time, Vallejo—it's about thirty miles out of San Francisco. We lived in the projects, a government project, and I had a lot of friends there. There was a mixture in the projects at that time of whites, blacks, Chicanos, Filipinos, Japanese, Chinese. So things were okay for a while. But

then we moved from there to downtown Vallejo and I got caught up
with some pretty rough guys. And my stepfather told me, none of
that. These guys would go into movies without paying, or pick up
comic books, or just stand on the corner and make noise—as any
boys would do. But my stepfather didn't want me to be part of it.
He was a very strict person with me. Very strong. A very
handsome man, a big man. Most of my strong characters, I think,
are built around him. When I first left here, I was lonely for my
friends, my family. Then my stepfather in Vallejo told me to get off
the block, get off the street, you know, and do something else. I
went into the library in Vallejo and started reading—I read a lot.
But I wanted to read about the South, and I wanted to read about the
rural South. But at that time you had very few people writing
anything that was in any way complimentary about blacks or the
rural South. So I decided to write a novel myself. I wrote it in one
summer, the summer I was sixteen. (Laughs) It was probably the
worst novel, the worst number of pages that anyone could possibly
call a novel. I'm sure it was. I sent it to a publisher in New York
and they sent it right back. I knew nothing though. I had not read
anything, I had not had any kind of help or any kind of direction
toward the proper way of reading. I had nothing like that.

    Laney: Did you talk to anyone about it?

    Gaines: Oh, I think my mother, or my stepfather when he'd come
in from the sea. But he thought I was crazy because I was
spending like twelve, thirteen, maybe fifteen hours a day doing that.
I first wrote the whole thing out in longhand, then I got a
typewriter—one finger here, one finger there. At any rate, I went
through high school and then junior college, and then I did not
have a penny in the world to finish college. Junior college was free
if you lived in the town—Vallejo—but it was not top education, just
an extension of high school, really. Then I was drafted and spent
two years in the army. When I came out, I got the G.I. bill, $110 a
month. I finished college in that way. And that's when I really got
into studying writing. When I came out of the army, I moved to
San Francisco and went to San Francisco State, and graduated in
two years. And I worked a year after that. And then I got a
fellowship to Stanford, and that's about the education I've had.

    Laney: The fellowship was the Wallace Stegner award?

Gaines: Yes. I was at State from '55 to '57, and I wrote some stories while I was at San Francisco State College which were published in the college magazine. I had heard about the creative writing fellowship at Stanford, so when I got out in '57 I went to work for one year. While I was working, I submitted the two stories that I had written at State, plus another one. I think you had to submit three stories or part of a novel, something like that. So I wrote another story and submitted those three stories to Stanford and I heard that I'd won a fellowship.

Laney: You mentioned at the lecture you gave yesterday that you had based your first novel, *Catherine Carmier*, on *Fathers and Sons*. When did you discover Turgenev?

Gaines: I discovered Turgenev at State. I mentioned that I had been trying to find books about the South. Then I began to read anybody who would write about the earth—Steinbeck, Willa Cather. For some reason, reading these writers led me into discovering the writers of other countries who wrote about the same sort of thing. I think in this way I discovered Turgenev's *A Sportsman's Sketches*. That was about hunting and meeting people in rural life. And then, the clarity and the beauty of his writing, even in translation. Then I discovered *Fathers and Sons*. It was a simple, small book—I know I could never write a big book. And this small book had just about everything that a small book can have. And, too, at the time I discovered Turgenev I could almost see myself in Bazarov's position, you know? When you go back, what? Not that I'd become a nihilist, but I could understand the nihilistic attitude after someone had been away awhile. But I think the major thing I liked about him was the structure of his small novels. My *Catherine Carmier* is almost written on the structure of *Fathers and Sons*. As a matter of fact, that was my Bible. I used it on my desk every day. It was the same novel I had written when I was sixteen in the library that summer. I started writing it again when I was at Stanford. This time it took me five years because I did not know how to really write.

Laney: Did you ever have times during this period when you felt you'd never be any good at all, you might as well give up?

Gaines: Yes, yes. But then I'd feel, I can't do anything else, I don't want to do anything else with my life. I mean, right now I

don't know what I would do—I'd probably be teaching. And I
would hate to teach because I couldn't do anything else. If I were
to teach, I'd want to teach simply because this is what I want more
than anything else, you know? When I graduated from State in
'57, I gave myself ten years. I said, in ten years I must be a writer
or I don't know what else I'll do with my life. I didn't know what
I'd do—become a farmer? *Catherine Carmier* was published seven
years after I made this decision, it was published in '64, but
nobody ever heard of the book, nobody ever read it. But exactly
ten years later, in '67, I published *Of Love and Dust*, which was
rather successful; it began to get some notice. And during that time
I published three stories, "A Long Day in November," "Just
Like a Tree," and "The Sky is Gray." I had published these stories
by the time my second novel came out. Then I published the
collection of stories, *Bloodline*. I always knew my stories were
better than anything else I had written. When *Of Love and Dust*
was published I told the publishing house, give me a two-book
contract because these stories are going to make it for me. They
might not make money, but they will make my name. So they gave
me a two-book contract. And they have been successful. "The
Sky is Gray" has been anthologized twelve to fifteen times.

Laney: Could you tell me about the technical aspect of your
writing?

Gaines: Well, I get up every day to work, to write. I try to get to
work by nine, and I try to get in four good hours. I usually write
longhand a couple of times, then I'll type fast, then I'll clean-
up type.

Laney: Do you ever start thinking a lot about a character and let
a story evolve from the character?

Gaines: Not really. *The Autobiography of Miss Jane Pittman* was
supposed to be just a series of conversations after Miss Jane has
died. But those conversations would have had a wide range of many
subjects, and Miss Jane would have been just part of it, to give it
some kind of order. The book was not begun as a book about just a
single person, a character. But the events around her life and her
interpretation of them is what I wanted—a folk autobiography.

Laney: I'm interested in how you feel about the character Tee

Bob in the *Autobiography*, as the white man who falls in love with a black woman.

Gaines: I've always considered Tee Bob as being one of the men in Miss Jane's life. Whenever they talk about the men in her life, they would mention Ned, of course, Joe Pittman, and Jimmy—the three. And very seldom did they mention Tee Bob, but I think Tee Bob is very, very important as one of the men in her life. I'm very sympathetic toward Tee Bob, as that innocent person caught up in something he has no control over. His problem and Mary Agnes Le Fabre's problem are no worse than, say, Miss Jane's problem and the old man—what's his name, Tee Bob's parrain—Jules Raynard—in that, I'm pretty sure if Miss Jane were white, she and Jules Raynard would be much closer than just two older people who sat back in the kitchen. They might live together, you know, they might be—not lovers, but people so close that they would depend on each other all their lives. Tee Bob was a victim. He had no strength, he was not tough and hard. He loved, you know, but hell, you just can't make it on love. You got to be able to do other things.

Laney: I noticed that Miss Jane Pittman has been compared to Dilsey. There is a famous quotation from Faulkner's Nobel Prize speech to the effect, "I believe that man will not only endure, he will prevail." Dilsey is considered the character who endures. Miss Jane endures, living to be 110, living through so many things. At the end she seems to prevail—her courage, her refusal to back down at that point. Do you share that affirmative view—of man prevailing?

Gaines: I don't really know that I do. I think, in Miss Jane's case, yes. But in the book I'm working on now, I don't know. Because he has his doubts about himself. He's a minister—he has his doubts—he runs into situations that make him doubt whether or not he will survive.

Laney: Does this reflect any change in your own views?

Gaines: Oh, no, no, no. Not at all. I think that, as I said before, when I first started writing, one of the things that impressed me most about *Fathers and Sons* was Bazarov's feeling toward things. But I think I'm a mixture of all these things. I cannot write only about man failing. I write about both. I try to write about both of them. I don't know exactly what my philosophy is. My only philosophy is to write truly, as well as I can, for as long as I can, and about things that I care about. And of course I care about people, their failures, and their accomplishments. My philosophy, in a way, is that you must stand individually in order to stand with the crowd. Or in order to be able to lead, you must be an individual. I like Miss Jane because she's small, she has fantastic courage, and she is an individual. She's not orthodox religious at all—she'd rather listen to a baseball game any day. Well, she'd go to church, but not when the Giants are playing the Dodgers, you know. She isn't going to church; she'll stay home and listen. But I can understand the guys who fail and the guys who doubt. But there's no change in philosophy, no change in philosophy at all.

Laney: Could you tell me a little about your new book?

Gaines: I don't like talking about anything that I'm working on. But it's called *In My Father's House*. The old proverbial battle between father and son. A theme I play around with in almost everything I write. In the case of the black man, he and his son were separated in slavery and they have been trying to reach each other since then. That is the central theme in this particular book. It's a novel, and it takes place in Louisiana. Everything—all of my work—takes place in Louisiana.

Laney: Have you ever written any nonfiction?

Gaines: No, no. I write little talks, now and then, to give to a class. I don't have that talent and, as of right now, I don't have the interest in that sort of thing. As long as I can make it in fiction, as long as there's something that I feel is truly worthwhile to write about, as long as I feel that what I'm doing is honest work, I'm more concerned with fiction, the novel, and the short story.

Laney: Many people tend to look up to artists as having some kind of inside track on things. Do you have any sort of precept or code that you try to live by?

Gaines: I keep writing these codes down, but I keep forgetting them. People are always asking me these things, and I keep forgetting. I just try to live well, I want to write and write honestly, as I've said. I want to be a man toward my family, toward my woman, toward my friends. I wish I could help some other children, black or white, become writers—and better writers than myself.

Laney: What would you tell someone who came to you and said, I want to write?

Gaines: Well, first I'd tell him to do a lot of reading, a lot of reading and a lot of writing. And I'd try to prepare him in that I'd tell him that it's a very lonely job, terribly lonely job, he has to sacrifice much. If he's poor, he's gonna have much, much to sacrifice, and be hungry a long time. But if he really wants to write, there's nothing in the world I feel would be greater for him than to write. If that's what he wants. But I'll try to show him what he has to face. But the number one thing I'd tell him is to read as much as he can and especially read the classic things, the things that have stood so long. Those are things you must read. But then, you tell him, read other things, too, much of other things—everything.

Laney: What books have greatly influenced you?

Gaines: I would say Faulkner's *The Sound and the Fury*, maybe *As I Lay Dying*, not quite as much, but some. Then you get into the Hemingway thing—I'd say, maybe the stories much more than any one particular novel. Of course, Turgenev's *Fathers and Sons*. Twain's work, especially *Huck Finn*. Chekhov's stories, de Maupassant's stories. Flaubert, *Madame Bovary*. Tolstoy. Shakespeare. Cervantes' *Don Quixote*. Gogol's *Overcoat* and *Dead Souls*. These are a few. Joyce's *Dubliners*, Joyce's *Ulysses*. Fitzgerald's *Gatsby*. *All Quiet on the Western Front* by Remarque. *Red Badge of Courage*. And I could give you a reason why I would choose each one of these, but that's not necessary.

Laney: What about your contemporaries? Is there anyone writing now whom you particularly admire?

Gaines: I have a good friend whose work I admire very much. His name is James McPherson and he wrote the collection of stories called *Hue and Cry*. I think he's a fantastic writer. I know he was, and I think he is now, a contributing editor to *Atlantic Monthly*. He's a person whom Ralph Ellison likes very much and I do too.

Laney: Do you like Ellison's work?

Gaines: Oh, yes, yes, definitely. But I don't consider him my contemporary. I think he's just a little bit older.

Laney: What about Baldwin?

Gaines: I like Baldwin. I like his essays, especially, much more than I do his novels. I think his first novel is much better than any

of the others, but his essays, I think, are his best. Just as I like
Ellison's novel *Invisible Man*, but the collection of his essays, I
think—*Shadows and Acts*—is a fantastic thing. He articulates so
much like I wish I could in that form of writing, which I can't. When
you asked me would I consider writing nonfiction stuff, I can't
because others can do that so much better than I can. When I'm
dealing with my Louisiana dialect, I think I'm on the same par with
the other guys. Dealing with my backyard, you know.

Laney: Do you ever resent being lumped in a class with other
black writers?

Gaines: Oh, no, no. I never take them seriously. They put me
where they want. I know *Time* magazine and a couple of others
have said that Ernie Gaines is the best, quote, black writer, unquote,
in this country today. But that doesn't mean a thing in the world
to me. Even if they said I was the best writer in this country today,
it wouldn't mean anything. It wouldn't mean anything if everyone
said it. I don't know who the top critic is in the country today, but
if he said, "You're the best writer there is," it wouldn't mean
anything to me. It would mean just that I gotta work harder the next
day to maintain that top thing, which I don't believe in doing. I
believe in doing my work as well as I can do it. Now, you can say
I'm the worst writer. I think I feel good when people—just the
average person—say, "I love that." I was down by the Parlanges',
who own probably the oldest house in Louisiana, the house is
over two hundred years old. On False River. I was there just
yesterday. And Mr. Walter Parlange, Jr., who owns the place now, he
and I were talking in the living room—one of the front rooms—and
he was saying that—we're so proud that you come from this kind
of background, and what you've done. And he said, I read that
book, and Lucy, his wife, had read it. No, I think he said he read
half and Lucy read half—and they talked about it. And he says, I
really love that book. And I had met his mother when I was there
at the place about a week earlier, and she had read it and she loved
it. Now, for people like that to say this to me means so much. Or for
people who don't read much, say like many of my people, to say I
read that and I liked it. That's what does make me feel much
better. I mean, of course, you want the New York critics to say,

this is it, you are that good. But if they say it, and your family and
your friends say that it isn't anything—that hurts, that hurts.

Laney: What writers are you most frequently compared to?

Gaines: Oh, everybody sees the Faulknerian influence, and the
Hemingway influence in my earlier stuff, especially *Of Love and Dust.*
Or the very early Erskine Caldwell, somebody said. A lot of people
notice the Faulknerian influence. I definitely have been influenced
by Faulkner, I read much of his stuff. He has made me listen to
dialects over again. I find that so many of my contemporary black
writers probably don't listen well to dialects around them. They use
whatever the other writer has used. Whereas the dialects from
the part of the country I come from are distinct from, say, the
northern big-city ghetto dialect—unless those people come from
that particular area that I came from. So reading Faulkner just
makes me pay more attention to dialect, to dialogue. Originally, I
even had it broader than it is in the book, but then you have to
make it readable, you know, you just cannot stick too totally to the
way people talk. Because if you stuck to the way people talk along
where I come from, I don't know who could read it. I couldn't
read it, if I wrote it exactly like that.

Laney: How politically involved do you think a writer should be?

Gaines: Well, it depends on the writer, whoever he is. I'm very
objective in these things—I don't know if that's the right word. I
can be quite involved, but I'm not really totally involved in politics.
But I can get quite moved by these things. There are certain
governors and senators and a few other people I think should be
shot tomorrow morning. But when it comes down to writing, I
feel that it has to work into a form of art. Now, if you can go out
and shoot everybody and make it a form of art, it's okay with me.
But I think I have a lot of protest in, for example, the story "Just
Like a Tree." After all, a woman dies because she is moved out
of her home. It's nothing more than that. But she's uprooted. The
bombings going on—well, you could go into a long, long dialogue
about things like that. But I think one gets the message, one gets
the feeling from it. And if I cannot move you by dramatizing a
situation like that, then I'm not going to try to move you by all the
rhetoric in the world. I just am not that kind of person.

Laney: Do you feel, as a writer who does have influence, that you

have a certain responsibility as far as ever taking a stand or using
that influence to some social purpose?

Gaines: Well, people have been trying to make me do it, but I
never thought about doing it. I feel that I'm going to write and write
well, and I think if I write well and truly about, you know, the
human condition, I think I'll leave the politicking to someone
else. I'll say yes to certain things, and no to certain things, but as
far as my writing, I'm gonna write what I want to write. But there
are some magazines that, because I don't take their particular
stand, ignore me.

Laney: Do you think you'll ever come back to Louisiana to live?

Gaines: If I did, it could not be before, say, ten years from now,
simply because I don't know how I would react to a given
situation. I don't know whether I would explode and hurt someone,
or get hurt myself. I suppose you know what I'm talking about. I was
talking to a lady just yesterday down where I come from, the
plantation where I come from, and she asked me, "How in the
world can you leave God's country like this? What in the world are
you doing in San Francisco?" And I said, "Well, I'm writing about
Louisiana." She said, "Why in the world don't you come here and
write about Louisiana?" But the distance, I think, is definitely an
advantage. But it's necessary, at the same time, to be able to come
here, which I do every year. I come here; I usually come at Mardi
Gras and spend about two or three weeks then. Go down to New
Orleans for Mardi Gras and travel all over this part of the state.
I've never really settled down in San Francisco, to say to myself,
this is definitely going to be my home. Because I live in a small
apartment and never thought of buying a home in San Francisco or
anywhere. And if not in San Francisco, nowhere else in California, I suppose, I'd want to live. I mean, permanently, you know, as
saying to myself, okay, this is going to be it, this is where I'll be
buried, and all that sort of thing. Whenever I think about my death
or anything like that, I just hope that the place where I was born and
raised, that I can still be buried there. But I'm pretty sure that there
were many other writers, like Turgenev and Joyce, who thought
about their homes and could only write about their homes, but
could never live there again. I suppose I'm in that same sort
of situation.

Laney: What is the thing in your life that you're proudest of?

Gaines: Being able to work, do my work—that I'm proud of. I think one of the greatest things that has happened to me, as a writer and as a human being, is that I was born in the South, that I was born in Louisiana. Because when I grew up on a plantation in the late thirties and the forties, I'm pretty sure it was not too much different from the way things could have been when my ancestors were in slavery. Oh, we could do a few little things more. But that I went through that kind of experience—there's a direct connection between the past and what is happening today. I'm very fortunate to have had that kind of background. I think that Louisiana's probably the most romantic and interesting of all southern states—the land, the language, the colors, the bayous, the fields—all these things together, the combination of all these things, I think, make it an extremely interesting place. If I were to come from any southern state, I think Louisiana is the one that I would choose. And I'm glad I came from here. I'm glad I came from here.

He Must Return to the South

Margaret R. Knight / 1974

From the *Baton Rouge Sunday Advocate* 7 April 1974: 3F. Used by permission.

"I have to come back to the South again. I can write in San Francisco, but I could not stay in San Francisco and write without coming to Baton Rouge. I must go back to the plantation where I was born and raised. I have to touch, I have to be, you melt into things and you let them melt into you . . . the trees, the rivers, the bayous, the language, the sounds."

Ernest J. Gaines, author of the overwhelmingly popular *The Autobiography of Miss Jane Pittman,* pauses in his reflections on his early childhood in New Roads.

"I had no choice as to where I would be born, but since I was born in the South, Louisiana is the greatest place I think any artist could be born because of its romantic history. I think coming from the South, I have experiences that maybe blacks or whites of any other race or nationality would not have if you were born and raised up in the Midwest. I think I'm closer to the earth, I'm closer to nature, I'm closer to the different attitudes 'both good and bad'."

Gaines' early childhood was spent surrounded by people who could have walked from the pages of his novels. On the plantation were grown sugar cane, corn, potatoes and cotton. At the age of eight, he went to the fields to pick cotton for fifty cents a day.

"I felt that people treated me as someone who was very smart," remembers Gaines. "I knew I was doing things that other kids were not doing at that age. I wrote letters for people and I'd read papers for the older people when I was a child. So, I did the things that a kid like Jimmy in the book did when I was a youngster."

Leaving Louisiana at age 15, Gaines moved to California near San Francisco. Homesick and missing his brothers and sisters, he started hanging around the streets. His stepfather advised him he

would have to find something better than that to do, so Gaines
went to the library.

"I read constantly, especially Southern fiction." Gaines continues, "I didn't see my people depicted in fiction as I knew them to be
in the South. I decided then and there I would become a writer. At
16, I wrote my first novel and it was awful. It was rejected by
publishers, as have many other later works of mine."

Entering the Army, Gaines served on Guam. After discharge, he
entered San Francisco State College, received his degree in 1957
and his graduate degree from Stanford University.

Seventeen years of daily writing for Gaines has resulted in five
published books, among them a children's book, *A Long Day in
November*. Gaines' favorite is a collection of short stories,
Bloodline.

In starting to write his most famous novel, Gaines decided on a
series of conversations and having a central life, Miss Jane
Pittman, to sort of connect everything together.

How does one go about breathing life into a character, and is it
all plotted before pen meets paper? Gaines has his own method.

"When I started *The Autobiography of Miss Jane Pittman,* I
knew that she would be a young kid, and I knew she would be
moving away from that original plantation.

"I knew that because I had read Booker T. Washington and I
knew the three things that motivated the ex-slaves at that time
after the war was changing of names, movement—even if they
moved away from the original plantation and were coming back
to it—and learning to read something.

"I did not know what the little girl, the little boy, the people they
would meet on the road might say or do. When I started out, I
knew nothing about the hunter or the people they would meet
coming back into the South, back to their original plantations, such
as the woman serving water over the fence.

"When I started the first chapter, I did not know these things,
but as I went along, I read enough to know what could have
happened at that time. I was reading at times, and I would see
things like that which would flash into my mind, and, of course,
the mind then would begin to move, move, move."

Gaines readily admits that writing is very hard, lonely work, but the thing he'd rather do than anything else in the world. He confesses, "I fall out of bed, throw some water on my face, drink two or three cups of black coffee, go to my little table in the hall and start writing. I don't sit there waiting for trumpets to sound and rockets to blast. I get up to write."

Spurning the typewriter till later, Gaines first brings his characters to life in longhand, where he can "think and strike out" faster. He re-writes countless times before the finished story satisfies him.

These finished stories, running the gamut of social problems, politics, human experience and conflict between young and old, have placed Gaines in the forefront of important American writers today.

"I hope when I die," Gaines chuckles, "they won't put on my tombstone, 'He wrote *Miss Jane Pittman.*' Put anything else, but don't put just that."

How would this Louisiana author like to be remembered?

"I want to be remembered as a guy who tried to write as well as he could and tried to be fair. Fair toward my characters and fair to other people. I just want to write as well as I can about the people I know."

The Other 300 Years: A Conversation with Ernest J. Gaines, Author of *The Autobiography of Miss Jane Pittman*

Jerome Tarshis / 1974

From *San Francisco Magazine* June 1974: 26–28.

On May 28, when the National Academy of Television Arts and Sciences announced this year's Emmy awards, one program led all the rest: *The Autobiography of Miss Jane Pittman,* a film made for the CBS television network. It had starred Cicely Tyson, who won an Emmy; the director, the scriptwriter, and the composer of the music also won Emmys. Hardly mentioned in the publicity was Ernest J. Gaines, the author of the novel on which the film was based, and one of San Francisco's best writers.

The Autobiography of Miss Jane Pittman is the story of a 110-year-old black woman, born into slavery in Louisiana, who witnesses the ordinary lives of ordinary black people from immediately before the Emancipation Proclamation, in 1863, to a civil rights demonstration in 1962. According to its introduction, the book has resulted from tape-recorded interviews with Miss Jane. At first she had been unwilling to talk, and her friends ask the interviewer, a young black school teacher, why he needs the material.

"What's wrong with them books you already got?" someone asks.

"Miss Jane is not in them," says the young teacher.

And that, neatly put, is the story of Ernest Gaines and his life as a writer. Gaines has been torn between two worlds. He was born in 1933 on a plantation in Louisiana, not far from Baton Rouge. According to a biographical note in one of his books, he remembers working in the fields at the age of nine, for fifty cents a day.

After the war his mother and stepfather moved to Northern

California, and about a year later, when he was fifteen, he
followed them. He went to junior high school and high school and
junior college in Vallejo, and after two years in the Army, studied
writing at San Francisco State College and at Stanford, where he
held a Wallace Stegner Creative Writing Fellowship. He has won
the Joseph Henry Jackson Literary Prize. In these terms he is a
Northern California success story.

And yet, although he has lived here for 25 years, his only subject
is black life in the rural South; specifically, in the part of Louisiana where he grew up, and where his brothers and aunts and uncles
still live. "That I still write about Louisiana is proof that I have
not found complete roots here," he told me, "and yet I go to
Louisiana once or twice a year, but I must come back here."

His first novel, *Catherine Carmier,* was about a young black man
who returns to his home in Louisiana after having been educated
in California. He finds that he can no longer live in the rural South,
but also that he cannot feel truly at home in Northern California;
it isn't Louisiana, but it isn't the Promised Land, either. The title
character is a young woman of mixed blood whose father will not
allow her—or himself—to fraternize with either whites or blacks.

Gaines himself is caught in a comparable set of conflicting im-
pulses. I met him at a wine-and-cheese party at a bookstore on Union
Street, where a group of nice and literary people had gathered to
honor Leon D. Adams, author of *The Wines of America.* Gaines
bought a copy of the book, and the author signed it.

I had known and admired his writing for several years, and had
been hoping to talk with him, for a book of my own, so I arranged
to visit him at his apartment, which is on Divisadero Street, in a
largely black neighborhood; he lives a very long distance from
Union Street.

As I might have known, Ernest Gaines looks back. He went to
predominantly white colleges in the 1950s, when Hemingway and
Faulkner were enormously admired in creative writing classes, and
he has not been carried away by the furies of the 1960s, in dress
or demeanor or prose style. On the walls of his work room are
portraits of Faulkner and Hemingway, and moving and even beautiful

photographs he has taken himself, of the buildings and the Louisiana countryside he grew up in.

The job he has set himself as a writer is, as I say, precisely to look back. I told him I thought he had written *The Autobiography of Miss Jane Pittman* at least partly so that Miss Jane's experiences, and her perceptions of the truth, would not disappear. "Is that a fair reading of your intention?" I asked.

"I suppose it is," he said. "I wish I didn't have to write it; I wish no one had to write it, because I think telling a story and talking is so much better. It's too bad that we don't have tapes of those older people talking, so we could listen to this without ever having to read it. That *is* one of my aims—for them, in their folk way, to tell what happened.

"Much of our history has not been told; our problems have been told, as if we have no history. So much of our literature deals with the big-city ghettos, and we existed long before we came to the big city. We came to this country as slaves, primarily to till the land.

"Much of this has not been written about sympathetically. Many of your white writers have written about black field workers who were clowns; they had strong backs, and they could pick a lot of cotton, and they could sing and be happy, but they did not have brains.

"Most of your black writers who have left the South have ignored the black peasantry, the people who work the land, as though they want to forget that completely. I think too many of our black intellectuals who have left the South put down those experiences, do not think those experiences are worth writing about. There's too much hurt to go back and do it.

"There *is* hurt, but I think there's much beauty there, much strength there. We've only been living in these ghettos for 75 years or so, but the other 300 years—I think this is worth writing about. I think we've made tremendous sacrifices, we've shown tremendous strength. In the ghetto you see a lot of frustration; you see very little strength.

"The majority of young black writers have concentrated on this one thing, as though there were nothing else to their lives; it gives me the feeling that they are ashamed of things in the past, or that they are ashamed of the people of the past.

"The more popular things you can read about black people today are about black militants, but nothing really true about our lives. The militant thing is true, sure, but there are other things, too; screaming is good, but I don't think it has any lasting force unless one knows himself.

"The books I read, by most of the younger black writers, are almost on the same level as the movies that are coming out, almost on the same level as much of the music that is coming out. Even within the big cities, our experiences are different from these things.

"There are blacks in the city who are not pimps or pushers, who are not in jail and getting beaten up by white cops every day. There are people who work every day, people who don't know what a jail looks like, people who struggle every day, for something.

"Those things are truly worth writing about. What I find in these books is not all that is happening; I think this is as false a view to give as the white writers' interpretation of our lives."

Gaines has been concerned for a long time with finding in books the truth of his own life and his family's life. When he was a lonely fifteen-year-old in Vallejo, his stepfather told him to stay off the streets if he wanted to stay out of trouble, and Gaines took refuge in the public library.

"I'd never read books; I'd never seen so many books. I read and read and read, but I didn't see my people or myself in what I was reading. At that time—'48, '49—you had very few books by black writers in a library like that one in Vallejo. So I read white writers, but they did not write about my people as I knew them.

"I would read about people from the earth, farm people like I was, like my people were. Steinbeck, *The Grapes of Wrath* and *Tortilla Flat*. Willa Cather, who wrote about the Middle West. Chekhov, or Turgenev, anybody who wrote about peasants or outdoor life. So I read and read, and then I thought I could write."

He chuckled. "That's when I tried to write something about what I did not find in the books, about my experiences and the experiences of my people as I knew them. I tried to write before I went into the Army, but I knew I knew very little about writing."

After the Army, he studied writing; to judge from his style, Hemingway and Faulkner must have been as influential as any of the teachers he saw in the classroom. "Hemingway is the great technician, and I think I've been impressed by his lifestyle and of course his style of writing.

"Faulkner, being a Southerner, can help any Southern writer to write. He can make you hear things; he can see things that you might not be able to see, or he can remind you of things. Mississippi borders Louisiana, and much of the way he would say things, his dialogue and the way he would tell a story, I can remember from my part of Louisiana.

"You see, I always knew what I wanted to say; I had to find ways to put it down on paper. I did not have black writers as models when I started out, but after reading the white writers, I could see that even they could show me how to write about my own experiences. Reading *Winesburg, Ohio,* showed me that the place I came from could be made into stories; reading Joyce's *Dubliner,* was the same thing. I used this plantation quarter as Joyce used Dublin, or as Sherwood Anderson used Winesburg, Ohio."

Gaines's work room is lined with books. Next to the chair on which I sat were rows of books on Africa, and on black life in America; for a while I asked myself if Gaines could possibly have narrowed his reading so drastically, but then I looked around, and saw that he had arranged his books by nationality or ethnic group. I asked him what he reads that he likes or approves of.

Nodding at the portraits of Hemingway and Faulkner, he said, "Oh, I read the two old men there all the time. I can read Tolstoy anytime; I can read Dostoevski sometimes. I can read Turgenev, whom I love very much. I can read Camus, whom I don't think I understand too well, but I can read him. I can read de Maupassant.

"I can read Joyce; I'd read *Dubliners* before I'd read the novels. 'Ivy Day in the Committee Room' I think is one of the greatest short stories that I've ever read. It's the most universal of his work; it's the kind of thing I'd like to do, the barber shop type of thing: you get together and everybody talks." He told me later that he had originally modeled *Miss Jane* after "Ivy Day in the Committee

Room," but later decided that Miss Jane herself, rather than a group of her friends, would have to tell her story.

To retrieve us from Dublin, I asked about novels of rural black life. "Well, the book that I read quite often is Jean Toomer's *Cane,* which I think is a masterpiece, and a lot of it has to do with the rural South. I suppose Georgia is the background there, and mine is Louisiana, and the sugar cane thing is definitely a part of my life, because I came from a sugar cane plantation. So that's the best book on rural life that I can think of, by a black writer."

He also knows Ralph Ellison's *Invisible Man,* and the novels of Richard Wright, and feels that Wright's *Native Son* has had a disproportionately large influence on younger black writers. "So many of our writers have not read any farther back than *Native Son.* Too many of our novels deal only with the great city ghettos; that's all we write about, as if there's nothing else."

In his own writing, Gaines seems divided between his love of old people telling stories and his love of telling history in a more didactic way than the human voice will normally support, and I wondered aloud if he had ever thought of writing history as non-fiction. As it turned out, the idea had been put to him, most recently by three African students visiting the United States who had suggested that he might wish to visit Africa, and write a book of non-fiction based on research. He had rejected the idea; he'd never published anything but fiction, not so much as a book review.

"I suppose I would like to go to Africa in order to move my writing back farther; *Miss Jane* takes place from 1863 to 1962. O.K., so I would like to go back to the 18th century and write up what tribe she could have come from. Or I come from. What actually happened? What about the wars, the tribal fights?

"How did I actually get to the boat? I want to know the exact thing, and so I'd have to go back there to do it, but I would still put it into dramatic form: the short story form, the novel form, the play form, something like that. But to go back there to write a non-fiction book—not now. Maybe when I'm tired of writing fiction, which I hope I never will be, I would try something like that."

I asked him about the book he is working on now. "It's very cynical—not the novel, but some of the characters. The main character is a searcher. He's looking for his son, both physically and philosophically, but the people who surround him are quite cynical. In *The Autobiography of Miss Jane Pittman* you found a hope, I think; although they were getting shot down, there was still much hope.

"Joe Pittman, who must ride the horse, or Ned, who must build schools for young people, or Jimmy, in the demonstration at the end, they all die, but they all keep striving, striving, striving, whereas in the book I'm working on now you find so many of the younger ones who are quite cynical.

"*Miss Jane Pittman* ended before even Jack Kennedy's death; the book I'm working on now is after Martin King's death. It takes place in a small town in Louisiana, and it deals with the attitudes of many of the young people who were sitting-in at lunch counters, and marching, and so on, who have changed so much now, like they don't give a damn, or something else must happen."

Gaines had told me that *Miss Jane* is being taught from Mission High School to Yale, and I asked him about his acceptance by young people. When he gives readings, he told me, more white kids than black kids come up to talk about his work. "In this country there are more white people than black people," I said.

"No, it isn't that," he said. "I can go to universities where there are several hundred black kids and find none of them coming to the reading. I went to the University of North Carolina at Chapel Hill, and this was, I think, in December of 1969. There were two or three hundred black kids on the campus, and Anthony Burgess and I were on the program, and there were no blacks at the program.

"If you were going to write a book, you had to write a *Soul on Ice* or Leroi Jones-type stories to get attention from the black kids on the campus. I don't know whether it was fortunate or unfortunate that my books were beginning to be published at the time when a lot of the militant demonstrations were going on, and I wasn't considered part of that crowd. I wasn't writing in *The Black Scholar,* or *Black World,* or some of the more militant papers, so I was not accepted as that kind of writer."

Looking around me again at the photographs of Louisiana, hearing the police and ambulance sirens from Divisadero Street, remembering the wine-and-cheese party on Union Street where I had met him, I asked to what extent he writes for some real or imagined public, white or black.

"Oh, no, no, no, no, no. I try to write a book that I think is true. I think that I am my own severest critic. My agent, and my editor, those are the people I've listened to. But as for a white public or a black public—I don't care what they think. I care about what they think as far as buying the book is concerned," he chuckled, "but nobody tells me how to write.

"Writing is too goddamned hard for me to think about a soul in the world. I get up in the morning, and when I sit down to work—all my stuff is done longhand—I don't think about a soul, but just try to get those goddamned characters to act right."

Ernest Gaines

Tom Carter / 1975

From *Essence Magazine* July 1975: 52–53, 71–72. Used by permission.

After 15 threadbare, relatively obscure years of writing, Ernest Gaines scored with *The Autobiography of Miss Jane Pittman.* The timing of his book was totally unplanned, but it was right. Now Miss Jane's story has touched, in one degree or another, more than 51 million people. Small, solitary, book choked and record strewn, this three-room apartment in a redeveloped section of San Francisco would seem to be an ordinary writer's home. Ordinary except for the severe visual prods that daily jab Ernest J. Gaines' memories of the deep South he left in the late forties. For among the portraits of great authors on his walls are moody black and white photographs he took while visiting home in Louisiana in 1968. They are of the muggy bayou country outside Baton Rouge, particularly the stark, sugar plantation where he was born in 1933 and lived for 15 years.

Most of the photographs are not of people but of ghost-like, weathered houses and lean landscapes. One is of a mammoth oak tree growing by the side of a lonely dirt road, the road Gaines' characters walk down.

His characters, Black, rural deep South peasants, had not been popular. That is, not until Gaines created Miss Jane Pittman. After 15 threadbare, relatively obscure years of writing, Gaines scored with *The Autobiography of Miss Jane Pittman,* a novel that took him about three years to complete. The book is a fictional account of the life of a 110 year-old ex-slave, who tells her story into the tape recorder of a history teacher/editor.

Since its publication in 1971, *Miss Jane* has sold 850,000 copies in paperback and over 26,000 in hardback, far overshadowing Gaines' first three published books. As a result of selling the book's TV rights, Gaines for the first time in his life, received a sizable amount of money and months later became famous.

His reaction to Hollywood's initial interest in the book tells a lot

about Gaines' single-minded approach to his work. When his New
York agent told him the Tomorrow Entertainment Company wanted
the book's movie and television rights, Gaines quoted the price
he'd accept and refused to see or talk to anybody until they met it.

But once Tomorrow Entertainment had the rights to the story,
they had trouble finding financial backers for it. "Nobody wanted
to buy the story of an old Black woman talking into a tape recorder
about her past life," Gaines says. "They felt it was too episodic;
they had to cover 100 years in 110 minutes and couldn't concentrate
on anything very long. I couldn't have written the screen version
and I had my doubts that anybody could." But CBS chanced it.
The TV special, filmed in Louisiana, starred Cicely Tyson in a role as
memorable as her Rebecca in *Sounder*. Forty-three million viewers
saw her portrayal of Miss Jane in January of 1974. The special
received rave reviews in hundreds of newspapers coast to coast, as
well as in *Time, Newsweek,* and *The New Yorker*. It was named
"outstanding special of the year" and won nine Emmys.

Credit for the prize-winning screenplay goes to Tracy Keenan
Wynn, son of actor Keenan Wynn. His TV version differed from
the novel in many respects, but Gaines curiously, is unperturbed.
"I had no control over the film. Professionally it's another man's
work. I'm a struggling novelist, and once I've finished a book, you
can say or do anything you want; my book is there. I hope people
will credit me or damn me for the book, *not* for the film."

Gaines says most people who were familiar with the book felt the
TV movie didn't measure up to it. Nonetheless some of Wynn's
inventions were powerful, especially the ending. In the book, there
was no march to the fountain.

"Television is a different thing," Gaines explains. "In the book
you can have this little old lady saying 'I will go to the demonstration
even if I can't come back here to the plantation,' and that's a
dramatic enough ending. But in television you've go to punch people
in the stomach. I heard Tracy was adamant—the march to the
fountain *had* to be there." With a rare laugh Gaines adds, "That's
what people remember more than anything, and that's what I didn't
write! But you know, it doesn't matter to me one way or the
other."

The oldest of eight brothers and three sisters, Gaines began

working in the plantation fields outside of Baton Rouge at age
nine, earning 50 cents a day picking cotton, Irish potatoes and
onions. He played games with the other children but was basically a
loner. Withdrawn, he often went off alone to pick blackberries along
the road or to take long walks—as he still does—or to sit with his
aunt Miss Augusteen Jefferson.

His mother, who was separated from her husband, worked in the
fields; his grandfather was the big-house yardman. His grandmother, like Miss Jane, was the big-house cook. Many in the family
were humorous storytellers and clever imitators, but they considered Ernie brilliant because, having attended a nearby church
school, he could read and write. The family and their friends, which
combined spanned four generations, often called on Ernie to write
their letters. Once he wrote a humorous play and staged it at church.
The experiences in it paralleled Jimmy's *Miss Jane*.

Gaines' Aunt Augusteen, who died 21 years ago, influenced his
life more than anyone. "She was crippled from birth so she never
walked," he explained. "While my mother worked in the fields,
Aunt Augusteen did everything—cooking, washing, and ironing.
She completely ignored the wheelchair that welfare gave her (we
kids played with it). She'd crawl over the floor like an infant,
down the steps and into the garden to weed and hoe, then to the
backyard to collect pecans and back into the house. When we misbe-
haved she made us cut the switch that would punish us. If it wasn't
the right size, she sent us back for another one."

"My aunt never felt sorry for herself," Gaines says slowly,
studying the somewhat sad, surrealistic photo of her on the wall.
"And the people did not feel sorry for her. She had a great moral
strength. I know the kind of burden she carried trying to raise us and
I feel any character I wrote about has to have a burden. The main
character has to have a heavy burden, one that can knock the
average person down; sometimes it does but he has to get up. This
is the philosophy I have, if I have any at all, because of the struggle
of my aunt, the struggle of my race, the struggle of people in
general. Any person who's worth a goddamn must really
struggle."

In 1948 when Gaines was 15, he joined his mother, who had
remarried and moved to Vallejo, California. He hung around

street corners with his buddies until his stepfather told him he
would get into trouble if he didn't get off the streets. Gaines went
to the library.

He wanted to read about familiar things but couldn't find any.
There were no books by Black writers in Vallejo's library; the
stories he found closest to American rural life were by John Steinbeck and Willa Cather. But in that same library he discovered
Chekhov and Turgenev, Russians who wrote about rural peasantry
and outdoor life. "The peasantry of America is Black, but any
peasantry touches me," he says. "I found them in foreign literature.
Southerners didn't write about it. They weren't up to portraying
Black peasants as humans instead of clowns."

Having attended a junior college for two years prior to joining the
army, Gaines entered San Francisco State College as a junior in 1955
determined to be a writer of those experiences he hadn't found in
the library. But he flunked an essay-writing course until he
suggested substituting fictional work. The instructor consented and
was impressed with the resulting short stories. Gaines passed the
course and one of the stories helped him win a creative-writing
fellowship at Stanford University.

In the ensuing years, Gaines developed style, but his literary
pursuits were not "timely." "Northern liberals and radical whites
were the only people who bought the works of Black writers, and
they didn't care for tales about Black peasantry. I think they were
much more concerned with the Black problem than with the Black
character," says Gaines. "Richard Wright's *Native Son* is a good
example. It was almost a blueprint of what you had to do if you
wanted to be published at all."

Gaines, however, never wanted to be anything but a writer of
peasant tales. After graduation he gave himself ten years to
"make it." He almost didn't, writing diligently in the morning,
working at jobs he didn't like in the afternoons, making inspired
notes at work on paper scraps and toilet paper. He lived on $175 a
month and had no phone.

"It was hand to mouth," he says, dismissing it with a wave of the
hand. "But 99 percent of the people who write have gone through
that. No one twisted my arm to be a writer, I chose it."

Gaines' first novel, *Catherine Carmier,* published in 1964, won

the Joseph Henry Jackson Literary Prize but it didn't sell. He
continued working at temporary jobs until, finally, a modest book
contract in 1966 (one year before his ten-year deadline) gave him
some independence that allowed him to form better working habits
and not sweat the rent. *Of Love and Dust* (1967) and *Bloodline*
(1968) were published but paid nothing in royalties. It was a time of
militancy and a literary scream came out of the ghetto. Books
like *The Autobiography of Malcolm X* and *Soul on Ice* sold a
bundle. When Gaines gave readings from his works at nearby colleges,
crowds were sparse and few Blacks attended. If Black students
didn't consider him an Uncle Tom, the best they could consider
him was out of touch.

It wasn't that Gaines had no anger, but rather that his approach
to anger was different. "Growing up in the South, I know the last
thing in the world that whites wanted to see was humanity in
Blacks," he explains. "I knew the way to show that humanity
was to do something positive. Some guys get angry and go to a
punching bag. As they're jabbing at it they're developing their
muscles; they're getting sharper. I try to use the anger in a positive
way, to create a lasting punch, one that will have a longer effect
than just screaming or calling somebody an MF or son of a bitch."

Nor was Gaines' head turned by the lure of big bucks that writing
in vogue material would bring. Compromises were out of the
question. Fortunately his determination and self-discipline pre-
vailed. But he admits, "those first ten years of writing were hell."

The times did slowly change, "especially since the TV special.
More Blacks and a new group of white intellectuals in their
thirties appreciate what I'm trying to do. I don't think the book will
sell any three or four million, but I think the book will be taught
in schools for quite a while. It's time."

It is usually very difficult for a man to write a book narrated by a
woman. Gaines read history, century-old slave narratives and
books about women. He called on his aunt's voice too. "I worked
her voice, plus the ex-slaves' voices, over and over until I got the
one I liked. It took a while but it was no problem. I could look at
my walls and remember."

Because of Gaines' concentration on peasantry in the deep South
and the fact that he studied in the fifties, white writers have been

a greater influence than Black writers. "Probably the only Black writer who has influenced my work is Zora Neale Hurston. But if I had read Jean Toomer's *Cane* before I developed my own way working and writing, it probably would have influenced me as much as Faulkner, Hemingway or Turgenev."

Yet all manner of art and excellence affect the author. Excellence, itself, is a message, a challenge to emulate in hard work and substance. Modest Mussorgsky's composition *Pictures at an Exhibition*—musical interpretations of pictures the composer sees, linked by a promenade theme—so inspired Gaines during the writing of *Miss Jane* that he played the album daily.

The success of *Miss Jane* doesn't seem to have changed Gaines. He does worry, however, that new demands on his time—which he guards closely—take a certain toll in daily discipline. Writing is still hard and somewhat painful.

"It was more painful in the past, but I can buy better whiskey now," he says with a smile. "Instead of worrying over something, I can get a good drink and maybe it'll be better the next day. I don't take a drink every time I have a problem, but I do have more money now and I don't have to press as hard. If something doesn't come out right away, I can get it a little later on."

He writes longhand at a nondescript kitchen table amid the careless clutter in his tired apartment when he can now afford better. That's not important nor, in a way is money. He's had offers to become a Hollywood writer with a handsome salary but he's completely uninterested.

Nowadays the chapters scattered in a semicircle around the table are part of *In My Father's House,* a novel he's been working on for four years. The setting is a small Louisiana town. The time is after Martin Luther King's death and it deals with young people's attitudes. It's deadline is two years old. "I hate to sound like I'm complaining, because I hate for anybody to complain to me," he says with a set jaw. "But it is giving me more hell than anything I've ever written."

Problems or no, Gaines continues listening to the whispers of his pictures and writing about the deep South.

This Louisiana Thing That Drives Me: An Interview with Ernest J. Gaines

Charles Rowell / 1976

From *Callaloo* 1 (May 1978): 39–51. Used by permission.

The following interview was originally taped in Baton Rouge, Louisiana, on March 6, 1976, a few days following Ernest Gaines' YWCA reading. During the summer of 1978, I, with Gaines' assistance, edited this interview extensively. In fact, Gaines himself retaped most of the interview, which I edited further. As presented below, the interview is, among other things, the product of a genial collaboration by telephone and mail.

Rowell: Ernie, you were born here in Louisiana on a plantation near New Roads. For the past few years I have observed that you return here ever so often to give readings and visit your family. Do you also return here for a spiritual renewal with the people and the land?

Gaines: I have brothers here. Aunts, uncles and different relatives, friends whom I'd come to visit. I also come back here to be with the land—not only with the people, but to be with the land. I come back not as an objective observer, but as someone who must come back in order to write about Louisiana. I must come back to be with the land in different seasons, to travel the land, to go into the fields, to go into the small towns, to go into the bars, to eat the food, to listen to the language. As I said, I don't come back as a scientist, strictly as an observer; I come back to absorb things.

Rowell: You said you must "absorb things." Does that mean you have not absorbed California, or does it merely mean that Louisiana interests you as a place to write about?

Gaines: Well, Charles, I'm not one of those intellectuals who can explain the creative mind, but I do feel that the early impressions on the artist are the most lasting. I'm thinking of such writers as

86

James Joyce who left Ireland but who could not write about anything
except Ireland. I'm thinking about the Russian writers who were
exiled but who could not write about anything except Russia. About
California—I have written several books about California. I suppose
I have written four or five novels about California, but they are
not very good books. They have not been published. They will not
be published during my lifetime, if I have anything to do with it.
Maybe sometime in the future I will write a good book, or publish a
good book, about California. But I doubt that I will be able to do it
until I have gotten rid of this Louisiana thing that drives me, yet I
hope I never will get rid of that Louisiana thing. I hope I'm able
to write about Louisiana for the rest of my life.

Rowell: In your reading last week, you mentioned that *In My
Father's House* will deal with relationships between father and
son. What specifically about that relationship do you deal with in
the novel?

Gaines: Charles, a pet theme I deal with in so much of my fiction
(and I just think I took it a little bit farther in this particular book)
is that blacks were taken out of Africa and separated traditionally
and then physically here in this country. We know that on the
slave block in New Orleans, or Washington, D. C., or Baltimore, or
wherever the slave ships docked, families were separated. Mothers
were separated from their children, husbands from their wives,
fathers from their sons, mothers from their daughters. And I feel
that because of that separation they still have not, philosophically
speaking, reached each other again. I don't know what it will take
to bring them together again. I don't know that the Christian religion
will bring fathers and sons together again. I don't know that the
father will ever be in a position—a political position or any position
of authority—from which he can reach out and bring his son back
to him again. I don't know where that thing which is needed will
come from. That is something I suppose some other writer will
have to deal with. Anyway, that is the main theme that is running
through the new novel—*In My Father's House,* the novel I'm
working on.

Rowell: At your reading, you also talked about point of view of
In My Father's House. You said it is different from that in your
other works.

Gaines: *In My Father's House* is told from the omniscient point of view. Everything I have done, except *Catherine Carmier,* is told from the first person point of view. That is the only difference.

Rowell: You mentioned some difficulty you've had in writing in the omniscient point of view.

Gaines: In the first person point of view, it seems that my characters take over very early in the book—or I should say that when I start a book in the first person point of view my characters take over very soon and then carry the story themselves. From the omniscient point of view, it is harder for me (for the characters to take over), because it seems that I'm always interrupting them. I seem to think it is necessary to add things that they might not. Sometimes I feel that they don't see enough or that they don't know enough. I'm constantly adding things, and adding things sometimes gets in the way of the novel. It slows the novel down too much; it impedes the progress, the movement. Quite often it throws things out of the line in which it travels; form gets in the way of development. This is where the problem lies. I had the same kind of problem when I was writing my first novel, *Catherine Carmier,* my only other book in the omniscient point of view. It was a very small book, but still it gave me trouble developing the character as well as putting some form in the book. I usually don't have problems when writing dialogue—whether I'm writing it in the omniscient point of view or the first person. But the other things like descriptive passages or exposition or development of theme—things like that—have given me a lot of trouble when I'm involved in a book dealing with the omniscient point of view. Usually I think of myself as a storyteller. I would like for readers to look at a person telling the story from the first person point of view as someone actually telling them a story at the time. But when you are dealing with the omniscient point of view, you are not being told a story; you are reading a story, I feel. Now maybe what I need to do is sit in a chair on a stage and just tell people stories rather than try to write them. I wish I could do that. I wish I could be paid just to sit around and tell stories, and forget the writing stuff. But, unfortunately, I am a writer, and I must communicate with the written word. And, of course, certain books require that you write not from the first person but from the omniscient point of view. *In My*

Father's House is just such a book. You cannot tell that story
from the minister's point of view because the minister keeps too
much inside him. He does not reveal it—he won't reveal it to
anybody. It would be totally impossible to tell this story from
anyone else's point of view—or should I say, have anyone else
tell the story. So the story has to be told from that omniscient point
of view. That is, I, the author, must tell the story rather than let
a character tell it for me.

Rowell: In your interview with John O'Brien, you spoke of your
characters, Tee Bob and Jackson, as victims of the past, and you
also talked about their efforts to escape the past. Is it really possible
for anyone to escape the past? That is to say, the past is, in my
opinion, always present and shaping the future.

Gaines: I think Faulkner says something like the past ain't dead;
it ain't even passed. And I agree with you all the way. I don't know
that you can escape the past. If it were possible, I would have
escaped it myself, because Louisiana is definitely not only my
past but my present also. I believe I, myself, and my writing are
good examples to support that observation that you can't escape your
past. There is a difference between living in the past and trying to
escape it. If you do nothing but worship the past you are quite
dead, I believe. But if you start running and trying to get away from
the past, you will, I think, eventually run yourself out of whatever
it does to you. It will run you mad, or kill you in some way or the
other. So you really don't get away. It's there, and you live it.
That is especially true with the artist.

Rowell: You also said that Catherine Carmier could not exist
outside the South. Why?

Gaines: Just as so many other people cannot exist outside the
South.

Rowell: What is there in her character that would prevent her?

Gaines: Her family, the problem of her family. And you must
remember that Catherine is nearly white. Her family is nearly
white—her father and sister. But they are not white, so there is the
problem between her family and blacks. And the problem between
her family and whites. Her family does not fit with the whites or
blacks. But Catherine is the strength of the family. The family
could never exist without her. She is the conscience. She is the one

who communicates with the family because of the problem they
have had in their past. That is the thing that would prevent her from
staying away. Oh, she could leave, she could go for a while, but
she would have to come back because they could not exist without
her. That is the reason so many people stay in an area. They are
trapped for one reason or another. Catherine is trapped because of
the family conflict. She is trapped because of the color of her skin
and the color of her parents.

Rowell: Why did you call your second novel *Of Love and Dust?*

Gaines: Because dust is the absence of love. Dust is the absence
of life. Man goes back to dust when he dies. There is a little line
of dialogue in the original draft of *Of Love and Dust* where Louise,
the little white girl, tells Marcus, my hero, that without love
everything is dust, or something like that. Then, of course, the
whole story takes place in the dust. When Jim meets Marcus for
the first time, he sees the dust coming toward him, even before he
sees Marcus in the truck. When the truck stops in front of Jim's
house, Marcus walks away from it while the dust drifts all over the
plantation. Each time Marshall Hebert, the man who owns the
plantation, goes by the house in his car you will notice how much
dust is flying all over the place. Because in the end it will be this man,
Marshall Hebert, who will bring death. So this is the meaning of the
story. There are two love stories in the book: the story of Marcus
and Louise, and the story of Sidney Bonbon and Pauline. Because
they are black and white, they cannot love as they would want to.
Eventually, death does separate—separates them all. I think even
when Marcus falls dead, he falls dead in dust. Dust is the absence
of love, the absence of life. These people wanted to love, but
because of the way the system is set up, it was impossible to
love. Dust.

Rowell: I want to go back to the subject of influence, because
certain critics keep writing about your influences. And in the
interview I mentioned earlier, you are compared to William Faulkner. You also said that both Ernest Hemingway and William
Faulkner influenced you.

Gaines: Faulkner has influenced me, as I think he has influenced
most Southern writers. But I'd like to make this clear: Faulkner
has influenced me in style only, not in philosophy. His philosophy

is a completely different thing. Faulkner can write, and he has an
ear for dialect, like few writers have for Southern dialect. You might
not agree with his philosophy, but he can capture that Southern
dialect, both the white and the black, like no one else I know can.
He shows you a lot about rhythm in sentences, the long sentences as
well as the shorter ones. His capturing of time can be compared to
parts of a great symphony. He can really capture a moment, put
everything into the moment. He knows how to stop time and make
you see how long a second can be. I've told this to many students
in high school as well as college who've asked me how can a white
man influence me. You know, in the 1960's you had to go through this
all the time if a student in the classroom didn't know what to ask
you. He would ask if you were a writer or a black writer? And he
wanted you to give him a definite *yes* or *no,* whether you were just
a writer or a black writer. If you were a writer, he had very little
interest in whatever you were talking about. I tried to tell them that
I consider myself a writer and tried to show them how a person
like Hemingway could influence me. I would say when Hemingway,
whose major theme was grace under pressure, was writing he was
saying as much about the black man as he was about the white man,
although very seldom were his black characters given any kind of
sympathetic roles. Still his writings of that grace under pressure,
his writing about the white characters, made me see my own black
people. For example, who had more pressure on him than Jackie
Robinson when he was playing baseball, or when he first broke
into baseball with the Brooklyn Dodgers? Who had more pressure
on him than Joe Louis? No man has had more pressure on him
than Martin Luther King. But look how gracefully these men stood.
These are the things I tell a young writer he can learn from
reading Hemingway's stories. Hemingway's characters are white,
that's true, but we can learn how to write about our own black
characters by reading what he has to say about his white characters—because, as I said, the theme that Hemingway uses is more
related to our own condition than that of white Americans. Good
examples of Hemingway's themes of grace under pressure can be
found in "Fifty Grand," the story about a boxer, and in *The Old
Man and the Sea,* where the character fights sharks and is defeated—
physically defeated, but not spiritually defeated—when he loses his

great fish. There is the story, "The Undefeated," which is about an old bullfighter who is just about washed up but goes for one more try. Our people go back for one more try all the time. We get up day after day after day and try again. With all the pressures on us, we, some kind of way, force ourselves to try again. We have survived by trying over and over and over. A writer like Hemingway can show you how to write the story about your own people. But there were influences on me when I was in college other than Hemingway and Faulkner. Sherwood Anderson was an influence because I had to study his *Winesburg, Ohio*. James Joyce was an influence, his *Dubliners*. I also learned from Anton Chekhov. I learned from the great nineteenth-century Russian stylist, Ivan Turgenev. His *Fathers and Sons* was a great influence on my first novel, *Catherine Carmier;* I used his novel as a Bible when I was writing *Catherine Carmier*. These men and many, many more were influences in those early years when I was trying to be a writer.

Rowell: Much good came out of the Black Arts Movement of the 60's and early 70's. But I think that too many of the advocates of the Black Aesthetic de-emphasized the importance of craft. That is, at the expense of good writing, too many critics and creative writers argued for politics as if how you said what you said were not of equal importance. Do you agree with my charge?

Gaines: Yes. And I think it's too bad they did that. But you can understand why. At that time the point was to get something over. Too many of the writers did not realize that you don't get it over with bad writing. To be a writer, one ought to strive to write well. If you want what you say to last, you should write it as well as you possibly can. Now I have been criticized like hell in certain magazines, whose names I don't want to mention here, because I insist on writing well. I've never insisted on not criticizing. I've never insisted on not writing protest. All I've said was write whatever you are going to write as well as you can. I don't know any other black writer who has written a scene which showed the brutality of the system any more than I expressed in the violence of the massacre scene in *The Autobiography of Miss Jane Pittman*. But I was after writing the scene as well as I possibly could. The violence is there. No one can deny that. But still accuracy was the thing I had to try to achieve. I had to rewrite and rewrite that scene in order to get it the way I wanted it. I suppose you know what scene I'm talking about. It's the scene in which the blacks, after they hear of their emancipation, try to leave the South. They try to leave that particular plantation where they have been slaves, and on the second day of their journey a group of Klansmen and defeated Confederate soldiers find them in the swamp and murder all of them, except Jane and the little boy Ned. I don't know of any other writer who has done a more violent scene than that. At the same time, my aim was to write well. My aim was to get the dialogue that was going on at that time, as well as the swinging of the clubs, as well as the noises made in the bush, in the shrub, in the trees, and among the leaves. I wanted to get the sun coming down through the trees, on the ground where the men lay dead, and a woman lay dying with a child clutched in her arms. This is what I mean by doing it well no matter what you're doing—no matter what the politics, or what the violence, is. You must write it well. Write it over and over until you do it well. I don't think there is any more respected black man in this world today than Muhammad Ali. I think we all love him; we worship him. But when he gets into the ring he's a fighter. He's as graceful as anybody we've ever seen. He's talking, but he's fighting. His punches and his jabs know exactly. He uses punches and jabs like nobody has ever done. He's directing them where they will have the greatest effect. Each one is calculated. Now we worship that in him. We respect that in him. That's the kind of thing I would like to see in writing. If you are going to use words, put them where they are going to have the greatest and most lasting effect. I've always felt that the white man out there would rather we did not use the proper language. He would rather that all we did was scream and make noises. He would prefer that our aim was not perfection. My aim in writing will always be at perfecting a sentence, just as the aim of the great fighter (or any other athlete) is perfecting his style, making the right move at the right time.

Rowell: A few years ago, when you spoke at Southern University (Baton Rouge), someone asked you what do you advise black writers to study to help develop their writing. I think you said they should listen to music. Why?

Gaines: Well, I feel we have expressed ourselves better in our music traditionally than we have in our writing. The music (blues, jazz, and spirituals, for example) is much better than our prose or poetry. I think that we have excelled in music because it is more oral. We are traditionally orally oriented. What I'd like to see in our writing is the presence of our music.

Rowell: I not only see black music as being important in your work, but it seems as if a lot of things—more than in any other piece of your fiction—went into the making of *The Autobiography of Miss Jane Pittman.* I hear, for example, the voice of the slave narrative. I also hear the voice of the tellers of folk history. Will you talk about the kind of research that went into the making of *Miss Jane Pittman?*

Gaines: When I wrote *Miss Jane Pittman,* my Bible was *Lay My Burden Down,* a collection of short WPA interviews with ex-slaves recorded during the 30's. I used that book to get the rhythm of speech and an idea of how the ex-slaves would talk about themselves. Remember I wanted a folk autobiography. *Miss Jane Pittman* is a folk autobiography. Miss Jane must tell things from memory. Miss Jane has not gone to school or done any research work. What she does is talk about the things she can remember and what others have said year after year after year. Of course, I had to do a lot of research, especially a lot on slavery. I also did a lot of research on the Reconstruction Period—I read book after book: books by black historians, books by white historians, books by Northern historians, books by Southern historians. I had access to the Archives at Louisiana State University. I went to the State Library uptown and to the Southern University Library. After I went back to San Francisco I could write back to these libraries and ask for additional information. While I was here I would go out into the fields and talk to the people, talk about Huey Long, talk about the flood, talk about Angola State Prison, talk about Jackson Mental Institution. We talked about everything. I remember just before I began writing *The Autobiography of Miss Jane Pittman* I went up to talk to Al Aubert. He was living up on East Boulevard at the time. While we were sitting in his living room, I asked him to discuss with me some things. I said, "Let's talk about twelve things that could have happened nationally that a woman who lived to be 110 years old might be able to recall." I wanted twelve things that

could have happened state-wide that a 110 year old woman might
be able to recall. I remember we began by talking about things
like, of course, the Civil War. We talked about the Reconstruction
Period. We talked about the Depression. We talked about Abraham Lincoln. We talked about Huey Long, of course. We talked
about Jack Johnson, Jackie Robinson, and Joe Louis. We talked
about the Dodgers and the Yankees. We talked about many, many,
many other things. For example, we talked about Roosevelt. We
talked about the floods of both 1912 and 1927. We talked about the
Civil Rights Movement. We had to talk about Martin Luther King.
We talked about all the younger people who were caught up in the
Civil Rights Movement that a lady who was 110 years old would
know something about. After Al and I had discussed this, I then
had to do the research work to give Miss Jane this information, to get
accurate data on this kind of information. Although she could
distort the information, I had to be aware of its accuracy. For
example, when dealing with the Joe Louis-Schmeling fight, which
she would talk about, I had to know exactly what round Louis lost
the first fight and what round he won the second fight. So this is the
kind of research I had to do. Of course, after I went back to San
Francisco I had people here in Baton Rouge to xerox that kind of
information and send it on to me. I had to put this information
into the mind of someone who was illiterate, who was very intelligent, of course, but who was illiterate because Miss Jane had had
no formal education. After doing the research work (knowing exactly what she should know), I then had to find a voice for her to
give that information in her autobiography. That is how the *Lay My
Burden Down* interviews were so valuable to me. After reading
so many of them (I forget how many I read, maybe a hundred), I
got a rhythm, a speech, a dialogue, and a vocabulary that an ex-
slave would have had. Miss Jane, as you know, was an ex-slave.

   Rowell: At your reading last week, you talked about the importance of love in *Miss Jane Pittman*.

   Gaines: At that reading, Charles, someone asked me why was
Miss Jane important. I said anyone who had lived 110 years in a
country like this, under the conditions she lived, and could love
God, could still love baseball, and ice cream, was worth writing
about. I went on to say that, if she could come out as a whole

human being after living 110 years with the kind of life she had to
live, she is worth writing about. Survival with sanity and love and a
sense of responsibility, and getting up and trying all over again
not only for one's self but for mankind—those achievements I find
worth writing about. Miss Jane, not generals who had killed
thousands of people . . . Miss Jane, who loved humankind so much
she did not have to kill one person to continue life. . . . So when
I mentioned the love in *Miss Jane Pittman,* this is the kind of thing
I quite possibly could have been talking about.

Rowell: What do you think of the TV filming of the novel? I know
everybody has asked you that question.

Gaines: I like the film. I liked what they did with the two hours
that they had. Remember this book covers 100 years in time. The
film covers 110 minutes of time, giving us about a minute to a year.
So the film could not depict the book as it was. No film ever can,
and this one definitely did not. But I think the two hours did give us
an idea of what the book was about. If we had had more time (say
three hours or four hours or five hours), we would have had a much
better film. I'm not saying we did not have a good film, but we
would have had a much better film. Even when we were shooting
the film here around Baton Rouge, the aim was toward shooting a
bigger film, more than a two-hour film. I wish the viewers could see
all the good footage that was done which had to be edited out in
Hollywood. So what you have in the film now is peaks—a lot of
peaks. But you don't have the valleys and slopes as you would
have had, had the film been longer. But the film as it is, I think, is
quite good. I want to go back to what I was trying to say a moment
ago about peaks and the difference in peaks and valleys and slopes.
For example, in the film after the Cajun Albert Cluveau kills the
professor, you never see Cluveau ever again. (The professor is Miss
Jane's adopted son, and Miss Jane, as you recall, is Cluveau's
closest friend.) In my book, after Cluveau has killed the son of his
closest friend, he gradually goes mad. In the film, before it was
edited, you see him going mad after he had killed the professor. The
actor, Will Hare, who plays the part of Albert Cluveau, does his
best acting in the mad scene. But, of course, when the footage went
back to Hollywood all this was edited out. So what we get is the
assassination and nothing about Cluveau's madness. This assassina-

tion is a peak, but the gradual madness is a slope and a valley. And
that is what I think is missing in the film. I am not saying that the
film is not a good film. But the slopes and valleys are missing.

Rowell: I want to go back to the late 60's and early 70's, when we
heard so many black writers and critics arguing that black writing
should be politically functional—that is, to aid in the liberation of
black people. And many critics argued that black writers should write
to the black community. Looking back at that time and looking
back at that position, will you comment on the period?

Gaines: I have always felt that the writer, regardless of what he
writes about, should write it well, and that's final.

Rowell: When you write, do you have an audience in mind?

Gaines: I never write for any particular group. I try to write well
enough so that anyone can pick up my book and say "I like this."
A black child in this country can pick the book up and say "I like
it." The same I hope of a Chinese child, or a Russian child, or a
Russian teacher. I never think of any particular audience. But I
think of writing as well as I can—writing cleanly, clearly, truthfully, and making it simple enough so that anyone might be able to
pick it up and read it. I've been asked what people would I rather
have read a story of mine. And I've answered that if I had to write
for one group, then I would want that group to be the black youth
of the South. If I had to write for two groups, I would like for those
groups to be the blacks and the whites of the South. Of course, I
want the world to read my work. But I don't write with the world in
mind. Writing to me is tough enough. It's hard work, but I try to
write clearly about my experiences, whether direct or vicarious.
Other people who have had that same kind of experience might
be able to recognize themselves in the work. But I never write for
any particular group, surely never with critics in mind. They are
the last people I think of when I'm trying to create a book, a story
or a novel.

Rowell: Ernie, one final question. If you were asked to give
advice to black writers, what would you tell them to do in
the 1970's?

Gaines: I don't know what to tell a writer to do. One of the things
I believe in is that the writer should be free to do whatever the
hell he wishes to do. I only hope that he writes about the human

condition. If he is black, he should write about the black condition. I don't know how in the hell he can avoid writing about white
conditions if he is an American. If he is a black Southern writer, how
can he avoid writing about the Southern condition? If he is a
Northerner, how can he avoid writing about Northern conditions?
As long as he writes truthfully about the human conditions, his
experiences, whether these experiences are direct or vicarious,
I'm pleased. I don't know what else you can tell a writer to do. But
I would give this same advice to a young man who wanted to play
football, who came out and asked my advice. I'd say, play the game
as well as you can possibly play it. Or if you are studying to be a
dentist, I would say study as hard as you can to be a damn good
dentist. Or if you are going into law, read as much as you can;
know law, know the Constitution, know everything there is that
you can possibly know about your subject. Sacrifice time; put a
lot of time into your work. In order to do it well you are going to
have to sacrifice; you are going to have to put a lot of time in. If
you are a writer, read good writers, whether they are white or
black, Chinese or Japanese, or Russian, or writers from Mars or
wherever. Read the best to see how they do things, because any
writer can help you—any good writer can help you. I don't give a
damn who he is or who you are. If he is good, he can help you.
Faulkner can help you. Hemingway can help you. Joyce can help
you. The great Russian writers (Tolstoy, Turgenev, and Chekhov)
can help you. The great French writers, Flaubert and de Maupassant, can help you. So study hard, and spend a lot of time at the
desk. You sure can't become a good writer unless you spend time at
the desk. I don't know of any writers who have written anything
worthwhile unless they read. You must read, and you must write. The
same thing goes for a fighter. A fighter watches films, a fighter
works, and a fighter listens to his manager, no matter whether
that manager is white or black or green or gray. It takes a lot of
work, a lot of discipline, and a lot of studying in order to
accomplish anything that you want to go into. So I'd say the same
thing to a young writer of the 1970's as I would to anyone else.

Ernest J. Gaines

Dan Tooker and Roger Hofheins / 1976

From *Fiction!: Interviews with Northern California Novelists.*
New York: Harcourt, Brace, Jovanovich, 1976. Used by permission.

Ernest Gaines lives on the second floor of a large apartment building at the corner of Golden Gate Avenue and Divisadero Street in San Francisco. About six feet tall, and stocky, he greets us dressed in a sweat suit and sneakers, a towel wrapped around his neck. We pass the small white writing table which stands against a wall between the two doors leading off the small square foyer. Beneath its legs yellow sheets of legal paper lie scattered like leaves.

In the living room a barbell lies on the wooden floor in front of a divan. There's a stereo across the room and hundreds of stacked records: Lightnin' Hopkins, Mississippi Fred McDowell, Gershwin, Schubert. He settles into a cushioned chair facing the overflowing brick and board bookcases beneath the windows. Behind him the glassed-in upper shelves of an old oak china cabinet hold more books, and the cupboards beneath are crammed with old manuscript pages, some handwritten, some typed.

We begin the interview, and at first, his answers seem stiff and uncomfortable as he sits with his arms lying flat on the armrests and his feet firmly planted on the floor. After a few minutes, however, he relaxes. He leans forward, then back. His hands begin to move, spreading apart, palms up, or pointing for emphasis. Though he speaks without a trace of a Southern accent, the South is present in him and in the room. He refers often to a number of framed black and white photographs taken during his yearly trips back to Louisiana. At the end of the interview he shows us each picture in turn, closer up: a huge old oak, "Miss Jane's oak"; a cypress; a pecan tree stripped bare in winter; a portrait of a small boy in the dark cavern of a barn door; his aunt who "never walked a day in her life"; and finally, the buildings on the former plantation where he lived as a child—the plantation store, the white church, and the house, a wooden house with a sloping tin roof, where he was born. He is writing a new book called *In My Father's House* which he has started many times before and which has, he says, "been kicking my ass around for ten years."

When you start a book, where do you start? Do you have an idea, an event, an ending, a character?

Well, I don't know. I have different ways to start different books. *Catherine Carmier,* my first novel, took me so long to write that now I've forgotten how I started. I wanted to write about the place that I'd come from and the people I knew, so I made up a story about what I knew as a child.

Of Love and Dust, my second novel, started with an idea. A white man can go with a black woman in Louisiana, but it's against all the rules for a black guy to go with a white woman, and I had known many different cases where this had happened, and certain little things reminded me of what I wanted to do. I was in a nightclub once where I saw a knife fight between two boys, two blacks, young men, and the fight was stopped before either of them got really hurt. Now, I also know an incident where a friend of mine got in a fight like that, and he killed a guy. Three guys jumped on him, and he killed one of them. He was sent to prison. He had been working for the white man, and this man could have gotten him out if he wanted to come out, but he said, "I'd rather spend my time because I killed this guy." So, he went to jail; he went to Angola, the state prison of Louisiana, and he spent five years.

Then, I listen to music. I play records all the time. I have a large collection of jazz, blues, and folk music. Lightnin' Hopkins, one of my favorite blues and folk singers, sings something about the worst thing that a black man ever done was moving his wife and family to Mr. Tim Moore's farm. Mr. Tim Moore's man, the overseer, would never stand and grin: "You keep out the jailhouse, nigger; I'll keep you out the pen."

When I started writing of *Love and Dust,* I thought of this boy who could have been taken out of that prison and put on this farm to work under a man like Lightnin' Hopkins was singing about. So, the Lightnin' Hopkins song reminds me of what could have happened to my friend. Of course, he would have been almost a slave to the man who had gotten him out, and he would have had to do everything the man said.

This is very chaotic, it doesn't make any sense, but when you ask how a novel begins in the mind, a little incident like this makes the novel. When I started writing the book, I had one guy kill another, and I had him bonded out of jail and put on a plantation to go through all the hell, but as soon as he could run, he runs. One incident led to another, and then it was up to the imagination. I suppose it's up to the writer to use his own experience, what he has heard, seen, tasted, touched, felt, and make a novel out of it.

In the case of *The Autobiography of Miss Jane Pittman,* I wanted to write a folk biography. At first, a group of people were going to tell about this one person's life, and through telling of this one person's life, they were going to cover a hundred years of history, superstitions, religion, philosophy, folk tales, lies—they were going to cover all this. After I'd written it like that one time, it was untrue, so I broke it down to one person telling the story, the individual herself telling the story, so instead of a short biography of Miss Jane Pittman it became *The Autobiography of Miss Jane Pittman.* I wanted to get it as a series of conversations, and what led me to that, I suppose, is that I grew up in the South around old people. My aunt—her picture's over there against the wall—was the lady who raised me. She never walked a day in her life, she was crippled all her life, and she raised us, me and my brothers and sisters. People used to come to our house because she couldn't go to their houses, and what they would talk about was something that I had thought about, that was worth writing about. But, of course, the actual writing was my imagination, what they had probably talked about, and more than they talked about because they couldn't know all the things I put in the book. These are the kinds of things that lead to novel or short story writing.

Is Miss Jane modeled after your aunt?

Oh, no. Miss Jane walks all the time. My aunt never walked a day in her life. But, morally, her strength, her moral strength, yes, and my imagination and my conception. . . . You know, here's a black woman who is on her toes. Not all black women are like Miss Jane. In a few of the records there are a certain number of women who went through the things that Miss Jane did, but not all the things that she did. On the other hand, Miss Jane didn't go through as much as some others did. My imagination is limited.

Miss Jane *starts out very much as a physical odyssey—*

Absolutely, it's supposed to be that way. I wanted several levels of literary form, several levels, with journeys, hard, physical things, and then it develops. In the beginning she's young, so it's her strength against nature. Then she goes on and becomes experienced. That's when she gets involved in other things like superstitions, and dreams, and the old voodoo woman. Then there's the symbolic thing of the horse, and the romantic thing of the beautiful octaroon with the son of the plantation owner which is a different level. Maybe I did not really go far enough, but these things are the things I was trying to aim at in her story because when people are telling stories they become realistic, naturalistic, fatalistic, romantic. . . . At the very end, Miss Jane becomes a different thing altogether. She becomes almost a recorder of history. When she talks about Jimmy and the quarters, she's not directly involved in anything that happens. Jimmy is The One. So, she's gone from action in the first part to just sitting down and observing things in the latter part of the book. There's several, I think, literary approaches running about in the book.

Do you think this shift in focus, on her at first and then opening out to include all Southern blacks, is a particular strength of the book? Did you do what you wanted to?

Well, I feel I did what I wanted to do. I didn't do as much as I wanted to, but I had it completely under control. I knew what I was doing at all times. Maybe, I didn't do enough, but I knew what I was doing, and the only thing I would do if I wrote it over is do a little bit more, concentrate a little bit more.

On what specifically?

Oh, really think more about the horse and the Joe Pittman thing, her travels, her conversion from sinner to religious person. I'd read much more on folklore, black folklore, on religion and the ministry, on the interpretation of religion. I would go further into the voodooism. I'd try to learn much, much, more about history. But I knew what I wanted to do. I wanted to start with an individual, with the problems that an individual confronts and then spread it out to the problems of the race. It didn't accidently happen.

The reason I ask all this is that Faulkner says that if you do your work right, your characters stand up on page 275, and all you have to do is take notes on what they do.

Oh, yeah. I agree there, that lots of times Miss Jane would take over, but I had to have an idea. When I was writing this book, I did a lot of research. I did a lot of reading in history, by black as well as white historians. I read a lot of black folklore. I read a lot of interviews with ex-slaves, the WPA interviews with ex-slaves in the Thirties. By the time you get to page 275, if you've really developed the characters well and put them into action, they'll take over, but you have to deal with direction. You must invent some incidents along the way, and when Miss Jane gets into the incident, she'll develop it for you. I'm not saying that I knew when I was writing page 50 that I knew what I was going to say on page 60 or page 65, but I had an idea of which way I was going. I don't just sit down without any idea. A novel is like getting on a train to Louisiana. All you know at the moment is that you're getting on the train, and you're going to Louisiana. But you don't know what the conductor is going to look like; you don't know who you're going to sit behind, or in front of, or beside; you don't know what the weather is going to be when you pass through certain areas of the country; you don't know what's going to happen South; you don't know all these things, but you know you're going to Louisiana. You know you're going by train, and that it's going to take so many hours, days. . . .

Your dialogue is remarkably true to the ear. It seems to us, as readers, to be exactly the way those people talk. We were wondering

*whether that came from memory. Did you have to spend a lot of
time making your characters sound as they sound?*

Well, memory, work, a lot of work, and then I go back South all
the time, I go South every year. I go for the Mardi Gras, and I
stay two or three weeks. In 1963 I stayed six months. I go back all
the time, and I had my grandmother, who just died a couple of
years ago. She had never forgotten her Southern attitudes, or
Southern ways, or Southern language. There are always relatives
or friends going South, and most of the people here are first
generation Californians, really transferred Southerners. And I read
Southern writing. Faulkner was great at interpreting the Southern
black dialogue. He's as good at catching the Mississippi dialogue
and putting it down on paper as anyone else I've read.

I really read my dialogue. I check it out to see if it sounds exactly
that way. And I've always been influenced by reading plays. I've
always liked listening to the radio. I grew up on the radio, rather
than television, and I used to spend hour after hour listening to
the radio. So, you're listening to dialogue, you're listening to
dialogue all the time, and you're hearing the good dialogue as well
as the bad. I remember when I was a child, *Gunsmoke* had probably
the best dialogue. I can still remember that. I could follow the story
well just by listening. That's one of the reasons why in a lot of my
books there's somebody listening through a wall to somebody
talking. Somebody's always talking in another room. Maybe that's
the radio.

In dialogue writing you've got to listen, and you've got to read,
and you've got to come to the point as quickly as you possibly
can. Hemingway can use the word as well as anybody. When people
talk, they always leave out words, they always understate things.
Whether they are teachers, or farmers, or students, they always
understate things.

If I just had to write dialogue, I could write several pages a day,
but I like to go over it. All the stuff you see back there on the
floor is writing I did last week that I have to rewrite this week. I
might write five pages one day, and then I might rewrite them the
next day to perfect the sound, the dialogue, as well as try to get the
descriptions down.

Do you find it harder writing descriptions?

Yes, I think everybody sees that in my writing. It's very hard for me to write descriptions. I like the sound of people's voices, and I think what a man says can very well tell what he's thinking, whether he's lying or not.

Just by the sound of his voice?

Well, not by the sound, that's not exactly true, but I think you can develop a personality by listening to the sound of the voice. It says a lot of things. You can listen to the voice and tell, at least I try. . . . This is my best weapon, the dialogue, and I try to do as much as I can with it. And I use the description when I cannot get away with the other thing. I'm not good at it, and I know it, and I have to work harder at description and straight narrative than dialogue. Dialogue is much simpler for me. My aim is to perfect it as much as I possibly can.

You said there were five pages on the floor from last week. How do you physically go about writing. Do you write every morning? Do you use a typewriter?

No, I write longhand. That's the longhand stuff. I write longhand once, twice, or three times, and then I type two or three times, and then I consider that a draft.

Do you write every day?

Oh, yes, I write every day. I get up to write.

Early in the morning?

I try to write about nine, and work until about two. I stop for coffee, maybe eat a bowl of soup and some crackers. I try to get four hours in, five if it's going slow.

You said you re-write a lot. Do you feel that you have to get one thing right before you can go on to the next?

Recently, I've been doing it because I'm getting older. When I first started writing, I would go through an entire book before I started writing one line over. And I don't know, now I'm a bit more conscious, and well, since critics are beginning to notice what I've been doing, I try to get things done well before I go someplace else.

Your last story in Bloodline *is told from multiple points of view. Is this just an experiment or were you really trying to work something out?*

Oh, no, no, it's nothing original, because if you read Faulkner, you know Faulkner has done it and that other writers have done it. I wanted a different interpretation about this lady's life, how others in the community felt about her life, and I wanted them to tell it from their point of view.

Don Stanley, who used to review for the *Examiner,* said that *Bloodline* wasn't just a series of stories, but an episodic novel. You begin with a six-year-old child whose view is limited. He's this tall and can interpret so much of life, and the whole action takes place on this plantation. The eight-year-old boy in "The Sky is Gray" goes into a southern city where he discovers the race thing and white people. "Three Men" is a little broader. That is, because of Southern life, one black is taking the life of another, and he has to pay for it in the same way. Oh, *Bloodline* is something else. In each story, I use a different kind of stylistic approach. The last story is just a different way to look at the situation, I suppose. And, as I said before, I wanted people around to give their own personal views. And of course the sound of the language, I like the sound of individuality, and this is one of the things I've used. Different people tell it differently: the little boy, the guy from the city, the white woman, the old people. I want sounds, different sounds, different angles, as when you set up a camera.

In Of Love and Dust, *the white overseer's children by Pauline, the black girl, are strong and healthy, while Tite, his child by Louise, his wife, is weak and ill. Is this symbolic?*

Yeah, that's when you play with symbolism you hate later, the decadence of the West, the decadence of an idea. If Bonbon and

Pauline had married, they would have had the most beautiful, productive and strong children, but he must stay with Louise. This is the kind of crap you hate later on, but at that time, I was pretty hungry.

How did you decide to have a detached narrator, Jim Kelly, tell the story in Of Love and Dust *rather than Marcus, the hero?*

When you get to Marcus, you get a one-sided thing. It's like trying to get Gatsby to tell the story of *The Great Gatsby*. You can't do that. I needed a guy who could communicate with different people. I needed a guy who could communicate with Bonbon, the white overseer, with Aunt Margaret, with Marcus. Marcus could never communicate with the people around him, and Jim could. I had to get a guy who could fit in like that. Fitzgerald used Nick because he could communicate both with Gatsby and with the real rich. Some of the younger blacks have criticized Jim as being an Uncle Tom, but I had to get a guy who could communicate with different sides, with the most conservative as well as the most radical and militant. And all through this, he must be able to learn to love, to try to understand. Even though he does not, he must try to. . . . Marcus said, "The hell with it, let the world burn; I don't give a damn."

Is the character of Marcus modeled after the friend you spoke of earlier who knifed a guy and went to jail?

My friend did not come out of jail. Marcus comes out of jail. But if my friend had come out of jail, he might have been like Marcus. I wrote the story "Three Men" before I wrote *Of Love and Dust*. In "Three Men" he stays in jail. I kept thinking of things, and eventually I went back to "Three Men." I said, "What would happen if my boy comes out of jail? What would he do?" And I said, "With this guy's attitude about things, he isn't going to give up five years of his life on this plantation to work and to pay for his bond if he finds a way of escaping." And my imagination began to race.

Marcus is a person who doesn't believe anything is going to happen to him. The rebel must have this: "Nothing in the world can ever happen to me. I'm not going to believe in anything else in the world but me and what I can do for myself." You see, Marcus was pre-revolutionary, pre-Civil Rights. Marcus looked after Number One. He was always Number One, and unless I have him thinking like that, I don't have a book. So, you play along a little. I know that doesn't answer, but that's the way it works in the book.

When you read another writer are you consciously aware of looking for things you might be able to use?

Well, usually when I read, I read because I like to read. I love to read just like anybody else who loves literature. But I think I read carefully, and I see how a guy develops a scene. For example, I've hunted, but I like to see how it's done by other writers. Turgenev did it so well in *A Sportsman's Sketches.* Hemingway has done it. And Faulkner, you know, what he does with the smell of the trees when the weather is hot or when there's been a light rain, things like this. Every now and then I might read a woman writer to find out how a curtain should hang. I don't know these kind of things. You put a carpet on the floor that way; drapes should hang that way, two inches off the floor. I might read a woman writer or a man who can describe these things, and I would pay careful attention. Tolstoy did things with the eyes, you know, the batting of the eyelashes, which other writers could not do, so I look to see how Anna Karenina bats an eyelash, that kind of thing.

What writers have influenced you the most?

Hemingway and Faulkner are my two heroes, I suppose, in American literature.

Why?

Well, Hemingway has influenced every American writer since Hemingway, and Faulkner has influenced every Southern writer since Faulkner, and I'm a Southern writer, I suppose.
I admire Hemingway because of this grace under pressure thing which I think is more accurate of the black man in this country than the white man. Hemingway, without his knowing it, without

a lot of the younger blacks realizing it, was writing as much about Joe Louis or Jackie Robinson as he was about any white man. The bull ring, the fight, the war, blacks do this sort of thing all the time, daily. Not all of them come out gracefully under pressure, but many of them do, especially those who accomplish anything.

It was Forster who said that Hemingway only wrote long short stories, that he didn't write a real novel because he was always finished in such a short period of time. He said there was not enough time for the characters to develop and this sort of thing. I would disagree because if enough pressure is put on a man, anything that can happen in the world can happen in twenty-four hours.

I've read a lot of Greek tragedies, so I know what it means to be confined to a day's space and time. When I wrote "A Long Day in November" I used certain rhythms, simple rhythms confined to a day. My life, my people's lives, have always been in limited spaces, limited areas, and there's always been a limited time of happiness, a limited time of this, a limited time of that, so my life can fit very appropriately in limited time, in limited area. I come from a plantation. Most of our activities were on this plantation, this road with houses on either side of it, the church there, the grocery store owned by the plantation owner at the front, and we worked in the fields, and most of the people I knew, their lives were confined to that area. Greek tragedy is confined, and it fits well with my experience because I was confined, my people have always been confined. And this is the kind of thing I do, although I've been criticized by, I think, Granville Hicks. He said Gaines always seems to round things off at the end. Ah well, what's the use of prolonging the goddamned stuff?

Has Ralph Ellison influenced you?

No, I'm afraid he hasn't influenced me in any way.

Do you mind commenting on why?

When I went to school, first at San Francisco State and then Stanford, the emphasis was on styles, on how to write truly, on how to write well. Most of your teachers knew that you had something to say, and they were trying to help you bring it out.

But in all the creative writing classes I took there were no stories by black writers. You must realize, at the time, Ellison was not the big man he is today. In the mid-Fifties *Invisible Man* was out but nobody was assigning it, nobody was reading this book. You were just beginning to read Baldwin's essays, *Notes of a Native Son,* you were just beginning to read these things. There was very little emphasis upon writing by black writers. So, since I could not write what the white writer was writing about, I could learn how to write technically from what the white writers were doing. The emphasis was on how to write. Many younger blacks are influenced by different concepts, the "black is beautiful" thing. Well, I knew that, you know, years ago when I first started writing. All I wanted to know was how to bring it out. These books weren't available in the Fifties so, of course, I didn't read them. By the time I read them, I knew what I wanted to do and the way I wanted to do it.

Do you ever get writer's blocks?

Oh, yeah. The novel I'm working on now is a novel I tried to work years ago and never could. It defeated me every time I tried to work it, it just defeated me.

I spent five years writing my first book because I didn't know how to write a book, five years. My first book was published in '64. My second novel was published in '67, three years later, but it only took me eight months to write. Between '64 and '67 I was trying to write novels, but I just couldn't get another novel written. I wrote three or four books set in California, these unpublished things in here, different drafts of four or five books.

Would you say more about the problems of writing about California?

I've been here now over twenty-four years; I've been here twenty-four years this month. I think it's the Southern thing in me that I just cannot—I must get it out whether it takes another two or three years or the rest of my life. I think I must really get that out of me before I can do the California thing. It's like Caldwell, who fell apart once he stopped writing about Georgia. Joyce would probably have fallen apart once he stopped writing about Dublin. Or

Richard Wright, who did not write anything really great once he left the American scene. I doubt that Faulkner could have written anything great after he left Mississippi. I don't think *The Fable* is one of his greater books. So, maybe we're only made to write one book, I mean about one thing. Maybe that's why I haven't written a California thing. I think for the rest of my life I'll have something to write about Louisiana. I haven't touched the surface yet. I have so much to do.

Ernest Gaines: A Conversation
Paul Desruisseaux / 1978

From the *New York Times Book Review* 11 June 1978: 13, 44–45.
Used by permission.

When prosperity came around the corner, Ernest Gaines moved two doors up the street. The success of his novel *The Autobiography of Miss Jane Pittman* changed from three rooms to six—but not their location. Mr. Gaines has lived in California since he was 15, and the last half of those 30 years has been spent on Divisadero Street in San Francisco.

"This is where I've done all my work," he says. "This is considered the ghetto, but most of the people here are just hard-working, middle-class folks. They'd be *embarrassed* if they ever saw a rat."

The living room of Mr. Gaines's second-floor flat overlooks the street. His office, however, is at the back of the house, where it's quieter and, with an only slightly obstructed view of downtown San Francisco and the bay, more scenic. The walls are papered with maps that state out the author's personal geography: Louisiana, California, the United States and Africa.

Mr. Gaines was born and raised (the oldest of 12 children) on River Lake Plantation, Pointe Coupee Parish, LA., in 1933. He has, as evidenced by his writings, a reverence for the past, and throughout this house his own history is illuminated by a series of photographs: the plantation where, as a child of 9, he chopped sugar cane for 50 cents a day; the house in which he was born and brought up; the church and school he attended; and, of course, that pathway of possibilities, the road to Baton Rouge.

There are books in every room of this house, and there seem to be just as many records. Mr. Gaines says his writing has been influenced by music—jazz, blues, Negro spirituals and other kinds—almost as much as it has by literature. And this house always has music: when I arrive it's Rubinstein and Beethoven and, when I leave, B. B. King and the blues.

112

A strong body, Mr. Gaines believes, helps the mind get its work done, so he starts each day with a three-mile walk. He then settles in for five hours of writing. Except, of course, on days when he's interrupted by an interviewer's questions, which he answers in a warm, hearty voice that still has in it more than a bit of the bayou.

Q. Where did the idea for *In My Father's House* come from?

A. In my books there always seem to be fathers and sons searching for each other. That's a theme I've worked with since I started writing. Even when the father was not in the story. I've dealt with his absence and its effects on his children. And that is the theme of this book.

It just seemed time—after five books—to write a book about that. And if I've failed, then I've failed; but it's something I've wanted to do for a long while, long before I did *The Autobiography of Miss Jane Pittman,* or even the *Bloodline* stories. It just happened that I didn't do it until now.

Q. It's your smallest book, but it took you longer to write than any other. Special problems?

A. I knew what I wanted to write; it was a question of bringing it off, a technical problem. Usually, once I develop a character and "hear" his voice, I can let him tell the story. My writing is strongest when I do that. In most cases when my books are giving me a hard time I am not using *that* voice but my own, the omniscient narrator, the voice of God looking down on things. Which is what I did in this book. It was necessary because so much of the story is due to what Philip Martin is thinking. He does not tell anyone what's on his mind, so it would have been almost impossible for another character to tell the story without it sounding false.

Q. To what would you liken the experience of writing a novel?

A. When I start writing a book I never know exactly all the things that will happen in it, but I know certain things. It's like taking a train to Louisiana; I know I'm going to go through Texas, and that I will arrive by a certain day, but I don't know how the weather is going to be, who will sit next to me, what the conductor's going to look like. These are the little details you don't know when you start writing. Of course, there are some *major* details you probably won't know either!

Q. Is writing a novel essentially coming up with a story?

A. Oh no, no. Content is probably only 40 percent of it, no more than 50 percent, as far as I'm concerned. If a book doesn't have *form*, then damn, it ain't no novel. We can go down the block right now and find a guy on the next corner who'll tell the biggest and truest story you can ever hear. Now, putting that story down on paper so that a million people can read, and feel, and hear it like you on that street corner, that's going to take form. That's *writing*.

Q. What do you look for in a novel?

A. I must find immediate action. I look for something going on right from the beginning. I believe what Poe said, that if you don't grab the reader right at the start, you've already lost him. It must touch me. Look at how Pushkin starts his novels; that's how novels should begin.

Q. What part of writing do you most enjoy?

A. When I deal with dialogue. Once I develop my characters I can hear their voices quite easily. Not that it's easy writing, but for me it's easier than writing straight narrative, or descriptions, or anything else. When it's going well, I just love hearing those voices. Of course, when it's *not* going well I don't like hearing them at all.

Q. Do you ever have to force yourself to write?

A. No, I don't have any problems showing up. I can go to my desk. Sometimes I have to stare at the blank paper for quite a while, but I get up every morning to work. I first write long-hand, fast, then again slowly, then I do two more revisions on the typewriter, so anything my agent or editor sees is a fourth writing, which I consider a first draft.

Q. In your books there's a high price attached to bravery.

A. You must understand that the blacks who were brought here as slaves were prevented from becoming the men that they could be. They were to be servants of the whites, nothing more. A *man* can speak up, he can do things to protect himself, his home and his family, but the slaves could never do that. If the white said the slave was wrong, he was wrong. These things happened even after slavery, in the South and here, too.

So eventually the blacks started stepping over the line. They said, "Damn what *you* think I'm supposed to be—I will be what I

ought to be. And if I must die to do it, I'll die." And for a long time
they did get killed. Once they stepped over that line there was
always that possibility, and quite a few of my characters step over
that line.

Q. You list Hemingway among your influences. To what extent?

A. I think he influenced everyone who was trying to write in the
50's. I've always liked the way he understated things, and I
admire his writing style, which told me I did not have to use
adjectives and adverbs, and that's the damn truth. Also, he wrote
about people who always came through gracefully under pressure.
Now *nobody* has experienced as much pressure as the black in
this country, and nobody has come through more gracefully. I'm
afraid I give most of my characters a heavy burden to carry, and
then expect them to come through with dignity. This is why I
admire Hemingway: he showed me how to write that kind of thing.

Q. When did you first feel you'd be a writer?

A. When I was about 16. I come from a place where there were
no books. When we moved to California I was lonely, so I went
to the library and began to read a lot of fiction. But the books I read
did not have my people in them, no Southern blacks, Louisiana
blacks. Or if they did it was by white writers who did not interpret
things the way I would have. So I started writing about my people.

When I graduated from college in 1957 I said I'd give myself 10
years. I had some jobs, in the Post Office, at a print shop, just to
get by. After I published my first book, *Catherine Carmier,* in
1964—although I didn't make a damn cent—I knew that I would
spend my life writing.

Q. Do you consider yourself a Southern writer?

A. Southerners consider me a Southern writer, blacks consider
me a black writer, I don't know. My Southern experience certainly
made the greatest impact on my life, that's what I draw on in my
writing, so maybe that makes me a Southern writer, even though
I've lived in California twice as long. I really don't think about it.

Q. What is the job of the black writer in America?

A. I don't believe in telling anyone what he or she ought to write;
the job of any writer is to write truly about what he knows and feels.
But I do think—and I've been criticized for saying so—that too
many blacks have been writing to tell whites all about "the

problems," instead of writing something that all people, including
their own, could find interesting, could enjoy. And in so many cases
they leave out the humanity of their characters. Black writers have
to do more than work out their anger on paper.

I like pride in people. I try to show the strength of black people,
but I was criticized when I was writing *Miss Jane Pittman* because
blacks were expected to write novels of protest, it was your "duty"
as a black writer. I stuck to my guns and wrote what was true to
me, and if you read that book you'll see that there *is* protest in it.
Every novel has its own protests—if you're not commenting on
the human condition then what are you doing but playing with
words, shuffling paper?

Q. All your books have been set in this fictional locale you've
created along the St. Charles River. Are you going to write only
about Louisiana?

A. I could be happy doing that. Everything I've published has
been set there, but I've probably written as many books about
California that have been unpublishable. I find a closeness with
Southern characters, their language, their habits. When I try to
write about California it just doesn't ring true.

Many writers have done their best work when dealing with things
that impressed them early in their lives. There's something about
those early impressions that pulls you back. And if the place you
come from is rich with tradition, stories, myths, superstitions,
that's more of an attraction. Louisiana, of course, is rich in these
things; it also has a very romantic history. But all of this may be
incidental—it's still the place that I come from.

Q. You left there when you were a boy. How had you learned
these things?

A. Working in the fields, going fishing in the swamps with the
older people, and, especially, listening to the people who came to
my aunt's house, the aunt who raised me. She was a cripple and
could not go visiting, so people came to visit her. I'd be there to
serve them icewater, or coffee. There was no radio, no television,
so people *talked* about everything, even things that had happened 70
years earlier. I learned about storytelling by listening to these
people talk. The idea behind *Miss Jane Pittman* was based on

things I'd heard as a child, and from the life I come from, the plantation.

Q. Do you think a book defining the black experience in America should be set in the South?

A. Yes, of course. No period in this country's history can better depict it—good and bad—than the decade between 1958 and 1968 in the South. More people from, more levels of society were involved in what was going on in this country during that time than at any other. Not necessarily more people, but more kinds of people, from the lowliest black peasant who could not read his name in boxcar letters to the President. And I think that period in the South has the makings of a great American novel. Of course it would take someone with the talent of Tolstoy, and a 1,000-page book. And, I've always said, a black.

Q. Is this a book you're planning to write?

A. I will write parts of such a book, slices of it, but not *that* book and maybe no others; it would take all the energy I have. I think I have the imagination for it, but you'd need to do a tremendous amount of research.

Q. What's next?

A. Right now I really don't have a book that I can say for sure I'll be working on for two years, or five years. I don't have a *Miss Jane Pittman* or an *Of Love and Dust* in mind. I do have things that I know I'll work on, but I don't know what they will become, if anything. I'll definitely be working on something, I know that, and for a long while.

Q. How do you respond to criticism?

A. I really don't lose sleep over anything anybody says about my work. I don't think anything is going to affect my writing, or my attitude toward it. I've got a lot of work to do, and I'm going to keep on doing it.

Q. How do you feel when you finish a book?

A. Great. Whether the book is going to be accepted by people who read it is not as important, and does not make you feel as good, as actually finishing it. Because you always feel that you've failed, that you did not say in this book what you wanted to say, and you're happy the damn thing is done so you can move on to some other book to try to say in it the things you want to say, and maybe do a little better. You're forever going to that next book, and you're forever happy when it's over with.

That's how I've felt after every book I've written. Hell, if I'd have put everything I wanted to into *Miss Jane Pittman* there would have been no point in writing *In My Father's House*. Faulkner said that once you're satisfied with everything you've done, you might as well break the pencil and cut your throat. I mean, the whole damn thing is over with. So you never really finish. Not if you are a writer. And it never gets any easier.

An Interview with Ernest J. Gaines

Patricia Rickels / 1978

From the *Southwestern Review* 4.5 (1979): 33–50. Used by permission.

SR: It seems to me you have had an ideal sort of background for a writer. Coming from a place where you had roots in a rural ethnic community that had been there for a long time, and then to have the experience of a really fine higher education, and living in a cosmopolitan place like San Francisco, don't you feel you have the best of two worlds?

Gaines: I definitely have. I come from Louisiana and California, the best states, I think, for writers. I should say they are perhaps the two most romantic states. They are very similar and very different. They are similar in having two cities that are very cosmopolitan—San Francisco and New Orleans, and they are two states that have existed under different flags. They have different languages, nationalities. And Louisiana is different from any other Southern state—our religion, our French-Spanish influence, the different classes—the white, the very fair, the blacks. And I come from that kind of background, that Creole, that French culture along the False River. I came from a Catholic-Protestant background. I came from the plantation system. And when I came up, in my early years, in the late '30s, early '40s, the plantation wasn't too much different than it had been for even my *great* grandparents, even in slavery, because we did the same kind of work in the field. We worked just as long.

SR: And the old caste system was still there?

Gaines: It was still there. It was still there. And so I have a good idea of the historical condition of my people, the plight of my people. And I was fortunate enough at an early age to go to a place like San Francisco to be educated, a place so different and yet at the same time so conducive to the imaginative mind. It encouraged me to work. I had people there who were writers around me, poets, musicians. I'd come up in a place that was oral, we *talked* stories, we talked because the old people could not read and write. This was the background that I took with me. I've told students many times that in order to come out of a classroom a writer you must go in there a writer. You must take something in in order to bring something out. If you don't have the imagination, or you're not tried before, you might come out as a journalist, but I don't know that you could come out as a creative writer. You have to take it in there and then that teacher will help you mold it, I suppose.

SR: It does seem that coming from an oral society as you did, where the history of the people and their literature was by word of mouth, provided a great richness for you, but, of course, only because you were the kind of kid that took it in.

Gaines: Yes, yes.

SR: It was there for everybody, but you were the one who took it in.

Gaines: Yes. I was very close to an aunt who raised me. She was crippled. She never walked. She had to crawl every place she went. Maybe I already told you about her?

SR: I recall you talked about her several years ago at Southern University. I wish you would tell it again for the SR. It was very memorable.

Gaines: She would crawl on the floor. Very strong physically, morally, mentally very alert. She did all of the work for us. My mother was working in the fields at that time, or she was working in New Orleans, and later she followed my stepfather to California, where I would later go. But in the meantime we were living with my aunt, my brothers and sisters and myself. And she would do the cooking and the washing and the sewing. We had to bring all the things to her, you know. She would sit by the stove and we'd bring the food to her, and she'd cook. Or she would sit on a bench and lean over and wash our clothes in this old wash tub, with a washboard. In the afternoon she would go out into the garden. She would crawl over the floor and crawl down the steps and into the garden to do a little work. She loved working in the earth, she had to put her hands in the earth. I say that's why I write about the earth and still love it.

SR: No wonder you have such strong vital women in your books.

Gaines: My aunt was very, very strong though she couldn't walk at all.

SR: Was that Miss Augusteen Jefferson?

Gaines: Yes. That was the lady I dedicated *Miss Jane Pittman* to.

SR: I always tell my students about your aunt because I think those are the kinds of relationships that mark a young person's character. Don't you think so?

Gaines: Yes. I was asked that today by a television interviewer. She asked me (It was a good question, by the way), "What was the one thing as a child that most influenced you as a writer?" For a few seconds I couldn't think of anything else *but* my aunt. She had the *greatest* impact on my life, not only as a writer but as a man.

SR: I remember you telling about reading letters and writing letters for the old people as a child.

Gaines: That's right, I did that.

SR: You said it gave you a feeling for the flavor of their language. I wrote down almost every word you said in my old copy of *Miss Jane Pittman*. You said "the sound of my people talking," and that phrase stayed in my mind. Would you recall a little bit of that?

Gaines: Well, of course, I come from a plantation where most people couldn't read or write. I was pretty precocious as a child—being precocious then was someone who could read and write—and I was someone who was willing to do it for them. Of course, my aunt made sure that I did. She told me to go out and do this. I would go to these people and read their letters for them and write their letters for them. In most cases they didn't know how to form the letter. They'd give me a little piece of paper, you know those small, narrow tablets and pencil and say "Tell Viney" or "Tell Clara I'm all right. We're doing ok., and the garden's all right." Something like that. Then I would have to form the letter. I'd just write it, and re-write it, and re-write it until I got it right. Then I'd read it back to them.

SR: You didn't know you were doing your apprenticeship as a writer.

Gaines: I did not know it. I did not know it, and I'm sure they did not know anything about it either. It was just one of those things.

SR: Did you read much as a child?

Gaines: There were no libraries. I did not go into a public library until I went to California. There was no public library for me. But I went to California when I was fifteen, and I started going to the library when I was about sixteen. The reason why I went into the library was because my stepfather told me to get off the block because I could get myself into a lot of trouble. So I went to the library and I started reading books. Of course I wanted to read about blacks because I was a long way from the people I had left—my aunt, my brothers and sisters, friends, relatives—and I wanted to read about my people here. But at that time—this was in '48—there were no books, there were no books, there were no books by blacks or about blacks in any California libraries. I tried to read anything else, though. If I couldn't read about my people at all, I would read about the rural South. I had to read about the rural South. And then I would read about the rural life in any country. I discovered the better writers who wrote about this thing. From then, I tried to write. And that's one of the pieces of advice I would give to a young writer. He should read and just read and read. Try to read the better things, and if he can't get the better things, read something else. But just read and see how someone will form a paragraph, form a sentence, describe a sky at twelve o'clock and describe it at six o'clock in the morning or in the evening, or whatever. It is better to do a lot of reading and then, of course, do the writing. The next thing is to sit down and write and re-write and re-write. As I must have re-written those old people's letters many many times before I got it half way decent.

SR: I think you re-wrote *Catherine Carmier* a couple of times, didn't you?

Gaines: Oh, I wrote *Catherine Carmier* about twenty times. *Miss Jane* was probably one of my easiest books to write—no, *Of Love and Dust* was my easiest one, *Miss Jane* was the next easiest. This book I've just finished, *In My Father's House,* took me almost seven years to write, and it's not nearly what *Miss Jane* is, or some of the others.

SR: It did seem we waited a long time for it but then we're still waiting for Ralph Ellison's next book. There's another subject I would like to get into. It comes as quite a shock to a lot of white students

to discover that Cajuns tend to be villains for you, or for the
people in your books. As you know, we live in an area where the
Cajun has been romanticized out of sight: To be Cajun is to be
warm-hearted, good, loving, and so forth. We don't like to face the
fact that for another people the Cajun was the other poor person,
competing for the same things but having the edge because of
racism. But what would you say about the image you had of
Cajuns as you were coming up?

Gaines: Well, you must understand that they *were* our major
competitors. They *were* the share croppers, the people who were
on the next field over from yours. The blacks would have this land
here, the whites would have this land here. The Cajuns would have
the forward land, which was the better land and the blacks would
have the poorer land, because they were renting this same land
from another white man. For example, now, the place I come from,
there are no black renters, no black share croppers there. The
same Cajun family who were share cropping there when my uncles
were, when I was coming up, they are the people who now are
leasing the entire plantation. They made a heck of a lot of money.
They made enough money that they could demand and get better
machinery. And, of course, blacks started out having the worst of
the land, or the land that was not as productive as the Cajuns had,
the whites had. Those blacks who had better land than some of the
other blacks, produced better crops and lasted longer. It was
obvious whenever there was a problem between us the whites had
the advantage. This was the argument when I was a kid growing
up and this is still a thing that comes up when you talk about where
we live now, when you talk about a white. "Damn those Cajuns"
is what is said. You find a scapegoat. You've got to find a scapegoat.
And in the case of the people where I come from, if the scapegoat
was white, then he was a Cajun. That's all there is to it, whether he
was Cajun or not. He *was* our competitor. The blacks have been
put in the position of being the scapegoat in most of this country
and especially in the southern part of the United States. So, it's
one of those things that come about. Now the book I am reading
from tonight [*The Revenge of Old Men,* ms. of novel in progress,
read at Deep South Writers Conference, Nov. 22, 1978] has this
same sort of thing in it, but the narrator of the story is a Cajun.

He's going to be the hero of the book. Now, you know I'm saying
something now that maybe I shouldn't say, because I don't know
how the book is going to turn out. I've written now about 20–30
pages of it. But he's the narrator. I'm going to have him say
somewhere that he's a Cajun. He is the most *decent* person in the
entire book, as of right now. I don't know what's going to happen
later. He is the most decent person, but at the same time, there is
going to be Cajun and Black conflict. He is going to be the one to tell
the story exactly as he saw it. He is a newspaper man from Baton
Rouge telling the story. He is going to visit both black and white
and try to see just what the problem is. It involves a murder in
which a white man gets killed and the blacks are held responsible,
a whole village, a whole quarters. He is engaged to the girl who
owns or is one of the owners of the plantation. When this thing
happens, she calls him on the telephone and says, "Get over here
right away. I'm going to need you. All hell's going to bust loose."
So he is going to tell the story of exactly what goes on. Now in this
particular book—and I'm not trying to do that to pacify anybody.
I try to write a novel as I feel a novel, and I could not have written
this book, the one that I am working on now which I entitle *The
Revenge of Old Men,* two or three years ago because I was not
ready to write it. It was something that I thought about after I
finished *In My Father's House.*

It's not that I feel any kind of hatred personally myself. But I
must, in my writing I must try to write what I think the feelings of a
people are, and the feeling of people in rural Louisiana in the
general area that I came from, these were their feelings, the feeling of
both the black side and the white side. I don't romanticize it at all.
I don't even try to romanticize blacks. I *don't* romanticize blacks,
but I try to get strong black characters just as I would get cowardly
characters or weak characters or any other characters. I'm not
going to write any other way. The people whom I write about—you
must understand that Ernie Gaines comes from rural uneducated
people, and all they were were poor farmers, that's all they were,
or small town people. If they came into contact with anybody in
any kind of position, they usually came into contact with their
competitor first. And no matter who you are, these are the people
where the greatest animosity is, your nearest, the people you see

more often. People have more arguments with their brothers and their sisters, their mother and their father disagree more with them than with anyone else in the world.

SR: That's where all the murders take place.

Gaines: Exactly. That's where all the murders take place, among families, among people who know each other. And so, in a case like ours, that same thing must happen between the Cajun and the black, and it's going to happen. It's happening between the Jews and the Arabs right now because they're neighbors. If one lived in North Africa and the other in South America, there wouldn't be any problems because they'd never see each other. You're always going to have these conflicts.

SR: I think it's good to bring out this point and discuss it.

Gaines: Oh, I think it's good, and I hope people can understand it. I know where I am. I know I'm in this part of the country and I know there are a lot of French speaking, Cajuns or whatever, down in this area. But I must speak the truth on what I have written.

SR: Well, I'm pleased we have talked about it a little bit. As you say, you are trying to reflect and report honestly the perspectives. . . .

Gaines: The feelings of a people. Right. You know, if I were writing a story, a novel about the professors, or the educated people at Southern University, nothing like this probably would *ever* come up in the book.

SR: That would be a fine kind of thing for you to write about.

Gaines: I've never been to Southern. I was educated in California. I would know more about a white university in California than I would about Southern University. I've never studied at any black university.

SR: To turn to another subject, I'm sure you know that lots of people are convinced and cannot be unconvinced that Miss Jane Pittman was a real person and that she wrote the story of her life.

Gaines: I know that. I get that all the time.

SR: An elderly woman recently insisted on this point, and when asked who she thought Ernest Gaines was, said, "Well, I guess he edited the book for Miss Pittman." I thought this was just about the highest praise an author could have. I don't know why people

assume this, but I suppose because the language is so good. You
have captured in a way people find perfectly believable the perspective
that seems just right for Miss Jane.

Gaines: Well, I, from the beginning have had those kinds of
comments. *Newsweek* [Gaines suggested a major news magazine
instead of specifying the name.] when the book was first published
was going to do a review of it, and they called me for a picture of
the lady. They actually thought it was an autobiography.

SR: Yet you make it perfectly clear in the book that it is a novel,
and you set up the framework situation. I suppose you know Theodore
Rosengarten's *All God's Dangers?*

Gaines: Oh, yes. I haven't really read it all but have read parts
of it.

SR: If Jane Pittman has a male equal for strength and beauty and
stubbornness of character and mother wit, it's Nate Shaw.

We talked a little bit about your female characters being so strong
and so well drawn. Would you agree that your female characters
are generally better drawn than your male?

Gaines: You know, I've always been around very *strong* women.
My grandmother, dying of cancer, six days before she died, tried
to walk to the hospital. She walked down the stairs herself to get a
cab. She had intended to get herself to the hospital and admit
herself. Six days later she was dead. She had that kind of stubbornness about her. I talked about my aunt who had such a strength
about her. My mother is like that. I've known these women. The
father was in and out. I didn't see him all the time. He was in the
Merchant Marine and at home only occasionally. So I had these
strong female models and it was up to us, the boys in the house—
and I was the oldest male—it was up to us to go out and be the man,
do the hard work, go into the fields or whatever. And since it's hard
for me to write about myself, I suppose it's hard for me to make a
male character that strong a figure.

SR: It's not that your men are not good, and strong. It's just that
somehow, not just Miss Jane, but some of your other women stay
in the mind.

Gaines: Well, the girl in *Catherine Carmier,* Catherine herself.
SR: You know, I'm one of the people who like *Of Love and Dust*.
Gaines: I love that book.

SR: But it seems to get less attention, or is taken less seriously.

Gaines: It's going to be re-published, I think next spring in a quality paperback, the Norton Library.

SR: Isn't that the same series that recently did *Bloodline?*

Gaines: Right.

SR: They did a beautiful job with *Bloodline*. It's the same series that did *Cane* and I think the same person designed the cover. It's very effective. We had needed a paperback edition of *Bloodline* for a long time. I think maybe a couple of the stories in *Bloodline* are the best things you ever did.

But to get back to *Of Love and Dust,* don't you think it suffered from its presentation? That's a tacky looking cover.

Gaines: Isn't it, isn't it!

SR: The picture is really bad, and the nasty things it says on the back cover. "Magnificent scathing novel of forbidden desire on a Louisiana plantation in the heat of summer." It's true, but when I read that on a dust jacket, I don't usually read the book.

But it is a good novel. And Marcus and Jim seem to be exceptions to what we were saying about your male characters. They are both very memorable. And I like the way you use Jim as the narrator and develop his relationship with Marcus.

Gaines: You've got to have those kinds of narrators, who can meet the most conservative type mind, as a Margaret, and the radical, as Marcus. You know a lot of the students call Jim a "Tom," "a white-mouth nigger," that kind of stuff. All the guy is trying to say is that there's got to be some kind of balance between these two people, because they won't ever come together unless there's somebody more in the middle to sort of *bring* them closer together. He was needed, and he *is* used in all fiction. In *Gatsby* Carraway was needed. He has to be the kind of guy who can fit in with both crowds. Huckleberry Finn, you need somebody like that who can fit in with both Jim and the others.

SR: I like the ending, when he's saying goodbye to Aunt Margaret and she has already forgotten about the killing.

Gaines: She's managed to put it out of her mind.

SR: Jim says, "Some day I knew I'd be like her, but Marcus never would have been." The one who can't mellow can't live.

Gaines: Oh right, right. You've got to bend with the wind or you're broken.

SR: But yet we need people like Marcus.

Gaines: Oh yeah, yeah. If we didn't have people like Marcus, we'd all be like—I don't know who. We need the Marcuses. We've *got* to have them.

SR: And I don't know whether we have as many as we did a few years ago.

Gaines: They come up and go down. But they keep coming up. There'll always be a few.

SR: You know, another thing you do so well is the child's point of view. Those two marvellous stories in *Bloodline:* "A Long Day in November". . . .

Gaines: And "The Sky is Gray."

SR: What about the beautiful children's book made from "A Long Day in November"? Was it very successful?

Gaines: No, it was not very successful. They really didn't push that book at all. The girl who edited the book really wanted a children's book from me, but I don't think the Dial Press really cared about pushing it.

SR: Didn't it win some sort of prize for its illustrations?

Gaines: Yes, it did. They're very good.

SR: It's a story that has, along with the sadness and the real potential for tragedy, the most marvelous element of humor. And it seems so much in accord with what psychologists like Bettleheim tell us children really need, to confront the realities of bad things that happen in the world. The fact that the child in the story participates in the near destruction of the family and *survives* and the family survives, makes me consider it the kind of book children could get a lot out of reading.

I notice that your last book, *In My Father's House,* was not published by Dial.

Gaines: No. We went to Knopf, and Knopf isn't doing any better. In fact, I think that Knopf did not do as well as Dial would have done. My agent just felt that Dial should have put more effort and more publicity behind *Miss Jane Pittman,* pushed that book more. It was nominated for both the Pulitzer and the National Book Award, and she felt that if we had had the right kind of people behind us,

we could have gotten one of those. But that didn't work, so we went
to Knopf and this book was not the kind of book they are ready
to push. But it was the only thing I could write after *Miss Jane
Pittman*. Maybe five years from now I could have written it
better, but as of right now it was what I could do. And they are
doing nothing to promote it.

SR: I know it is not being well promoted. Of course, around here
we are particularly interested and we have been watching for it.
It's a good length; it's not over-priced, and it's certainly a timely
book. Where is and what is the black leadership after the death of
Malcolm and of Martin Luther King? To pick up a figure like Rev.
Martin in his dilemma—which way he should go, what he should
do—I don't think you could find a more timely subject. But then,
I'm very much interested in the legacy of Martin Luther King. I
like, too, the way you leave it at the end. We don't know what's
going to happen.

Gaines: I've been criticized a lot in bars for that. I go to a couple
of my favorite bars in San Francisco. We play dominos together
or shoot dice together. They read my books, you know, and they
complain, "Now, what the hell am I supposed to do? You stopped
the book half way. It took you seven years to write. Don't you think
you could have written another chapter?" That's the kind of thing
I've run into, but I felt it was complete once he went back into the
room, when she tells him, "We just have to start again, that's
all." To me it's complete.

SR: I think you stopped it at a very good place. You gave the
whole problem but not the whole solution.

Gaines: The problem is: here there are two men, and neither able
to stand at a particular moment in his life, neither father nor son.
The father hears the son knocking at the door, but he is unable to
say, "I love my children, my wife, and I'm going to be responsible
to them." And the son blames himself for not being able to commit
a murder, when his sister is raped. That novel is based on two
moments in life. If the first man had done what he felt later he
should have done, there would have been no problem.

SR: There would have been no Rev. Martin.

Gaines: There would not have been a Rev. Martin; there would
never have been any reason for them to go to California, so there

would never have been the reason for the rape. Other tragedies
could have followed, but it would never have been that. So this is
what the story is.

You know, there's an old lady in San Francisco, a very beautiful
lady, in her eighties who travels all over Europe by herself. She
and I play chess. She plays very good chess. Well, she beats me.
That doesn't mean very good chess. She called me after reading
In My Father's House. She said, "Ernest, let me tell you I think it
is a *very* good book. It's an odd thing. You know, there was a day
in *my* life when I was paralyzed like that. We must get together and
talk about this." There is a moment in everyone's life when you
become paralyzed to do the thing that you *should* do. You have
regrets later on. It can be a moment that can cause a complete
change in one's life, a moment that you should have taken to throw
on the lipstick properly or put some perfume behind your ear.
You know, that's what Chekhov would deal with, the little thing
you didn't do exactly right at the right moment, and you have to
pay for it later on. You can make that moment as important to one's
life as you want to, and I've tried to use it in this case, to make it
a point that would just *change* a man's life, completely change it
and lead to tragedy. I was writing it as a *play* in prose form. That
was my aim at the time. And, we have some people who are
interested in trying to do it.

SR: As a play?

Gaines: Yes, as a play. Interested. Not that we have signed a
contract or that we are sure there *will* be anything. But there are
people interested.

SR: I think that *Of Love and Dust* would make a very good
movie.

Gaines: Oh, I've thought that! Several people have taken options
on *Of Love and Dust,* but nothing has come of it. But I think it
would make an excellent movie. Of all the books I have written, I
think it would make the best movie.

SR: I saw movie scenes in my mind when I read it. To return to
My Father's House, I have a sense as I read it that it is the most
depressing of your books.

Gaines: Mmm.

SR: It doesn't have those moments of lightness, of humor, of the ridiculousness of existence. I thought it was going to, because I loved that woman. . . .

Gaines: Virginia Colar.

SR: Yes. I liked her. She is one of those women of yours. And you come close to the humor I'm talking about in the opening chapter when she makes excuses for taking Robert X into her home. She knows it's a dumb thing to do, but her heart is so big that she feeds him, with the excuse that she had made a mistake and cooked too much soap. There it is. But before that book was over, I found myself terribly depressed. It seems as if the options are running out. If the Civil Rights Movement, the Martin Luther King movement, *didn't* really change very many things, if he is dead, and the movement has petered out, and Robert X seems to be just a destructive, self-destructive. . . .

Gaines: No, no. I don't think I was saying that Martin Luther King didn't really *change* things. That's the *last* thing I would ever say.

SR: *You're* not, but a lot of the people in the book say that.

Gaines: Yeah, some people say it. But that's the *last* thing *I* would ever say, because he *did*. Billy is the one who says those things. And Billy says things out of complete anger, the little fellow from the war.

SR: The guerilla fighter?

Gaines: Yeah. What I am saying and what Martin is saying, what the story is saying, is all the things we've done—we fought to drink together, ride on the bus together, eat in the same places, but we have only recently realized that we are strangers. Martin and his son are strangers. We're not close. No, there's no way that I am criticizing Martin Luther King. Not me. Because King is probably one of three men of this century that I'll call heroic. A fantastic man as far as I'm concerned, for all that he did. But the movement was not aimed at fathers and sons. It was aimed at breaking down social conditions.

SR: In writing this book, did you have Turgenev's *Fathers and Sons* in the back of your mind?

Gaines: Yes, oh yea. That was not the original title, but that was what I always had in mind, the conflicts between fathers and

sons, the strangeness and strength of those relationships, the distance between fathers and sons.

SR: An estrangement?

Gaines: Yes, I would say so. I could go on and talk about why
you do have this distance between them, but that would take a
whole hour.

SR: Okay. I don't want to wear you out. But let me ask a few
more things. How come you don't write more short stories? You
do them so well.

Gaines: I have not written any short stories in about ten years,
for the simple reason that once I finish a novel I seem to have
another one in mind. But really I haven't thought of any good short
stories lately. If I do, I would write them, I'm sure.

SR: Your story "Three Men" is in the anthology *New Black
Voices* that we use in our Black literature course. The students
respond very well to it. They find it a strong and moving story and
representative of other dilemmas outside the prison situation.
May I ask just one more question?

Gaines: Sure, sure.

SR: Critics often compare you to Faulkner, and I am sure they
mean to be praising you. But don't you think it is a bad comparison?

Gaines: Why would you think it's bad?

SR: Well, for example, they say Miss Jane Pittman is the greatest
Black female character since Dilsey.

Gaines: (Laughter) Oh, yeah, Dilsey.

SR: Dilsey is nowhere compared to Miss Jane. You are much
better at your Black people than Faulkner.

Gaines: Well, I *hope* I am. I *hope* I am.

SR: And you're not really trying to do the same thing, are you?

Gaines: No, Ma'am! No way in the world. I want to write about
my people. I happen to come from Louisiana and I happen to
come from the land. My people did a lot of hunting, so I write about
hunting, the same with fishing. My people always talked about
the past and I try to write in the way that they spoke of the past. I
try to write about a certain place because when I was a kid in the
South my world was limited. Faulkner could write about his Jefferson, his Yoknapatawpha County, but I had to *live* in that place. I

had nowhere else to go. When I write about *a* given place, it's
simply because I never had anything except that place. There is
no way that I *try* to imitate him. I know I am connected with my
people here as much as he was with his. I think that most
Southern writers *are*, and I think it is a major theme in most
southern writers. And if you're going to write about the South,
there is always the past and present thing. Because you are constantly reminded of the past. That picture on the wall there
[photograph of an old Black man seated beside a very decrepit
cabin made of rough hewn logs]. If that doesn't connect us with
the past, what in the world can? And you see these things. You can
drive along these roads and . . . I visited a man today who lived
way back among the sugarcane fields. You couldn't *imagine* anybody being in those places back there. My brother and I had to
go back in there this morning, go by this old man's place out in the
fields. So I am constantly reminded of past and present.

You know Faulkner once wrote a story called "Mule in the
Yard." It's a funny, funny story about an old Black woman and a
white woman trying to get their mule out of the yard, about the
funniest thing you can read. Now, the same experience happened
to me. I'd gone to chop some weeds down and the weeds were like
a fence that kept the mule inside the yard. I chopped all those
weeds down, and the mule ran out. Now the owner had to get him
back in. He chased him *all* day long. The funniest thing you ever
saw. It wasn't funny to *him* at all, but it was funny to everybody
else. He'd chase the mule, the mule would stop and eat a little
while, then he'd run off again. Now, you know, everybody in the
South has seen this happen. You don't have to be in Mississippi.
This kind of stuff is something that I have experienced myself.
Now, let's say I had never lived in the South, had never seen anything
like this. Then you could say I was imitating Faulkner.

Now, we *have* been influenced by Faulkner, we *all* have. I think
in my story "Just Like A Tree" there is a definite influence of
Faulkner's *As I Lay Dying*. But as far as imitating him, intentionally
imitating him, I don't do that. People have asked me if Hemingway
has had any influence on me. He definitely did.

Hemingway's major theme, as I tell students, was "grace under
pressure." I ask them, who has had more pressure on them than

our Black athletes? And who's come through more gracefully than those who made it? Now Hemingway shows me how to put this on paper. That is the only thing I want him to do for me. To show me how to write about a subject that is true to my people.

SR: How about the Russians?

Gaines: Ivan Turgenev is *definitely* an influence. I read *Fathers and Sons* as a *bible* when I was writing my first novel *Catherine Carmier*. I've read him ever since. Definitely an influence.

But I suppose the reason I'm compared to Faulkner more than to anyone else is the Southern thing.

SR: And maybe because of what he said about "my own little postage stamp of ground. . . ."

Gaines: Yeah, right. You know most people feel that Faulkner has defined a world, has defined the South. Okay. This is it. Anyone else is imitating him. Just like anybody who writes about a bullfight is imitating Hemingway.

SR: Do you admire any of the other Black American Writers?

Gaines: I admire *all* the Black American writers. The man I think would have had the greatest influence on me had I read him earlier, is Jean Toomer, his *Cane*. To *me* that's the Black American novel. That *is* my novel.

SR: You know, however many times you read *Cane,* you never think you get it all.

Gaines: I think that there's nothing in Black literature to compare to it—that man is more original than any other Black writer. He is as original as any American writer. He was doing in *Cane* what—I'm sure Hemingway read *Cane*. You see *Cane* came out early, around '23, and Hemingway didn't start publishing his stuff till around '26–'27. What Toomer was doing, those chapters, and those little poetic things between the chapters, Hemingway does the same thing with the *In Our Time* stories—First he writes a story and then these little small passages.

SR: But *Cane* is full of terrific women, and Hemingway's women are not. . . .

Gaines: No, no. I mean form. I mean style. This is an influence. I'm pretty sure of it. Not only Hemingway, a lot of those people knew about what Toomer was doing. But even if Hemingway might not have known it, Toomer did it first. Much of what Hemingway did, Toomer did first. Much of what Gertrude Stein was doing, Toomer was doing also. This man has a combination of prose and poetry that we *ought* to have, Black writers ought to have. We're full of music, natural rhythm, you know music, music, music. And he has more music in his prose than any of us. Unfortunately for me, I discovered him after I had already sort of established a style of my own. But if I had not, I know without a doubt that he would have had the greatest influence on me.

SR: Is there any final comment you would care to make about your last book, *In My Father's House?*

Gaines: I wrote the book as honestly as I possibly could. I've gotten really high praises from some reviewers. *Newsweek* and the *New York Times* gave it a very good rating, both the daily and the Sunday *Times.* The *Washington Post* gave me a very, very good review of the book. The Baton Rouge paper gave me a very good review. Others have put it down. Jim Baldwin thinks it's a farce. He cannot support it.

SR: He's written a few farces himself.

Gaines: And just after Jim McPherson won the Pulitzer, my editor wrote him to get a comment, knowing that Jim and I were friends. You have this kind of thing going on, that those who compare the book say, "This is not the best thing you can do." That's what Baldwin told me. Baldwin said, "You must be the one to keep it up, keep it going. You can't fail." That's what he tells me. "We all have failed, but you can't. You've still got the potential to *not* fail."

SR: But it's not right for him to put that on you.

Gaines: I know it's not. But that's what he wants. Just like anything else, you might write a book that's not up to what the others were, not up to the expectation of what people wanted after *Miss Jane Pittman.*

SR: What people want is *The Return of Miss Jane Pittman.*

Gaines: Right, right.

SR: There is such a variety in your books. You've never just done the same thing again.

Gaines: That's been my aim, to try never to repeat myself, to never cheat and never repeat myself. I just hope I can keep going for two or three more books.

SR: Two or three more? You are just beginning.

Gaines: I hope so. I hope I can go on for another twenty years or so.

SR: I appreciate this interview very much, Mr. Gaines, and so will the students.

Interview with Ernest Gaines
Jeanie Blake / 1982

From *Xavier Review* 3 (1983): 1–13. Used by permission.

J.B.: You only spent the first 15 years of your life in Louisiana and yet Louisiana is the source of all your works, all of your books have Southern Louisiana as their setting. What's the reason for Louisiana's appeal? You have spent most of your life in California. Is it just because you were born here?

E.G.: No. It's the last 200 years, the people who have lived and died here. But I'm not the only writer who has ever done that—Joyce could not write about anything but Ireland.

I have younger brothers who were born here and left and they don't give a damn about coming back or even thinking about this place. We didn't all go to California. Some of the children stayed with my aunt. They sent me to California because I was the oldest.

J.B.: Your aunt was really very special to you, wasn't she?

E.G.: My aunt had the will to do, the will to survive. She never complained a day in her life. I loved my aunt very, very much. I think I loved her more than I've ever loved anyone.

J.B.: People have said that Miss Jane Pittman was your aunt. Was she?

E.G.: My Aunt Augusteen was not the model for Miss Jane Pittman; but Miss Jane had my aunt's moral strength. But my aunt never walked a day in her life. She crawled. She didn't even have a wheelchair until later, but she never used it. She'd crawl down the steps into her garden. She was the type of person who loved putting her hands into the earth.

My mother worked the fields. Later she followed my stepfather to California. She went from the fields of the plantation to New Orleans and from there to California. I lived with my aunt until I joined my mother.

I'm the oldest of 12 children. I have nine brothers and three sisters; and all are alive. Well, some are more alive than others.

J.B.: You were your aunt's favorite. Does that mean she spoiled you?

E.G.: No. I had to work harder because I was the oldest. People would bring their children to my aunt's before they would go to work in the fields. It was my duty to get up and light the fireplace so that it was warm when the people brought their children. We didn't have heaters then. I had to get up before sunrise to make sure there was water and wood in the house.

J.B.: When was the last time you saw your aunt?

E.G.: I saw her in '52. My aunt died the next year.

J.B.: How old were you when you began working in the fields?

E.G.: I lived on a sugar cane plantation, River Lake Plantation, on False River. I went into the fields when I was 8 years old and picked cotton and potatoes.

J.B.: Is it difficult to write about Louisiana when you live in San Francisco?

E.G.: I think I could write about hell if I concentrated enough. I could be on the moon and write about Louisiana. People ask me how can I do this, but if I were here, I might look at the buildings around me. I don't want to see those buildings; I want to see that plantation with the line of houses on both sides of the street in the quarters.

J.B.: When did you first experience discrimination?

E.G.: I started to understand discrimination at a very early age. We were trained to understand those things. Blacks could not afford to forget. I had pressure on me to know and to remember.

I felt the discrimination that any black Southern child would feel. New Roads was my little Bayonne. I couldn't eat or drink in certain places. I had to ride the back of the bus and I couldn't go to the bathroom in certain places. I've been hurt and insulted and I've seen the same things happen to my mother, sisters and brothers.

J.B.: Are you satisfied with the changes in the law?

E.G.: I'm not satisfied with the laws now. There are still miserable old men in Washington and Baton Rouge who are fighting against any kind of integrated society. The laws are there, but they can be broken. The Klan is just as much in effect today. They used to wear sheets; now they don't have to wear sheets. They can just parade down the street any time they wish.

There are some changes, of course. But I think a lot more can be done.

J.B.: Which novel gave you the most problems?

E.G.: My most difficult book was *In My Father's House*. It concerns a theme that I've always tried to follow in my books. I just carried the theme further in this one.

My most difficult character was Catherine Carmier. I had more problems with that damn woman, I can tell you that.

J.B.: You wrote *Catherine Carmier* when you were 16 years old, but the book wasn't published until years later. Why?

E.G.: I started to write *Catherine Carmier* when I was 16 and then put the book away for 10–12 years. But that manuscript is not the same *Catherine Carmier* that was published.

When I was 16 I wrote something that I thought was a book and I sent it to New York. It was sent right back. I then took it to the incinerator and burned it. After 10 years later I was writing short stories when my editor told me that I wouldn't make any money writing short stories and that the best way to gain recognition was to write a novel. It was then that I tried to think about the novel I wrote when I was 16. I started it again and it took me five years to finish it.

Catherine Carmier is told from the omniscient point-of-view which has always given me problems. I can handle the first-person point-of-view very well.

In My Father's House is also from the omniscient point-of-view and that book took me about seven years to write.

Miss Jane Pittman only took about two and a half years. In it I used the first person, which is taking the point-of-view of one of the characters. I have described *Miss Jane Pittman* as a "folk autobiog-raphy"; and by folk I mean it is not a story told by an educated person, but an uneducated person, an illiterate person, but someone with a tremendous sense of being, of knowing. Miss Jane is very intelligent from a folk, non-educated point-of-view. The format was verbal because Miss Jane couldn't write. That's why I created the tape recorder.

J.B.: Were you pleased with the way *Miss Jane Pittman* was presented on TV?

E.G.: I was pleased with much of it. Cicely did an excellent job and I think it's a good film, but it could have been a much better film if we had had more time and better secondary actors and actresses, but that would have cost more money.

I think the movie was almost an experiment for the producers. I think they knew they had good material, but they didn't know how the American public was going to take to it.

J.B.: What's your opinion of *Roots?*

E.G.: I'm not going to say anything about *Roots.* I think the book was so much greater than the film and that's all I'm going to say.

J.B.: In one article, you said that music is as important to your writing as literature. That's a pretty strong statement.

E.G.: I say anything sometimes. It all depends on how many drinks I've had. If I've only had two drinks, I can say intelligent things; if I've had none, I say nothing; and if I've had too many, then I can say some pretty dumb things.

I love music, all kinds of music. I think my stories are meant to be read out loud and I think that's because of the musical influence in my work.

In my work you see a lot of repetition: He said, she said Repetition of certain things and certain lines. Martin Luther King used a lot of this in his great speeches. It's a rhythmic thing that you develop in your speaking, which is a result of music.

Maybe I shouldn't have said music is as important as great books because it is not. It's a different medium, but music has been an influence.

I hear my books out loud in my head when I'm writing. When I was working on the *Autobiography of Miss Jane Pittman* I had music in the background. I played Mussorgsky's *Pictures at an Exhibition* over and over and over again. I thought of Miss Jane as picture of plantation life, sketches of a plantation. I have four books in that novel and each ends with something big happening.

In the first book, Miss Jane decides to go back South. There was no Ohio for her. The second book ends with the death of the school teacher. The third book ends with the death of Tee Bob, the son of the white owner of the land. Last is the death of Jimmy, the civil rights leader.

Nothing in the world is more dramatic than quick, violent death;

and it was listening to that music that helped me develop these sets, these scenes in my mind.

I was not so much aware of music when I was writing *Catherine Carmier*. But with *Of Love and Dust,* I played rural blues to help me capture the dust, the dirt and the sweat, the black nights and the white hot days.

J.B.: What's your main consideration when writing a book?

E.G.: The story has to be the thing. The story and the characters. I'm always talking against writing that is just political. The writer should be very detached from his work. I've always used the comparison that a writer should be as detached as a heart surgeon is from his work. To write well, you can't be crying as you're cutting someone's heart out.

J.B.: But you've written some very violent scenes, they must have affected you emotionally.

E.G.: Of course, but then I rewrite it. One scene in *Miss Jane* was the massacre and I had everyone killed except Miss Jane and the little boy. I remember a black student asked me, "How could you write that without total anger?" Now, I didn't say that I don't get angry while writing, but I created the damn situation. The important thing about that scene was getting Miss Jane alone in the swamps and the only way I could see to do that was by killing everybody off.

When writing the massacre, I wanted the reader to hear the sounds of people being clubbed to death, to hear how the small animals and birds leave. It was a Brueghel painting scene, a very violent scene, and I couldn't have written it if I were weeping all over the place. I had to sit down and write. I had to do that and do it well if it would make the reader angry; and then, maybe people would remember and not let that happen again.

People have accused me of being too goddamn cold. I don't think I'm cold. The work has to be done well. I'm a writer first. I can't get angry about things I created.

J.B.: You've been labeled a black writer, a Southern writer, a Louisiana writer, a California writer. Which are you?

E.G.: I don't care what the hell people call me. I just don't give a damn. By the time they start categorizing me I'm thinking about something else to write about. All I need is to have enough funds to keep myself going so I can write. I don't give a damn what category people put me in. If they buy my books, they can put me in any category they want. It doesn't matter.

I would like to write as well as the best and I don't give a goddamn what people say.

J.B.: When you begin a novel, do you always know what will happen. Is everything outlined?

E.G.: It's impossible for me to know everything when I start out. I discover things along the way just as the reader does.

J.B.: Do you know the endings?

E.G.: No, not always. I bet I wrote six, seven different endings for *In My Father's House*. I had everybody dying off in it. I just didn't know what to do with it; and it was for that reason that the book took seven years to write.

J.B.: Do you have a writing schedule?

E.G.: I try to write about five hours a day. I don't create at the typewriter. I first write in long-hand on yellow paper, then I retype it and retype it and revise all the time.

In San Francisco, I get up at 6:30 or 7 A.M., eat a little food, go out for a four to five mile walk, come back, shower and then stare at that damn desk.

J.B.: Why don't you just dictate into a machine?

E.G.: I write it out first because I like that physical part of writing. I started out by writing in pencil because I didn't have a typewriter. I don't believe in just dictating into a tape recorder. I believe in doing things for myself. I do everything for myself. My eyesight is going bad, but I'm not that blind yet.

J.B.: Do you talk about your book in progress?

E.G.: Once I start writing a book I very seldom will discuss it until I have gone through a complete first draft.

J.B.: You gave yourself 10 years to see if you could make it as a writer. When did you make that promise to yourself?

E.G.: When I got out of college in '57. I decided then that I would give myself 10 years to see if I was satisfied with my accomplishments. It was exactly 10 years when I began to make some money as a writer. *Of Love and Dust* was published that year. I made $1,500 on *Catherine Carmier,* which took me five years to

write; and that was the advance money—the book just didn't sell.
Now it's being republished.

J.B.: How much money have you made from your other books?

E.G.: I didn't make any money at all from *In My Father's House*.
I only had about $20,000 advance on that book, which is nothing.
That's it so far; and it took me seven years to write. Then my agent
gets her 10 percent and Uncle Sam gets his. I guess I made about
$2,000 a year on that book.

Miss Jane carried me on her back for a long time. I don't know
how much money *Miss Jane* made. We sold rights to television
for $50,000. That's outright. But I get a percentage of the royalties.

J.B.: If you had not made it, what would you have done?

E.G.: I don't know. The San Francisco Golden Gate Bridge is
famous for people who jump. But I don't know if I would have had
the nerve. I banked everything on those ten years, which were
going to either make or break me. I didn't have anything else. I
could have gone on to receive my teacher's credentials, but I don't
know if I would have done that. And that's the only thing I could
have done with my background.

J.B.: Do you have a favorite novel of yours, or is that like picking
a favorite child?

E.G.: I won't pick a favorite.

J.B.: You really enjoy writing dialogue, don't you?

E.G.: Dialogue is the meat of my writing. My challenge.

J.B.: Are you a religious person?

E.G.: I'm not orthodox. I don't go to any church. But I hope
there is something else. If man is the greatest thing in this
universe, then I pity this universe.

J.B.: Do you have a temper?

E.G.: Yes ma'am, I have a temper. At times I can get awfully
mad. I get mad at people I put trust in when they let me down.

J.B.: Do you keep a diary or a journal?

E.G.: I used to keep a journal, but I stopped. I don't write about
anything I can't remember. I might hear a phrase every now and
then that is so unique I will write it down because I might want to
use it later.

J.B.: Which writers have influenced your work?

E.G.: I've learned from Flaubert, who was a great formal writer;

from Turgenev, a great classicist; and the modernists, such as Hemingway and Fitzgerald's *Gatsby*. I don't care for Fitzgerald, but I love
the structure of *Gatsby*. I like some of James Joyce's short
stories; and I especially like the form of *Ulysses*, the one day thing.
I've tried to do that in my work, to get as much in one day as I can.
A Gathering of Old Men, which I am working on now, takes place
in one afternoon. You can do a lot of complex things in one day.
Anything that can happen in life can happen in one day, 24 hours.

J.B.: Does writing give you a feeling of immortality?

E.G.: I think my books will outlast me, but that's not why I
write. I write because I can't shoot lions. I write because I'd
probably be a pretty terrible bank robber or thief. I think one of the
reasons I write is to try and catch—and I don't know if this is it
either—to catch some of the things that I think are important in my
own America, the narrow little space that my people were allowed to
move in and out of. Maybe that's why. I suppose you're driven to
writing as ministers are driven to be ministers. I know I write because
I don't want to do anything else.

But I want to make money and I don't know if I would spend five
hours a day writing if I didn't make anything at it.

J.B.: You had so much in common with Jackson Guerin in
Catherine Carmier. Was that your story or was it total fiction?

E.G.: I think every work has a bit of your autobiography in it.

J.B.: Have you ever been to a writers' conference?

E.G.: When I finished Stanford, Malcolm Collier, [Cowley] one
of the top critics in this country, wanted me to go to a writers'
commune in New England and work. But my agent told me not to
do that. My agent said once you get involved, you'll do it forever;
keep away, even if you have to sweep the streets. You get depen-
dent, he warned, and will go from one to the other for the rest of
your life.

J.B.: Of the 16 students you are now teaching, how many do you
think will be able to support themselves with their writing?

E.G.: Maybe not one. I was just like these students. I just worked
eight hours a day, instead of four. I know what work is. I know what
it is to go to that desk and work.

But I'm masochistic in a way. I love the work. It's like getting in
shape for a fight. I've got to practice every day. I'm disciplined.

My stepfather, my aunt, being an athlete, all taught me discipline.
You've got to get up in the morning and work.

J.B.: What advice do you give your students?

E.G.: I tell them they have to do six things: read, read, read,
write, write, write.

J.B.: What is the most common mistake beginning writers make?

E.G.: They want to be published too fast. They want agents. I
believe in agents, but you don't need one until you have a book
ready. I think few writers with their first novel need an agent.
Unless, of course, the book really sells, then you need someone
to take over the business side for you.

But your average book-going author is not going to sell very well.
I don't need an agent to publish a book, but I need an agent to do
all the little things, to fight and argue for me. It could mean the
difference between getting $20,000 or $50,000 advance.

J.B.: What qualities must a successful writer possess?

E.G.: You have to be able to lie, to tell stories. Observation is
part of it, but not all great writers are visual. Some have a great
ear. Joyce was one.

I'm most comfortable with hearing and maybe seeing some
things. Some writers can describe how whiskey feels going
down—from the first inhaling of the fumes to the actual going down.
I can't do that, but I can hear it, the pouring of the whiskey into
the glass.

A real genius has all five senses working together. That's a
real master.

J.B.: You seem to be very demanding when it comes to your characters.

E.G.: People are constantly criticizing me for putting too much
pressure on my characters, like the little boy in "The Sky is
Gray." But I demand a lot from people, my family, my friends, my
woman, my characters. I know I demand too much: People can't
perform all the time. I damn sure don't always perform in the
proper way.

I make demands of myself. Of course, I fail and then I get angry.
But I do make demands of myself and my characters. You see, I
can make my characters do what I want. Others can tell me to go to
hell, but those damn characters better do what I want or I'll get

rid of them and put someone else in. But you can't really do that, you know.

Faulkner once said that characters usually take over on page 114, unless you end the book on page 113. You have to control your characters like wild horses, let them go and go and go with some minimum amount of control.

J.B.: Do you consider yourself an intellectual?

E.G.: I am not an intellectual and don't want to be. An intellectual studies books, not people. I don't know if an intellectual knows how to drink at a bar, and they don't know how to act with people who are not intellectuals. They don't know how to talk with them. They are either tense or being too Goddamn patronizing.

J.B.: Have you ever lived in New Orleans?

E.G.: I've never lived in New Orleans. I wanted to live there in '63, but my uncle persuaded me to live in Baton Rouge. I would like to live in New Orleans because I want to know about the city, if just for background information.

Eventually I'll have to leave those plantations and come to town. I can go to Baton Rouge in my stories, which I did in *In My Father's House,* but it's always just a little scene and then back across the river to Pointe Coupee Parish.

J.B.: Do you write poetry?

E.G.: I love reading poetry, but I don't write it. I wrote a poem once and everyone told me I should drive a truck instead, so I quit writing it.

J.B.: You've written several books about California that were never published. Why didn't you burn them, as you did your first novel?

E.G.: Maybe when I'm dead, people will see just how bad things can be for a writer. They are not good. Certain writers can only write about certain things and that's all they can do. I don't know if I could write about contemporary Louisiana.

J.B.: Have you ever been married?

E.G.: Never been married, but women have tried. But I've fought it.

J.B.: What type of women are you attracted to?

E.G.: Women who love bars. Fast women. I love them and they love me.

J.B.: All of your white characters seem to be racist, cruel and/or stupid. Why?

E.G.: I try to create the type of white character whom I can best understand. I might be prejudiced toward the character, but I try to do as well as I can with that character.

J.B.: Do you have any regrets?

E.G.: I regret that I don't have a 25-year-old daughter, someone to take care of me when I have a cold. A daughter would make me coffee and put a scarf around my neck.

J.B.: When you finish a novel, do you give yourself a break?

E.G.: I try to give myself some time, but my mind is never off writing. I just maybe quit for a couple of weeks.

J.B.: Do you write for a black audience?

E.G.: I think I have a God-given talent, but I don't believe in telling anyone how they should live. This is one of the things I've complained about. I have, in a way, refused to write for whites or blacks. I try to write as well as I can.

Now, if there were only one audience in the world to read my works, then I would like that group to be blacks or Southern blacks.

I know when *Miss Jane Pittman* first came out, some of the worst criticism came from blacks who did not see her as being important enough to write about. They thought that little lives did not make literature.

Miss Jane was written in 1968 when all the demonstrations were going on. At San Francisco State, the cops were bashing in the heads of the protestors and, instead of joining them and fighting the cops and dogs or carrying a placard, I was at home writing a story about a little old lady. But I wanted people to realize that she was very important, that her spirit existed during the past 100 years. We see her and take her for granted. No one writes about her, the average little old lady walking on the road.

I think the greatest writing takes something small and turns it into literature. This is what I try to do.

J.B.: Do you have doubts about your writing ability?

E.G.: I'm very satisfied with my work, but at the same time there is nothing more painful than to do my work well.

I have doubts. I have doubts all the time. Sometimes I will go back and read a part from one of my books and say, that was damn good, I was really good then. And yet, I may write something the next day and feel that it is the worst thing I've ever written in my life.

Every day is a day of recognition. Every book is a challenge. It doesn't get any easier.

I feel that there is only one big book, the complete thing, which I will never finish. The complete thing is your life as a man; then you die off.

I feel that *Miss Jane, Catherine Carmier, Of Love and Dust, Bloodline,* are all part of the big book because no one book ever captures everything. So you write another book. But that won't capture it. I know it won't. So you do a little more and never finish.

A MELUS Interview: Ernest J. Gaines—"Other Things to Write About"

Mary Ellen Doyle, S.C.N. / 1983

From *MELUS* 11 (1984): 59–81. Used by permission.

A writer who knows his own goals and methods, knows his right to maintain them, and does so with tenacity and good humor—this is Ernest J. Gaines in public and private interviews. As guest of the 1982 River City Contemporary Writers series at Memphis State University, Gaines was questioned by a panel from several Memphis colleges and by the audience. Later, he answered my further questions by letter and telephone and in three interviews in 1983 at his home in San Francisco.

Gaines was raised and worked on a sugar cane plantation near Baton Rouge, Louisiana, until, at fifteen, he moved with his mother and stepfather to California. Following the latter's injunction to "get off the streets," he made his first incursion into a public library and into a new world of vicarious experience. Searching in vain, however, for his own Louisiana experience and people, he received his stimulus to write.

His short stories were published first in college magazines, then in journals, anthologies, and a collection, *Bloodline* (1968). In 1964, *Catherine Carmier* became the first of five novels. Though public awareness of Mr. Gaines's novels was most extended by the televised version of *The Autobiography of Miss Jane Pittman*, his literary reputation rests on his growing stack of books—books which, like his responses to interviewers, reflect his humane, hopeful, zestful approach to all life.

Interviewer: My first question is really an invitation to speak of your own aims and motives. Your work was first published in the sixties, the era primarily of militant writers. Your basic tone seems significantly different from theirs, although you have several militant characters truthfully drawn, and you certainly "tell it like it is." Would you comment on this difference and on your aims?

Gaines: Well, most of the writers of the sixties were younger than I, and I started when I was sixteen—in 1949; and I haven't changed much what I wanted to do then. The sixties were just another time to continue what I'd thought about all through the early fifties, when I first got out of the Army and went to San Francisco State and later on a fellowship to Stanford. I knew I wanted to write about my rural Louisiana, the people I knew—their personal daily lives, their dreams, accomplishments. I began writing seriously, I'd say, about 1955, and I started publishing in college magazines as early as 1956. So by the sixties, I'd discovered—decided—what I wanted to deal with, and I never did alter it.

I was living in San Francisco in the late sixties, and I had friends and relatives and critics tell me I should be writing about what was going on at San Francisco State (when Mr. Hayakawa let the cops on campus—things of that sort). I was writing *The Autobiography of Miss Jane Pittman* then, and I know most people thought I should be writing something more contemporary. But I stuck to my ground—to writing my particular book. I felt I had already set the goals for my writing, and I intended to go on. I followed the work of the sixties, read a lot of it—criticized a lot of it. But I established my direction before they started.

Interviewer: Are you saying that you want to break with the tradition of protest associated with Richard Wright and his followers?

Gaines: What I've always been saying is that the blueprint for Black literature is not *Native Son,* that something existed a hundred years before Chicago in 1940. In my writing, I just refuse to accept the idea that everything started in Harlem or Chicago, that we must write only about the big city, urban northern ghetto life, say. I know there are other things to write about. I know there's bravery and courage, and love and hate and fear and singing and dancing. These things were happening many many years before the naturalistic novel came about with Richard Wright. Jean Toomer wrote about them in *Cane,* a fantastic book. Before Alex Haley called it *Roots,* I was trying to do something like that, to write about our past, where we come from. Each book I've written, except the last one, has gone farther back: *Catherine Carmier* starts with the sixties; the *Bloodline* stories were set in the forties up to the sixties; *Of Love and Dust* was a story of the forties; then *Miss Jane,* of course, went back to 1862. So I'm constantly going back and back and back, trying to show that all Black stories don't have to be in Memphis or Harlem or wherever.

Interviewer: This sounds like the concept of the novelist as ghost-writer of history. Does this concept interest you, and if so, what history are you trying to write?

Gaines: Well, I don't know that I'm writing history. I try to write about my background, the people I come from. They have lived in the same area, on the same plantation, for five generations, and they have not been written about. Most white writers treated only the romantic things of the South and I think many Black writers of the fifties, sixties, and seventies also thought rural life was not worth writing about; they preferred urban life, the big city. I'm trying to write about a people I feel are worth writing about, to make the world aware of them, make them aware of themselves. They've always thought literature is written about someone else, and it's hard to convince them that they are worthy of literature. I keep repeating this over and over, to convince them.

Interviewer: Do you try to educate white readers about Blacks?

Gaines: No, I think too many Blacks have tried to do that—to write to educate whites. No, I don't. I—really, I write because I must write. I write because I don't want to stay drunk all the time or don't want to climb mountains or start fights—or anything like that. So I write—I write to keep my sanity really. I'm always asked who I write for, and if I had to write for any particular group—if I *had* to do it—someone had a machine gun and said, "You'd better write for someone; tell us," I'd say, "Well, I write for Black youth, especially of the South." And if they said, "OK, give us two groups," I'd say, "For the Black and white youth of the South." But I'm not really writing for any one group of people—just as I never did join "schools." If I joined a school, I'd have to write according to what was going on around me, and I refuse to have to do that. So I just write as honestly as I possibly can and put it out there and hope you read it. It's a lonely position to be in, but there are lonelier, I suppose.

Interviewer: I'd like to comment that your work also reaches very significantly the northern urban youth, primarily Blacks, but also whites, because you deal with precisely that area of Black experience, from 1860 to 1960, that they cannot personally remember.

I knew I'd crossed the generation gap when I first met students who
had little or no living memory of Martin Luther King or the civil rights
revolution. And your work brings that experience alive for these
students who are not from the South and not from the time period
that you write about. But the inevitable question: if you choose to
write about rural Louisiana, why do you choose to live in San Francisco?

Gaines: Well, you see, I'm always in Louisiana even though I'm
not living there. And that's not unique. Other writers left a certain
area to write about it. I can shut my eyes and see—especially the
things I write about. If I wrote about the oil wells popping in Louisiana
right now, maybe it'd be better if I were in Louisiana. But if I'm
writing about something that happened forty years ago, I can face
the wall in San Francisco and see it as well or better than I would if
I sat in an apartment or a house in Louisiana and looked out at
oil wells; they would distract me. Looking at the blank wall, I can
see any kind of world I want to see there. But I do go back there
every year; I go back to be with the people, to be with the land, to
talk, eat the food, go to the bars—that sort of thing.

Interviewer: Do you ever write about other places?

Gaines: No, I can only write about Louisiana. I've written several
manuscripts about San Francisco, but they're very bad. I have
about five manuscripts—on the Beat thing, all kinds of live stories—
but they just didn't come out. So I picked my own back yard—and
there's nothing wrong with that. After all, Yoknapatawpha County
was good enough for Faulkner. I want to write about Louisiana
because I think we have enough material in Louisiana to outlast me.
I haven't touched it yet. So I concentrate as much as possible on
that little area. That's enough.

Interviewer: Then do you write from experience?

Gaines: Well, people ask me that, and I say, yes, I write from
direct experience and vicarious experience. I use the rural Louisiana material—rural and Baton Rouge. I can't even write about New
Orleans because I never spent enough time in New Orleans. I've
been there twenty-five times, I suppose, but I have not stayed there.
I can get a lot of books—history, travel guides—but I'd rather not
do that. So I can have characters go to New Orleans and do things,
but then they must leave because I don't know the structure of

things there. They have to go back to Baton Rouge, back out to the country as fast as possible, to the small town. I know that feeling there.

Interviewer: If you write only from your experience, how can you write about an old woman or whites? or, on the other hand, how can writers stick to their own experience and not be limiting themselves as artists?

Gaines: I don't write only about things I've done; I said I use both direct and vicarious experience. I don't know a woman's feeling about different things; I've read enough and heard them talk about it. I don't know living conditions before the forties, but I had to write about Miss Jane Pittman in the 1860s—through reading and reading and reading. I wrote about white characters during that time through reading and reading about what was going on at that time. I've been praised for some of the things. But I've had the same sort of criticism about my Black characters: they are too harsh or too mean, or they are bowing and scraping. I think the writer's success depends on how much talent he has, how much work he does, how well he wants to do this; if he's a poor writer, no matter how well he wants to do it, he won't write well even about his own situation, his own people.

Interviewer: Can you tell us about the research you did for *Miss Jane Pittman?*

Gaines: Yes. I went to the archives at LSU, the library at Southern, and the State library. I bought books, and the library in San Francisco got books from other libraries. I would read just enough of any books for the particular thing I wanted Miss Jane to know—just the passage I needed. The single book that I think helped me most was a collection of interviews by ex-slaves in the 30s, called *Lay My Burden Down*. Through that book, I got a common language; I got how the ex-slaves of a certain area spoke, what they ate, the number of pieces of clothes, what freedoms they did have—that sort of thing. The other books were technical histories. I also read biographies—autobiographies—journals. I even read *The Diary of Anne Frank* to see what a young girl would think about when she's alone—almost anything to try to get to Miss Jane.

I remember—speaking of research—I remember the Huey Long

chapter. I read three books on Long, and knew that when he was
shot, it was a Sunday and was raining; I knew that when he died on
Tuesday, it was raining. But no one had written what the weather
was on Thursday, the day of his burial, so I went out to the fields
and asked the people about it. Some people would say it was
raining, others that the sun was shining. So I went back to LSU and
asked the research librarian for all she could find on the days after
Huey Long's assassination. She brought out a pile of manila fold-
ers—yea high—and said, "Well it's somewhere in there." I went
through it for three or four hours, and a little passage in an Arkansas
paper, about three inches long said there were intermittent show-
ers. So both groups of people I'd spoken to were right. But I had to
find out for myself. And after I'd spent four hours in there, I
didn't even use the material because when Miss Jane came to
narrate her little chapter, the detail was not necessary. But I had to
get it. Using historical information like that, you have to digest it
and then give it back to a little lady who is illiterate—very
intelligent—brilliant, but illiterate. She's never read a book; she
cannot write. So that was a problem; I had to get all this information,
and then I had to come back and get a language for her. I remember
Twain said, "Read, then distort." You must know everything,
then give it to someone like Huckleberry Finn.

Interviewer: Let's go more into your reading. What contemporary novelists do you read?

Gaines: I don't read too many contemporary novelists. As a
matter of fact, I only read contemporary novels by friends of
mine—James Alan McPherson, Alice Walker, Maya Angelou. There
are so many other books that I like reading over and over. I can
always pick up *War and Peace* and read a chapter. I can't do that
with contemporary novels. Once I've seen them I don't read them
any more. (I shouldn't say that because I'm writing now!)

Interviewer: What reading would help a beginning writer today?
Would contemporary writing help most?

Gaines: If it is experimental writing, I think it would not be as
helpful to the young writer as good established past writers. I
can't think of a better book for a young writer to read about war,
say, than *All Quiet on the Western Front*. Tolstoy's *War and
Peace* might be too big. I think for structure, there's not a better

book for a young writer, whether he likes the subject matter or
not, than *Gatsby*—for first person point of view and the structure.
Or Twain's *Huckleberry Finn*. Or Flaubert's *Bovary*. Or Turgenev's *Fathers and Sons*. I think the young writer should know these
books. I think he should read them and then come up to contemporary novels. If the novel is going in a different direction (and I'm
not sure of that), I don't know when it's going to get there. If we
knew that in 1988 a novel would differ from what we know as the
novel form, I would say, well, maybe read the experimental books
today. But I think a writer should have a base of these other
established novels. I think he should have that.

But of course, I do something very different from the experimental novel; my characters still say "Yes" and "No" and they say it
in separate sentences, and I use commas and periods a lot. I don't
use way-out adjectives and adverbs and long, "subconscious,"
sentences and all. I still like well structured paragraphs and end
them with a period. All these dashes and parentheses and little
drawings and symbols—I can't do things like that. If anyone can,
let him do it. It depends on the individualism of the writer. I can
just give a few hints on how to get started:

Interviewer: Can we talk a little about process? Do you rewrite a
lot? How much can you write in a typical day?

Gaines: Of course, I rewrite a lot. Dialogue is very easy for me
to write; I can write, say, ten pages of it a day. Of course, I may
rewrite it ten times to get it exactly the way I want it, but I can
revise dialogue very fast. Descriptive passages give me some
problem; I might write only one page of descriptive work a day.
How much work I can do in any day's time depends on what the
situation is, whether I have a group of people I'm writing about, or
one or two people talking or moving, what part of a scene I'm
doing. Instead of trying to write a certain number of pages or a
certain number of words a day, I try to get in a certain amount of
time a day—about five hours. I start at nine in the morning and
work until about two in the afternoon. I stop in the middle for
coffee or water, but I try to get in that much time each day, five
days a week. If I get two pages today, maybe I get five pages the
next day, and the next day only two or three paragraphs. It depends
on the problem of the book that I'm working out.

Interviewer: Are there any things about the process that you fear?

Gaines: No, I don't have any fear of the process—I'm just trying to think—no, I just get up and I go to that desk.

Interviewer: Someone talks about how characters begin to take the writer over as if the personalities of the characters are floating around out there and the writer doesn't really always know what they will do or say next. Is it that way with you?

Gaines: I think Faulkner once said the characters take over on page 114 unless the book ends on page 113. I do think that they take over. Miss Jane took over. I have a problem with the omniscient point of view because I'm constantly overseeing everything. I had this difficulty with my first novel, *Catherine Carmier,* and with *In My Father's House.* But in those stories where I use the first person point of view, the characters do sort of get control. There's no way you can change them; there's no way in the world I could have kept that little old lady from trying to get to Ohio. I knew she would never get there, but I couldn't keep her from going. She had to go as far as she did till she got very, very tired, and I couldn't do anything about that. Yes, they do take over. But you have to get up every morning at nine o'clock and sit at the desk and write for five or six hours or they won't take over.

Interviewer: I'd like to pick up your comment on viewpoint because I find that to be one of the most interesting technical features of your writing. Usually first person narration is in the past tense; the event is over. But in several stories, you have narrators, including children, who use present tense, as if the event is in progress, as if they are "thinking their lives" as they go. For instance, in "The Sky Is Gray": "We stand and wait for the bus and the bus is coming. . . ." This is done even when the child is coming out of a waking dream. It struck me as a technical innovation. Is it, or is it a kind of dialectical use of the present tense?

Gaines: I never thought of making changes in technique. I think I must have read it somewhere. I think Faulkner uses it in the first part of *The Sound and the Fury,* with Benjy's immediate feelings. And it was a way to deal with a kid six or eight years old.

Interviewer: Well, Lewis in "Three Men," too, at least part of the time, is thinking-narrating as the action occurs. It does create tremendous immediacy. Whatever your technical viewpoint, your stories seem to use the mind's eye as a camera which is always very closely on the character.

Gaines: I think the best writers of the present are those who concentrate on the people very closely. And I do try to develop characters to make them as real as possible. My aim in literature is to develop character, not only the character in the book, but my character as well as yours, so that if you pick up the book, you will see something you feel is true, something not seen before, that will help develop your character from that day forward.

Interviewer: My students ask about some of your strong characters, especially your *very* strong, even tough, mothers. In "The Sky Is Gray," for instance, the mother insists her young son endure the bitter cold without his collar turned up. Not only does she not coddle him, she does not accept what most of us consider a child's ordinary demonstrations of affection. Why?

Gaines: In that story, the father was in the Army, and whether he would ever come back she did not know. She was just disciplining this kid to be able to face that tough life out there, and what she required wasn't any tougher than what many children have had to go through at that time, children who went into the fields at seven or eight years old, had to work whether it was hot or cold. But until I started going around to schools, I never thought she was harsh in any way. She disciplined him, and the kid could take it. But it was discipline with love.

Interviewer: I find that students recognize that love, and they recognize that James recognizes it and, in some very real sense, understands. But it is the other adults in his life who explain her requirements to him. What they come to is, "Ok, I understand, but why must it be *that* tough?" And another question they ask is why the mother in "Long Day in November"—another strong woman!—insists at the end that her husband beat her. That gives a lot of trouble: wife-beating under any circumstances is a bit hard to explain!

Gaines: She insisted on that because she knew the people would laugh and make fun of her husband for having to burn up his car just to get his wife back home again. And the last thing she wanted, I think the last thing any woman wants—I'm not up to date on what women think and feel, but I *think* the last thing they want is for someone to laugh at their mates. And she says, "Ok, if you put a mark on me with this switch and you hurt me, then they will not have anything to laugh at: they'll see that you are a man after all, 'cause most of them said you were not."

Interviewer: They acknowledge her motive but still ask why she had to use that method. That story ends in a clearly positive resolution. And most of your novels leave the reader, I think, with a strikingly positive view of human life. Yet, paradoxically, most of them end with ambiguous or very tentative projections of a better future for the protagonist—if he/she is even alive. Can you comment on this paradox?

Gaines: I think some of us will make it, due to the tenacity of our nature. And this is what I try to say in my books, and that is what my protagonists are saying: "I will make it, I will make it, I will make it." Ten percent or so do make it, the other ninety percent don't. For every Miss Jane Pittman who made it, nine other Black women either went insane or died inside long before they were physically dead and put in the ground. It is the ten percent I choose to write about. That is why most of my leading characters are super brave and must take risks—to help themselves or others, even though the risk may cause his or her death.

Interviewer: Before we turn to specific novels, will you tell us something about your still uncollected short stories? So far, I have found listed: "Boy in the Double Breasted Suit," "Chippo Simon," "Mary Louise," "My Grandma and the Haint," "The Turtles," and "The Comeback." Will you eventually collect some of these as you did those in *Bloodline?* Or have they been incorporated into later stories?

Gaines: The stories you mentioned were written while I was at San Francisco State and Stanford. They are the only published stories of mine other than those in the *Bloodline* collection. One day I should hope that a "small press" or a university press would take an interest in my "college stories." As of now, no one has requested permission to publish them in a collection. Too bad. Because I think they are pretty good stories, and they show the ideas of the young writer.

Interviewer: May we talk about specific novels now? *Catherine*

Carmier seems to me an amazing first novel. Was it written while
you were at Stanford?

Gaines: One version was written much earlier; when it came back
from New York, I just burned it up. Then, at Stanford, a visiting New
York editor told the class you could never make money on short
stories, which I was writing at the time. I thought I'd never have
a penny when I left Stanford, so I'd better write a novel. And the
only thing I could recall was the idea I'd had before. I wrote and
rewrote that for five years. Many more things were in it: more
background, more characters; the people in the quarters and
Catherine's aunts were more involved. It was about the problems of
Black and mulatto people on either side of a stream of water. And
it was the story of Jackson and Lillian coming home for the last
time to tell people they were moving out. In the original draft,
they had a long conversation on the bus without his knowing who
she was. But then I wanted to make them tragic lovers, and that
wouldn't work. The tragedy was not their love but what had already
happened to them. Lillian wasn't mature enough; Catherine was the
mature one on the place. My agent, who has done more for me as a
writer than anyone, said she could not see how Lillian and
Jackson could have anything mature, especially after she saw that
Jackson and Catherine had been very close as children but didn't
know they loved each other. Eventually, I saw them being close
again. So all these things made the book very big; I was developing them all, but nothing dramatic was happening. Finally, I cut it
down to size because I believe in form in my books, and I was not
getting it.

Interviewer: The title suggests that the story is Catherine's. Yet
in reading, I felt a balance of interest between Catherine and
Jackson, with Lillian in a supporting secondary role.

Gaines: It's titled *Catherine Carmier* because I finally couldn't
think of a better title. I called it "A Little Stream" once; part was
published once as "Barren Summer." But I don't see it as Catherine's story more than Jackson's or even Lillian's.

Interviewer: I think viewpoint affects our sense of its form. That
is basically omniscient, but in a few places, I wasn't sure whether
I was hearing the narrator's comments or Jackson's thoughts.

Gaines: You have both, also others. This novel was originally done from multiple viewpoints; Lillian, Della, Catherine, Mary Louise, different people in the quarters would each have a section. When I shifted to the omniscient, some of those voices or views were kept. But writers do that unconsciously; as you look over the shoulder of characters, you slip into their minds.

Interviewer: Then how much do you want the reader to see the old people and the quarters as Jackson sees them? Is the "deadness" in him or in them?

Gaines: In him—well, in both. The place is stagnant, and the people have their little lives and problems. But when he sees the garden drying up and says, "No more than my soul," that's true; it's in both. Catherine doesn't see the life around her as he does; why not take her viewpoint or Mary Louise's? I don't want any one character's viewpoint to be taken as the whole story, and Jackson has an obvious prejudice.

Interviewer: So when he described the old people as trees or rocks, "never understanding, never giving," that is his view?

Gaines: Yes, that's his view. I disagree with him.

Interviewer: What about Jackson and his aunt? He was evidently very close to her as a boy; now he can't talk to her.

Gaines: You come back ten years later and I don't know that you can talk to people. The religion that held you together, the place, the road and the river, all the old people—he can't relate to any of them. He loves Brother and Mary Louise, and he can't talk to them. Madame Bayonne's the only one because there he's dealing with reasoning, not emotion. And he can leave her; nothing keeps him. He can't do that with Aunt Charlotte. She wants him to be the typical Black schoolteacher, go to church, listen to the old people; he can't do that anymore.

Interviewer: He comes across as a character in great pain—very moving. You project in the book a very sensitive feeling for this difficulty of having gone to California for an education and then come back. Did that come to some extent from your own experience?

Gaines: I can tell his feeling, but his life and mine are not parallel. I left Louisiana, left aunt and friends, and I would not exchange San Francisco now; but that's all.

Interviewer: Why has Lillian kept coming back for six years or more?

Gaines: Well, she loves her sister, and she hasn't made a final decision not to come. Also, the people in New Orleans were worse on the "Creole, Creole" business than her people at home and she probably hated them worse.

Interviewer: At one point, Jackson thinks of her as "deep and evil," and this seems somehow true. She seems hard, stifled in feelings, and evil in trying to manipulate others' lives.

Gaines: Many people are like her, and she did not make the world that formed her character. I cannot criticize her; she saw Jackson's taking Catherine as revenge for all three of them—not only on her family but on the whole system.

Interviewer: Would you talk about the relation of Raoul and Catherine?

Gaines: People have interpreted that all wrong. Raoul depends on Catherine but not for sexuality, and surely she has no desire for him. After his wife becomes unfaithful, she's just dead, and his whole life is for his daughter. And Catherine knows that if she stays, she can put some sun in both their lives. Raoul needs her more than Della.

Interviewer: I saw Raoul as very possessive; I did not see real incest. Yet his sister's words suggest at least an unacknowledged substitution for a relation with a woman.

Gaines: I think she says that because he turned down Bertha. But that's the last thing that *I* had in mind.

Interviewer: Catherine's staying home to be the companion her father demands—it may look like unselfishness, but is it? And isn't it in some sense hurting Della? Suppose she'd gone with Jackson—might not Raoul have turned to his wife again?

Gaines: No, no. I don't know that just because Catherine left, Della would have had any better life. And she stays not only for her father but her mother too,—and Lillian, she keeps coming back. I know two women who lived like that with their families, and I think both cases were mistakes. But the South needs these women. Faulkner and Tennessee Williams and I wouldn't have anything to write about if these neurotics weren't there. Not that Catherine is neurotic; she's very strong. I have a brother whose wife had to look after her own family, her brothers and her children, her mother, who had only one leg, her father and an old aunt. Without her there, I don't know how they'd ever have gotten along. As a matter of fact, I based Della somewhat on her mother, a beautiful woman who used to laugh and talk a lot.

Interviewer: I'd like to talk about the ending. Della says that Raoul needs her now, that he will make Catherine go, and that she will send her to Jackson; that seems like a final word and judgment. But then the narration says Jackson waited for Catherine to come out and "she never did." And this seemed to be a wide "never" and a different final word. To me, it's ambiguous.

Gaines: Della says Raoul needs her; he hasn't said that. He probably will make Catherine leave, but then he'd just as soon die. Another thing—when Jackson and Catherine are driving back from the dance, he keeps saying, "I need you, it will be just you and me," and that reminds her that life and marriage can't be "just us"; Jackson could possess her just as much as her father. But all that's another story. When Catherine goes into the house, that's the end of the story. I suppose it is ambiguous. It may be the writer just wasn't mature enough at that time to know how to end it.

Interviewer: I was struck more on second reading with the beauty of the book, yet it does seem that the later books have greater depth of characterization.

Gaines: Oh yes, this is a very young man's book, a college book in which you try to put everything your instructors have told you to make viewpoint and form right. Later you write with everything you've learned from your reading, from baseball to bars, from all life experience.

Interviewer: I hope to see more critical comment on *In My Father's House,* which seems to me very significant in its themes and characterization. Will you comment on this novel, your purpose in it, its thematic meaning?

Gaines: That book is a hard one for me to talk about. I don't ever read from it when I go to colleges and universities. It is a book I had to write because I was haunted by the idea. It cost me more time (seven years) and pain than any other book I've written. It is the story of a minister and his son, one of the children he'd fathered as a young man but never even seen in the many years since their mother left him. Until he found God, this was just "something that happened," that happened to many Black males then. When he realized his responsibility, he tried to make it up by becoming the "new man" with a new family, and still forgot the old. When the past catches up, he goes to God for an answer but finds it can't be fixed in a few days. There is an old Negro saying, "God isn't always there when you call him, but he's always on time." But this Christian belief is shaken, cracked. God helped the minister to help other people, but when he needed God to bring himself and his son together, God failed.

Interviewer: And his work in civil rights is not enough to make him a success as a man.

Gaines: Not really. When Johanna left because he would not care for her and the children, he really wanted to get up and go after her. That's what he wanted to do, but being the kind of person he was at that time, he could not do it. And his dream says he still cannot do it; he runs but cannot catch up. When he falls, he cannot get up. He can lead people to a voting booth, to demonstrate in stores, but what she wanted, he cannot do, not with her. He can do it with the little family he has now, in a way he can.

Interviewer: And the civil rights revolution as such cannot repair the breach in families, between fathers and sons?

Gaines: No way! That's the next point I wanted to make in the book. Sitting at a counter with whites does not bring father and son together. Just because they are sitting there does not mean they are communicating. Billy says that: he and his father get along "average. . . . I don't bother him, he don't bother me." That's a main theme of the story.

Interviewer: The father-son relation is central to *In My Father's House* and to several short stories. Would you comment further on your ideas about it?

Gaines: The father and son were separated when they were brought to this country over three centuries ago. The white man did not let them come together during slavery, and they have not been able to reach each other since. Despite the revolution, the Black father is in a position of non-respectability, and the white is still in control. The Black man is seldom the owner, still is not the public defender in court, not the judge. The young Black man almost always sees a white in these positions, not an older Black man, not his father. You can always hear a professional football player say the most important male in his life was his coach—usually white; that was the father-figure who would stand by him in trouble. We expect the same in the military, a white officer. So the son cannot and does not look up to the father. The father has to look up to the son. That is not natural. And the cycle continues, and continues, and continues. A few of our Black fathers made it, but the majority do not—and I doubt they will in our time.

Interviewer: How do you react to reviews that see him as a weakened Martin Luther King?

Gaines: Some people thought I attacked King because I named him Martin. Martin is a common name along False River where I come from. If I have six heroes, Martin Luther King is one of them. Phillip Martin had done a lot. But twenty years earlier he had made a mistake with his own family, and when he had a second chance, he made the same mistake; when he fell, he didn't try to get up, he didn't explain. That's the whole story—not what he failed to do in the town.

Interviewer: A most interesting aspect of the book is his continuing inadequacy as a husband in important ways; he does not trust Alma enough to involve her; she says this to him: you want me for the bed, to take care of the children and go to church.

Gaines: That's most common, but he couldn't do even that much for Johanna.

Interviewer: When he's talking to Robert in the car after getting him out of jail, he says he couldn't do it because he went by the rules left from slavery. Isn't this his rationalization? In 1950, lots of Black men did take responsibility for their women and children.

Gaines: Yes, but Phillip Martin is not included in the "lots." He says I was never allowed to respect my woman; I just continued the rules. Until he finds God, he continues.

Interviewer: How did you intend sympathy to go in the scene of his demotion as civil rights leader? I found mine going back and forth; on one hand, he deserves what he gets. . . .

Gaines: Well, my sympathies were much more with the people than with him. I have no sympathy with a man who is supposed to be a leader, to take care of the people and puts one person above them. And yet, as a father, he had to go the other way. He'd done all the other things they wanted; now he had to catch up with what he'd lost long ago.

Interviewer: In the chapter of his search for Chippo, he seems to be making a journey into the past. Was that the purpose of prolonging that chapter, bringing in all those people? Why couldn't he just go to Baton Rouge and find Chippo?

Gaines: That would be too simple, just as it would be to cross the room to his son. The old preacher has to say, "Just pray," so he can say if that was all that was needed, the trouble would have been solved long ago. Then he meets Billy who says to just leave everything to the roaches and start over, and he disagrees with him. And waiting for Adeline is not the answer either. So on his search for his son, he has to meet all kinds of people—almost like what Miss Jane had to go through for her conversion.

Interviewer: He has to look at all the options of the past and reject them, also the future option of burning the whole place down. It seems to me Beverly puts the answer in front of him: you have done something for the people, they aren't afraid any more. And there's Patrick, you do have a son and a future. And she's young enough to represent the future.

Gaines: That's what I wanted Beverly to do. And Shepherd's name—he's sort of Shepherd of the flock. That's why I brought in the young lovers. You can't change what is gone by, but you can pick up and do a little better. They will do what Johanna and Phillip might have done at their ages. And I'm sure I had that symbolism in mind for his own Patrick.

Interviewer: One other question about the ending—one gap about it in my mind: was there any idea in your mind that part of this starting over would be to reach out to Johanna, to tell her of her son's death, take some responsibility for her present poverty and misery?

Gaines: I really don't know that. Maybe. It's over when Alma says "We have to start again." But I would think that after this he would reach out to her, go to California, explain to her, then come back and start over with Alma.

Interviewer: A few questions about structure. Why did you withhold any direct introduction to Phillip until Chapter 4? We hear of him from others, get a physical view of him, but don't see him act or get into his mind.

Gaines: The first few chapters are devoted to the boy: Martin's name comes up only to get the reader interested in his character. Until the confrontation it's not necessary to bring out what he really was.

Interviewer: It struck me that the withholding makes the reader hear first the positive views of him—Virginia's, Elijah's, Beverly's. Only then do you find out for sure his relation to Robert. I felt prepared to look at his past without just wiping him out of my sympathy because I'd seen what those people see, and that was necessary to balance the intense sympathy for Robert that is built up in that first part.

Gaines: (laughing) Well, you've just explained it better than I could. I agree, because they did see just one side, and the people who knew the other—Chippo and Nanane—were not there. And I wanted that positive side seen; he's done some very positive things.

Interviewer: Phillip's conversion was obviously central in his life. Did you ever put in a conversion scene of any kind?

Gaines: I did in the original and tore it up because it was narrated by Chippo when I was telling the story from multiple points of view. Then I found that was impossible because I could never have Phillip Martin or the boy as narrators. But if they couldn't be narrators, I couldn't tell the story because it's about them and no one else could tell it. So I had to switch to omniscient point of view and cut out Chippo's telling the conversion.

Interviewer: Could Phillip have remembered it as he does Johanna's leaving him?

Gaines: No, it wouldn't have been keeping the form together.

Interviewer: I have the feeling that it is formally right that the scene not be dramatized, but I haven't figured out why. A last question on this book. In a 1975 interview you said it was "giving me more hell than anything I've ever written." Do you want to say why?

Gaines: I don't know. It was like a cold you have to get rid of that takes a long time. It was something I'd always wanted to do—to write a tragedy that has a lot to do with the Black male and his history in this country.

Interviewer: Your last novel, *A Gathering of Old Men,* seems to have a similar theme: the second chance to be a man. Yet it seems to have no central character.

Gaines: The old men as a group are the protagonist. The central motif is that they had not acted manfully in the past, and here was God giving them a second chance to stand up one day. So it's not Mathu or any one person; it's the men. In an early version, a mulatto who is really a first cousin of Candy's was going to be the leading character. Then I realized I was playing something I didn't want to get into, that I really wanted the men to be important, wanted to concentrate on them. The other character would divide the interest.

Interviewer: I read about twenty-five pages of an early version in *Callaloo.* There it seemed that the narration was going to be entirely through Lou Dimes. Was that your original intention?

Gaines: The original idea was that Lou Dimes was a "liberal white guy" who's played basketball with Blacks, who sees a relationship between Candy and Mathu and between Mapes and Mathu, sees something about these old men, and from a liberal viewpoint is learning and trying to understand and tell it. So I began with the first-person viewpoint, but after going over it a few times, I realized that Dimes could not get all the information needed and especially not the language I wanted: the child's or the old women's, Janey's or Miss Merle's, or the men fishing. So I dropped Lou Dimes as sole narrator and went to multiple narrative.

Interviewer: In checking out the narration, I noticed that none of the "main," the most involved characters, do any of the narration. Candy, Mathu, Fix, Charlie, Luke Will, Gilbert—none of them do. It's Janey and Snookum, the whites in the store, and the old men.

Gaines: I just felt those people, as observers, could do much better than the people involved. Mathu and Candy can't narrate or the reader would know too much. It wasn't important for Fix to narrate because the young man tells what went on, and when he's visited by his son we know what he thinks and feels. In one draft, I

had Mapes narrating; he's on his way fishing when he gets the call
and starts talking and talking.

Interviewer: The order of narration seems significant. The first
several sections are Black-white-Black; then it's all given over to
the memories of the Black men, and then you switch to a series of
white narrators.

Gaines: In the first part, I didn't intend the Black-white-Black; I
was just building up the plot, and there was no better way than having
the boy run messages around. Once I got to the men, I had to
arrange their stories so I would not have two tear-jerkers following
each other but have it paced. I had stories for twice as many men,
but my editor said we can get the feeling of the thing with only four or
five of them. The point is that it's not just Fix; he represents
everything that has happened to these people whether he was
involved or not.

Interviewer: The long chapter of their reminiscences is one of the
most powerful in the book, and it is striking that immediately
after it you switch to the white Tully who goes to Fix's house. And
suddenly, just after all those horror stories, there is Fix with his
grandchild in his lap, grieving for his son. I expected to see him
organizing a lynching—which, in a sense, he was—but the impact
is of his grief. And even more powerful is the moment when Luke
Will, who has nothing to redeem him or what he's doing, asks
someone to take care of his wife and children. You never seem to
deny anyone his moment of humanity.

Gaines: My agent brought that up, too; she had seen all the drafts
and Luke had never said anything like that. It's a normal thing; I
think Klansmen could love their children. For me to be fair as a
writer, I cannot deny Fix or Will his humanity, and I don't know
anyone totally without feeling. Maybe I was feeling good that
morning. I know I had written several drafts and not written that
speech of Luke's.

But another thing—Fix is thirty years late. His son is playing
football now. The Klan doesn't come on horses as nightriders
now, you have pick-up trucks and CB radios. So Fix's kind of
vigilante vengeance is dying out, but there will be the new Luke
Will type. The Luke Wills are in the police department. Fix is

seventy or eighty and can't shoot straight, but Luke will do it for him.

Interviewer: In 1979, the story time, would a sheriff slap old men around as Mapes does, and would they answer him back as they do?

Gaines: They had not answered him back before, because before they were afraid to die. But that day, they came to live or die for a cause—"for once in my life, I'm going to do something and then I die." So they'll say anything. I don't know that Mapes would typically knock them around, but there are people like him who don't know any other way to get information. But I've never seen just this situation.

Interviewer: So this scene was the product of your creative imagination. Were any of the episodes based on actual events?

Gaines: None, really. Some of the ones I cut out were. I had heard of a fight between a Black and a white sharecropper racing to the derrick with their sugar cane. I had heard of a sixteen-year-old young man electrocuted for supposedly killing a white man; he was partially insane. A man there told me the electric chair didn't work and they garrotted him, choked him to death. I had that in the story once, and my agent advised me to change it. I had heard these stories not from Blacks but from whites. Another woman told me of going to town with her little girl, a fair-skinned child; an insane white woman tried to take the child because she was "too beautiful to be a nigger." They had a fight over it. I knew them. In the book, one of the mulatto men tells this, how they fought and fought until the white woman got the child and slammed its head on the ground and killed it. The killing did not occur, in fact, though the fight did. I cut that story out. The point of all the stories was that these things happen; if Fix didn't do it, somebody did.

Interviewer: I would like you to talk about the killing that does occur—the shoot-out. Obviously Charlie has to come out and take his stand. But does he come out to end this scene if Luke doesn't shoot him, so that they'd both be alive, or does he not believe what Luke said and come out to shoot to kill?

Gaines: Well, I sent him out to do that because he knew durn well that Luke Will would come out to kill. When he came back from the swamp, he didn't know Luke Will would be there with a shotgun, but he knew he was going to live as a man and then die. So he stood up to die at that moment rather than prolong it.

Interviewer: When Luke says, "Let us give up," does he mean it or is it a trick?

Gaines: No, no, he knew they couldn't get away so he wanted to give up.

Interviewer: Then my question is—and here's where I got stuck in that episode—wouldn't it have been the humane thing and just as much a victory to have let him give up?

Gaines: How does Charlie know what Will means? I'm telling you, but Charlie doesn't know that. He knows he's going to die, so Luke's wanting to give up doesn't mean anything to him, not now. He may believe in Lou Dimes, but he doesn't believe in any real justice. I cut out a part where Lou says, "Charlie, I got me and Candy here and we know what happened," and he says, "Yes, but you won't be the jury. I'm going to die anyhow." So he has to come out fighting. They chose the battleground, and he has to fight.

Interviewer: Then, were we to respond to all the shooting and killing as a sign of manhood over cowardice or as a tragic necessity that so many should die? Well, only two die, but the possibilities were enormous.

Gaines: Oh no, never was, because the old men couldn't see anything, and the other bums were drunk. I knew that; that's why I got them drunk. I could have had complete chaos, but I didn't want that; I just wanted those old men to stand one day.

Interviewer: After all the grandeur and tragedy, so to speak, of Charlie's stand, why the switch to the great comedy of the trial?

Gaines: The tragedy is over; it was told in eight hours, one day, as in Greek tragedy. The whole book meant one thing to me, that day of standing up. After that, I had to get them buried and have some kind of hearing; but as far as I was concerned, once they walk around and touch Charlie's chest, it's over. Gilbert is back sitting with his family, Candy leans on Lou, Mathu is back with the people and has achieved an independence of Candy, and Mapes will be embarrassed for the rest of his life; but these are sort of comic things. It was not their day; it was the old men's day.

Interviewer: It struck me that all those characters except Mathu have undergone some degree of change and progress.

Gaines: Mathu has too, and he says it at the end: "I never thought I would see a day like this. I always felt above you because you never did anything. I hated those people because they never let me be an American, and I hated you because you never tried."

Interviewer: Candy seems to undergo a learning process about Mathu and the people, to realize she can't be the old-time patron because they won't take her protection any more. She understands why Mathu goes home from the courthouse with the other people.

Gaines: I really don't think she does understand that. She knows she needs Lou for support; that's why she reaches for his hand when Mathu leaves. But Mathu's turned his back on her, and I don't think she knows why. Lou tells her in the car; that's why she slaps him, because she doesn't want to understand. In another draft, she gives a big speech, "When you needed medicine, who went to the store? When you went to the doctor, who took you? When you were hungry, who fed you?" And they must all say, Yes, Candy did it. I cut that out, but I hope people can still get the feeling of her role.

Interviewer: Mapes also seems to move from his kind of contempt to some respect at the end.

Gaines: Yes, I think so. He's always respected Mathu, but the rest were just darkies or niggers. They'd never do anything. But at the end, he has to give them, especially Charlie, some respect. And he means it.

Interviewer: Why did you change the title from *The Revenge of Old Men?*

Gaines: Well, I didn't see them doing anything for revenge. I thought "Gathering" sounded better, too. I've tried to use "Revenge" in several titles. I once called *In My Father's House, Revenge in St. Adrienne.* Just didn't work.

Interviewer: Do you see any changes and developments in your overall purpose and tone from your early work to your latest?

Gaines: None. Absolutely none. Just got better, I hope.

An Interview with Ernest Gaines

William Parrill / 1986

From *Louisiana Literature* (Fall 1986): 17–44. Used by permission.

My interview with Ernest Gaines takes place on the sun porch of the house furnished for him by the University of Southwestern Louisiana where he is writer in residence. Gaines is a big man with a commanding presence, a deep voice, and hair graying at the temples. He nearly always wears a beret. He seldom hesitates for a word and he speaks rapidly and forcefully.

Catherine Carmier (1964), *Of Love and Dust* (1967), and *A Gathering of Old Men* (1983) are set mainly in the "quarters" of a large plantation near Bayonne, the imaginary town which is Gaines's equivalent of Faulkner's Jefferson, and recount the changing lives of the people who lived there from Civil War times until recently, when their jobs disappeared and their houses were razed in the name of agricultural efficiency. Even those novels which are primarily in the quarters, *The Autobiography of Miss Jane Pittman* (1971) and *In My Father's House* (1978), are dominated, even obsessed, by its presence and its memory.

After the short walk from the English department to his house, Gaines gives us a tour of the house and of the converted garage in back of the house which serves as a study and where he does his writing. The shelves are filled with books, mostly on literature and history, which seem to have been read and casually replaced. Only the section on black literature and history is neatly arranged.

WP: How did you first become interested in writing?

Gaines: I probably started writing when I was only seven or eight or nine because I lived on a plantation at False River. Very few of the older people who lived on the plantation could read or write. Both their reading and writing was very limited, so I would always write their letters for them and then read the letters that they would get in the mail. I also read the Bible and things like that for them. I became interested in writing when I went to California at the age

of fifteen. I went into the public library at the age of about sixteen.
I got in the library because my stepfather told me I had to get off
the block. After school, I would hang around with the kids, and
he said, okay, off the block or you're going to get yourself into a lot
of trouble. So I ended up in the library, and that was the first time
I'd ever been in the library. I'd go about an hour. Of course the
public libraries you had in Louisiana in the False River area
where I came from were all segregated. So I went into the library
and I saw all these books and I started reading, and I read, and
read, and read. I did not particularly care for the way blacks were
depicted by many of the writers, especially the Southern writers,
the Southern white writers, but I would read them anyhow. I would
read any writer who wrote about the land. I went through Steinbeck, Willa Cather, the European writers, the nineteenth-century
Russian writers. Out of all this reading, I never did find my own
people in those books. It was then, about the age of sixteen, that I
began to write about the people I had left in Louisiana, about the
place and the people of Louisiana. That's what I started on.

WP: I read that you wrote the first version of *Catherine Carmier*
when you were sixteen.

Gaines: At sixteen. That was my first project. My mother had a
baby about that time, when I was sixteen, and I had to babysit
for her. His name was Michael. I had that entire summer, and I had
my mother rent me a typewriter. I didn't know a thing about typing. I
had never taken a typing class, but she rented it for me. I kept
Michael asleep. I made him sleep, and by the use of one finger at
a time I pecked away at it until I got a novel. I wrote about a
hundred and fifty or seventy-five or eighty or ninety pages,
whatever. I sent it to New York, and of course it was not a book by
a long shot. They sent it back to me, and I took it out into the
yard and put it in the incinerator. About nine years later, when I
was at Stanford, that would be in fifty-eight, I started on it again,
and four years after that, I finished it.

WP: As far as you can remember, how much of the original novel
that you did when you were sixteen was retained in the final
version?

Gaines: Very little, because in the beginning there was only the
love story between Catherine and Jackson. I don't even know

174 Conversations with Ernest Gaines

whether her name was Catherine then. I didn't know what the characters were all about then. I know it was a love story, and that was about all. But it did not have him going to the South for a little while and then going back to California. It did not have Lillian's leaving and going back, you know, passing for white. I don't think it had the murder of the small child. I don't think he was in there. It was just about a guy who comes back and sees a girl, the girl he was in love with when he was a little kid. I hope I can say that. I mean I was only sixteen when I tried to write it. I don't know what it was all about. I know it was about a darker-skinned family on one side and a mulatto family on the other side. That was the original idea, the conflict between them.

WP: After reading your other novels, the thing that amazed me about *Catherine Carmier* was how complete a representation it was of your themes and point of view.

Gaines: I think one of the things I discovered when I was quite young was that I knew what I wanted to write about. Of course, many things have changed since then. The Civil Rights movement came along since that book was written. I've done much more traveling and much more reading. But I feel that I knew from the beginning what I wanted to write about. What I've learned from the writers I've studied is how to write, but I knew all the time what I wanted to write about. I didn't need anyone to tell me what to write about. I didn't need the kind of topical subjects to write about that were popular during the sixties. I didn't need any of that.

WP: I remember when I was growing up I was much impressed by *Native Son* and by a novel which is almost forgotten now but which got an enormous press at the time, *Knock on Any Door*.

Gaines: Willard Motley's novel, yeah.

WP: When did you become aware of those important black writers?

Gaines: That is a good question because I did not become aware of the important black writers until after I left college. I grew up in California. I grew up around San Francisco. When I first went to California, I went to Vallejo, California. Then, after I had been in Vallejo for five years, I went into the service just after the Korean War, and then when I came out, I went to San Francisco State to study English lit and creative writing. Later I went to Stanford for an advanced degree in creative writing. During that time, black writers' works were only mentioned. We did not study Ralph Ellison, we did not study Langston Hughes, we did not study Willard Motley, we did not study any black writers. *Native Son* was mentioned; the other books were not even mentioned. I was in Alabama this last weekend, and they asked me the same sort of question about black characters and black writers, and I said, the only black character I ever studied in all my college years in San Francisco was Othello. I did not study any black novelists at that time.

And I was so far behind in most of my work that I had to spend most of my time catching up. In high school, junior high school and college, I had to spend most of my time catching up with the average student there. When I went to California, I think I was in the ninth or the tenth grade, and many of the students had read books that I should have read when I was much younger, so I had to read all those books and catch up. And later when I went to college, I had to read all those books that I should have read when I was in high school and had not read. So the writers I was reading were white writers. Instead of reading black writers, I was reading Faulkner, I was reading Mark Twain, I was reading Hemingway. We were reading English writers, we were reading French writers, these were the people we had to read. So I did not have time to go out and to read black writers. I had to read all the books that were assigned. Then of course I was trying to write at the same time. Between the reading and the writing, all my time was occupied. It was after I had gotten out of college, after I had left the university, that I began to catch up on the black writers.

WP: While your books show the destructive effects of racism, you allow even the unsympathetic characters a certain amount of room to move around. That is, they don't know that they're always bad guys. My feeling about James Baldwin, for example, is that he never had managed to get it right.

Gaines: Yeah, well, different people say different things about me. A person at a university back East I won't mention his name because I'll be going back there—a friend of mine just left there— and this guy who's chair of the English department said that Gaines' whites in *A Gathering of Old Men* are stereotypes, so my friend

said, well, what about the black ones, and he said, well, I don't
think they're stereotypes. A lot of whites have accused me, but not
all of them because most of my readers are white and my books
are taught all over this country and published all over the world. A
lot of whites have accused me of making my whites devils and my
blacks angels. I just don't agree with that at all. At the same time, a
lot of the more militant blacks have said I have not been hard
enough on my white characters. It's awfully hard to please everybody, so when anyone asks me who I write for, I just say that I
write for no one especially. I just try to write well.

I honestly think that I'm as fair with my white characters as most
of, as probably all, of our white writers are with their black characters.
I'm not trying to measure myself against them, not at all, but there
are certain reasons why you may not be fair.

You mentioned Baldwin a moment ago. I think that with a person
like Baldwin who grew up in Harlem, in a certain area where you
don't have this exposure to all people, your vision can be narrowed.
So much happened to so many Southern white writers. Their
visions are here; they see blacks but they don't know how to reach
them. They think they know the blacks. The writer says, I know
him, but he really does not communicate with him, or with people
on his level. He knows those who work in his yard or those who
work in his kitchen, or the ones who clean up the place, but he does
not know those people who are not doing that, so his views are
as narrow minded as someone who lives entirely in a single area.

The best thing that ever happened to me was that I went to
California at the age of fifteen. I had lived here long enough to know
a little, but I hadn't lived here long enough to become too bitter
about things. I had lived here long enough to have my mind really
open to learn. If I had lived here another seven or eight years, my
mind might really have closed down on things, but when I went
to California, I went to an integrated area in Vallejo, California,
about thirty-three miles northeast of San Francisco. This was just
after the war in forty-eight. I lived in an area in army housing along
with poor whites. All these people had gone to the west coast to
get jobs in army supplies and navy yards and air force bases and all
this sort of thing. So we were all housed in the same general area,
and I was there with poor whites, Japanese, Philipinos, Latinos,

and all of these people at that age. So I began to realize even at
that young age that people were different, that this person believed
this and this person believed that, and that people had different
languages and different philosophies, that this person loved his
home and that his home had an influence on how he thought. So
I began to see that at a very early age, at fifteen, sixteen, seventeen.
I knew these people. I went to school with them every day at an
integrated school. If I had moved into a completely black area, say
like Watts in Los Angeles where there is a completely black area,
or say the south side of Chicago, or Harlem—any place like that
where you had no other exposure—I maybe would have had that
kind of narrow view, or a more narrow view. I would maybe be
willing to see things but maybe unable to see things because no
light had come in, because there was not enough sunlight to let me
see all sides of things.

WP: What did you think about *Invisible Man?*

Gaines: It's a difficult book for me to read even now. It's a
difficult book for me to understand even now. I always preferred his
book of essays, *Shadow and Act*. But this is sacrilegious to say
things like that about *Invisible Man*. I'd like to say it's a great
book and I love it very much and it has everything in the world for
me, but I can't honestly say it. It's a very difficult book for me to
understand, although I read a lot about what others say about it. I
read what Ellison says about it, what black critics say about it, what
white critics say about it, but when I get down to reading the book
myself, it just doesn't give me that understanding of what's in it.

WP: I see that Ellison has a new book coming out called *Going
to the Territory*. I assume it's a book of essays and not his novel.

Gaines: I think it is. I spoke to Robert Penn Warren and to his
wife at the Southern Review Literary Conference a few months ago,
and they did mention that a collection of essays was coming out.

WP: I was interested in *Of Love and Dust* that after Marcus had
killed a young man in a fight he was sent back to work on the
plantation until his trial came up. I assume they used to do that sort
of thing.

Gaines: Yes, they did. I've known situations where that has
happened. The plantation owner could bind you out, and you
could work on the plantation until your trial came up, and then if

you were not sent to prison you could work for him because he had gone bond for you. I've known other situations where the white bosses have gone to the prisons to get the guy out and he refused to come out. I've known cases like that. I've known one of each.

I had a good friend—he's dead now, he was killed in San Francisco—who was sort of like the boy in "Three Men," who refused to go out with this guy who wanted to bind him out. Later he went to Angola to serve his time and when he came out of Angola, he was told to get out of Baton Rouge. Later he went to Houston and he was run out of Houston by the cops and he went to San Francisco. He was a pretty rough guy, and he was killed by a woman. She shot him point blank with a .38.

WP: I think you show the racist, paternalistic system very well in "Three Men" where the young man gives himself up to the authorities because he hopes that the man will take care of him. (Pause) I know this seems like it happened a thousand years ago, but what was your reaction to the enormous controversy about William Styron's *The Confessions of Nat Turner?*

Gaines: Well, I could see why the critics criticized the book exactly as they did. My criticism of the book was with its form rather than with the philosophy or context he was speaking of. I just did not think that a person of Nat Turner's background would have spoken in Styron's language. I can see why the book was criticized by those black critics who have all the right to feel and to believe that Nat Turner was a genuine hero and not this demented person that Styron depicts.

WP: Frederick Karl in his book on the American novel, *American Fictions, 1940–1980,* says that in his opinion the controversy was extremely unfortunate because he thought that it injured black writers, that it kept them from dealing with large and controversial subjects.

Gaines: I think he's nuts. I don't agree with him at all. I wrote *Miss Jane Pittman* after this. That's a large subject; it deals with life in the South for a hundred years. I think Alice Walker's book *The Color Purple* is a large subject. I think that if he means the naturalistic approach to the novel, then I don't know who else is doing this. But I don't think that has anything to do with taking on large subjects.

WP: *Bloodline,* of course, is a collection of stories which contains "The Sky Is Gray," which I have read is one of the most anthologized of all modern short stories. It's certainly one of the most loved stories and since the television version of it, it's been read even more.

Gaines: That story is so well known by people, black and white, Southerners and Northerners. I really don't know why. I think it's a good story, as I think all of them are good stories. I don't think it is so much better than all the other stories, but that's the only one that people really talk about, and they talk about it so much.

WP: I would try to answer that question. I think it gives pretty nearly the whole range of human experiences. It's got an openness and a fullness and a great-hearted quality that we associate with a certain kind of great art, with Dickens and writers like that. It's a wonderful story. (Pause.) Did you have anything to do with the movie version?

Gaines: No, nothing at all, just as I had nothing to do with *Miss Jane Pittman* when they made that film. They made it out there near Stockton, California, at a place where a lot of westerns were made and a lot of movies which deal with farm people, but I was not involved. I was invited to be on the set during the time of shooting. They shot about three weeks and I was there about two of the weeks, but I had nothing to do with it at all.

WP: All the people I've interviewed so far, with the exception of Shirley Ann Grau, have written screenplays. Have you written any?

Gaines: I've been invited to write them, but I got out of it. I told them I didn't think I could do that. I'm not going to do what they tell me to do, so I got away from it. I don't think I would ever write a screenplay which didn't have something to do with my own work. I would like to work on my own novel or short story, but I'm not interested in going to Hollywood and in doing what they want me to do. And I know how much they change things, and I don't want to do that.

WP: Also, all the people I've interviewed have had a background of growing up in the movies, which I basically don't see in your novels.

Gaines: I grew up with the movies, but I also grew up with the

radio, I think. We didn't have television, but we used to listen to
these great radio programs during that time. I think I learned a lot
about dialogue from listening to radio programs, especially the
plays. I think they had this show on Sunday evening, which had all
of these great plays, and I could imagine what the entire thing
looked like just from hearing people talk about it. I think that in
much of my dialogue, the short sentences or whatever—maybe a
writer shouldn't explain what he does or how he does it, and I really
can't explain it. Critics are constantly asking me what writers influenced me, and writers have influenced me, but I think that listening
to radio shows has influenced me. I used to listen to the old
Gunsmoke, with William Conrad playing Matt Dillon—I think he's
about five-seven or five-eight and he's about that wide (gestures),
so he couldn't make it in television—and I really thought it was
some of the best dialogue I had ever heard. So radio as well as
the movies had some influence on my work. I don't write for the
movies, I write to be read aloud.

WP: David Madden likes to associate his storytelling with the
oral tradition of the mountains where he grew up.

Gaines: I would rather tell a story than have someone read it. I
do a lot of reading. I was at Auburn in Montgomery this past
weekend, and people there had read the stories—they had read *A
Gathering of Old Men,* and yet they said, when you read it, I get
something else out of it. I write to be read out loud, especially when
I'm dealing with the first person point of view.

WP: When I read "A Long Day in November," the story about
the man who burns up the automobile, I was reminded of Ellison's
story, "Cadillac Flambeaux."

Gaines: I don't know that story.

WP: It's about a man who burns up his Cadillac, and it's one of
the stories he published, I think around seventy-two or three, and
which was part of this epic novel which never appeared, and I
wondered if he could have seen your story.

Gaines: Oh, he saw it. The *Bloodline* stories were published in
sixty eight, and he chose that book as one of his favorites for that
year. He knew all about that story, but whether or not that had any
influence on his story, I have no idea.

WP: Well, there aren't that many stories about people burning

cars. (Both laugh.) Which brings us to *Miss Jane Pittman,* a story
so real that a lot of people think she actually existed . . .

Gaines: I've heard that too.

WP: . . . and which was enormously popular. I assume that that
book has sold as many, or almost as many, as all your other
books put together.

Gaines: Oh, yes, many times more than all the rest put together.
That book has sold I would say somewhere in the neighborhood
of fifty thousand in hardback and continues to sell in hardback after
fifteen years. And we've sold a million plus in paperback. It was
the film that really sold that book. Before the film, it had about
three hardback printings and about three paperback printings.
Now have about fourteen, fifteen, hardback printings and about
twenty-three, twenty-four, paperback printings.

WP: What did you think of the film?

Gaines: I like the film for the amount of time they had to work,
two hours. That book covers over a hundred years in time, so
they're giving us roughly a minute a year. A lot of people don't like
it, but I do. It brought some things out. It changed too much, of
course, but it brought some things out. If we had had four to six to
eight hours, I think we would have had a major film, because it
would have taken the time to rewrite the script well, it would have
taken time to get better actors—there were three or four actors in
there, Cicely of course was great, but we would have had better
actors, better writing, more time, better camera work and everything else if we had had the time, but since it was made for television
and since the producers didn't know how the American public,
which means of course the American white public, would accept
the film, they made a fast quick film which didn't cost very much
money at the time.

WP: There is certainly an amount of oversimplification of the
novel, but I think that, for a television movie, for any kind of a
movie, it's certainly very good. You've been very fortunate I think
in the two adaptations of your work.

Gaines: Yes, I agree with you because I know others who have
not been so fortunate. Faulkner was never so fortunate.

WP: How many real people are there in your novels? Do you take characteristics of somebody you know and involve them in different actions or what?

Gaines: Well, let's take *Miss Jane Pittman,* for example. I didn't have anyone in mind for Miss Jane physically. I didn't know what anyone a hundred years old would be like. But I used some of the characteristics of my aunt too here. My aunt never walked in her life. She crawled all over the floor, but she cooked our food, washed our clothes, did everything. I gave Miss Jane her moral strength, her courage, but Miss Jane was not based on anybody. Catherine was slightly based on a girl I knew. Lillian was not based on anybody I knew at that time. I think I've known more Lillians since I wrote that book than I did before. In *Of Love and Dust,* Marcus had some of the characteristics of Muhammad Ali. He loved to talk, he said, I'm good and I can prove I'm good, like Muhammad Ali, Cassius Clay at that time. Marcus was slightly based on a guy that I knew, the same one who was killed in California. As a matter of fact, the boy in "Three Men" that kills and the boy in *Of Love and Dust* are the same. It's the same sort of story, it's the same story, except that in *Of Love and Dust,* he comes out of prison—he says, I'll take my chances outside—and in "Three Men" he remains in the prison. But my characters are not usually based on any particular person.

In "The Sky is Gray" now, much of what little James goes through—and my middle name is James, you know—I went through. But it's not me. I did have the toothache as a child, we had to ride in the back of the bus in the mid-forties, we could not eat up-town, we could not walk in a place and get warm or anything like that, and his mother was somewhat like my mother. I had to kill birds in order to eat, and I am the oldest of my family, so I had to look after my younger brothers and sisters. I went through all of that in a period of say ten years, but I crowded all of that into his life in a period of a daytime.

WP: I thought one of the most moving parts of *Miss Jane* was the story of the two brothers, Jimmy and Tee Bob, and of course that wasn't in the movie.

Gaines: They wanted to put it in the movie. If that movie had been longer, four hours, it would have been in there. But God, I'm glad what they tried to put in the movie, they left out. They had

Jimmy up there eating with them in the house. They had Robert
Samson coming down into the quarters and admitting that Jimmy
was his son to different people. They had all kinds of crazy things like
that. A white probably would have said that to Miss Jane, but he
never would have gone around boasting about it. And he surely
would not have had Jimmy sitting around on the patio eating with
him with Tee Bob and Tee Bob's mother.

WP: I assumed that they just left that out because that was just
too delicate a subject for them to handle.

Gaines: Well, they could not bring in all the subplots. They only
had two hours, less than two hours with commercials, so they
had to stick with Cicely, they had to have the camera on her all the
time. Miss Jane is in all the scenes in the first book of the novel.
In the second book she's in most of the scenes, but then the other
characters begin to take over. In the third book, "The Plantation," that's the love story between Tee Bob and Mary Agnes
LeFabre. In the last book you have the Jimmy story. So as she gets
older, as you move through the books, Miss Jane is less and less
involved in the direct action, but because the film is so short, they
had to have Cicely's face on the screen all the time.

WP: What is your feeling about the enormous success of that
book? I know that the writer is always happy to have a book
that's so successful, but some writers feel that such a success
detracts interest from their other works or makes it almost impossible
for them to live up to what the public expects.

Gaines: I don't think about trying to live up to anything. I just try
to write as well, to write better, the next day. People are always
asking me, what is your favorite book, and they expect me to say
Miss Jane Pittman. Certainly it's my most popular book, but I
don't have a favorite book, and if the world and the reading public
feel that *Miss Jane* is the one they want to read, it's okay with
me. I'm always more interested in the book I'm working on now, or
the book I will work on ten years from now, or twenty years from
now. I'm not interested in *Miss Jane* any more, other than in the
royalties which will come in from it. It has no effect on my trying
to measure up, simply because I think I have done that. I've written
as well in the *Bloodline* stories, in *Of Love and Dust* for a straight

dramatic novel, in *Catherine Carmier* for a delicate love story. I don't have a favorite book.

WP: My favorite of all your books is the one that you didn't mention, *In My Father's House*.

Gaines: Thank you for saying that. I was talking to a guy in Alabama the other day who said that was the least of the books he liked.

WP: It's got the stark inevitability of Greek tragedy.

Gaines: That was my aim. That was my aim.

WP: There's nothing wasted in that book. It's totally honest and almost foreordained from the beginning, from the first page.

Gaines: A great man falls, and what he's going to do when he gets up. He feels that even God had failed him. He could not even please God any more.

WP: But I can see how someone who reads *Miss Jane* and "The Sky is Gray" and then comes to *In My Father's House* would be put off by it because this is much more grim.

Gaines: Oh, yeah, I've met a few people who liked the book, who said, this is one of the better ones, but most people, the doctors here at USL, feel that no, this is not your best. They give different reasons; for one thing, there's a lack of humor anywhere in the book—there's no humor anywhere—and it is so grim, and we don't particularly feel with the subject. I think it's the least taught of all my books. When you said that it was in the style of Greek tragedy, that was my aim, but I don't know if you can do that. I think if I were a playwright—but no one has shown any interest in it, no one has ever put out any kind of money—I think I would really like to work with them and then I would try to bring out that idea of Greek tragedy in that story.

It's very difficult for me to read. I can't read that book. It took me longer to write that book than any other. When I read from my books, I never read from it unless someone requests it. I will read from *Miss Jane,* I will read from *A Gathering of Old Men,* which I was writing on afterwards. I think in order to read *In My Father's House,* you would need to read it in one sitting to get everything out of it. It's not a book you can read a part of and put down. You can section *Miss Jane* to read, you can section *A Gathering of*

Old Men, but with this book I don't know that you can pick out
sections to read and leave a satisfied feeling with your audience.

WP: I think *In My Father's House* is one of the most important
Southern novels of the past thirty years, and I think that, if people
don't like it, that's their problem. But I don't think it's totally
without humor. What about Chippo?

Gaines: Chippo, yeah, yeah, but I think people get so involved
with that father-son relationship that they overlook people like
Chippo and all the others. It's a book that I don't read.

WP: More than any other writer I've interviewed, and more than
any other Southern writer I can think of, you deal with the church
and its influence on the lives of the people you write about. I think
I'd be honest in saying that most white writers who wrote about
that kind of fundamentalist white church could not deal with it
without a touch of irony. But you seem to me to be looking at it
straight-on saying, well, this institution may have faults, but it's
doing a lot to keep this society together.

Gaines: A certain part of society, yes, I agree with you there. I
think that my younger people may not see it as the older ones
did. You know Marcus' idea was that he wanted to go to church
because there were a lot of women around the place. You have
the young man in "The Sky is Gray" who disagrees. Then you have
Jackson who comes back in *Catherine Carmier* and who says it's
all bourgeoisie stuff and that he doesn't go along with that. He's not
a nihilist, but he has sort of nihilistic leanings. You do have that;
however, I do have the church as the institution which has kept the
older ones going. And of course that's what Jimmy says in the
last book of *Miss Jane Pittman:* this is all we have. I have no flag, I
have no guns, I have nothing else, and I need this strength—the
church—in order to be able to continue.

WP: You know that Baldwin was a teen-age preacher in Harlem
before he moved away from the church. Do you think the church in
the city still has the same kind of viability you depict in your novels?

Gaines: I know that in San Francisco there's a church on every
corner. There's a bar on this corner and a church on that corner,
and it still seems to have its strength with the people. At least I see
them out there all the time. I don't go, but people pass right by
me, and I drive right by them, so I think the church still plays its

role in the cities. Take for example Dr. King's church in Montgomery—I went by it just the other day—the Dexter Avenue Baptist
Church just off the capitol, just a short walk from the capitol, from
Jefferson Davis' statue. I think the churches are just as strong as
ever with some of the people.

WP: The novelists that I've talked to seem to agree that religion
is not much of a preoccupation with the people they know or are
interested in.

Gaines: Religion is not a main theme that I'm interested in. It's
always there, just like the color of the skin. You can tell that this
person is black, you can tell the kind of house he lives in, you can
tell the kind of food he eats, you can tell how he lives. And so the
church is there at all times. Usually my male character has reached
a point where he has to make a decision: my decision is whether I
follow the man or I don't, and I don't know that he, except for
Phillip Martin, relies on the church to give him strength at the
particular time or on something else deep inside himself. The boy
in "Three Men," Proctor, tells the young guy whom he saves at the
end, whom he will stay in prison to save, okay, you pray, I can't,
but pray as a man would pray, maybe that will help me take the
beatings I'll have to take. I'll try to be a man, but I cannot get down
on my knees. And it's the same in my other novels and stories.
For example, in a comic novel like "A Long Day in November," he
goes to the church and the church fails him, so he has to go to the
voodoo woman. They go back to the more basic things, further and
further back, but the church is always there somewhere in the
back of all the stories and all the novels. I lived on this plantation,
and of course the church was right in the middle of the plantation.
The church is still there. I went to school during the week and
church on Sunday.

WP: You write about the relationship between the Cajuns, who
took over after the Second World War a lot of the land which the
blacks had been sharecropping for almost a hundred years, and the
blacks who were forced to farm the least desirable land and who
then were forced out entirely. The young blacks all moved away.
Has that changed?

Gaines: It has not. My people had been slaves on the place and
they had become sharecroppers when the owner of the plantation

turned it over to sharecroppers. But then the Cajuns became share-croppers as well. They got the better land. They got better machinery, and they produced more, and a lot of the blacks moved out because they could not compete. And of course the Second World War not only took a lot of young blacks into the service, but many others escaped and went to the North to find work, leaving the older people there, and eventually the Cajuns had all the land in that general area. During the sixties, something else happened. Larger companies took over and leased this place; soy beans took over and oil wells took over, and the Cajuns were moved out as well. In *A Gathering of Old Men,* that's what it is all about. The ones who loved the land, worked the land, and then were kicked off the land.

WP: Has there been much ideological criticism pro or con of your novels?

Gaines: By whom?

WP: By either the blacks or the whites?

Gaines: I've been criticized, but not really. I don't think I'm taken seriously yet as a writer to a point where there can be long articles or comprehensive essays about me and my work. I have known people who have done masters on my work. I have known people who have used me in their doctorate, but I'm not one of those people whose work is written about by the major critics. Every so often, something gets in one of the black oriented journals, like *Callaloo,* which is published at the University of Kentucky at Lexington. But I'm not taken so seriously that any books have yet been written about me.

WP: I think the problem may be that *Miss Jane* was too popular and the others haven't been popular enough.

Gaines: That's quite possible. I won't mention the name of this particular person or the magazine, but when *Miss Jane* first came out, this particular person said to me, I haven't read your book, and I want to tell you why. After *Time* and *Newsweek* and *Life* gave you such great reviews, I knew that the book had to be a waste of time, and I will never read it.

WP: Which of your books would you say has gotten the best reviews? I know that *A Gathering of Old Men* got some splendid ones. The one in the *The New Yorker* I know was super.

Gaines: I think *Miss Jane* got the best reviews out of all the books. Next was *A Gathering of Old Men* and the *Bloodline* stories. I had the lead review in *The Saturday Review of Literature* when *Bloodline* came out. I think that's what turned a lot of people about the book and then later, people started anthologizing "The Sky is Gray" and it hasn't stopped yet.

WP: I wondered about the technique of having so many voices tell the story in *A Gathering of Old Men.* Were you thinking of Faulkner's *As I Lay Dying* when you were doing that?

Gaines: I was not particularly thinking of Faulkner. I had done that in the last story in *Bloodline*, "Just Like a Tree," using multiple points of view. But Faulkner's *The Sound and the Fury* has had its influence on my work. I don't know that I would have ever been able to write from that multiple point of view had I not read Faulkner, but at the time I was writing it I was not thinking of Faulkner. The original writing of *A Gathering of Old Men* was done from a single point of view by Lou Dimes, who was the newspaper guy, Candy's boyfriend. Then I realized that Lou could not see these old men gathering because he was in Baton Rouge—he could only hear about them—and it was then that I decided to make the change for two reasons: number one, I wanted to see the gathering, and number two, I wanted language. I wanted a little boy running down the street bragging about the way to hit a horse when you want it to run fast. I wanted a litany as Janey went through the house calling on God: Lord have mercy, Lord have mercy, Jesus, what now, what now. I wanted her looking out onto the backyard at the old lady, then looking out to the major on the porch. I wanted a rhythmic language throughout the book.

WP: When I talked to Madison Jones, he said that he felt that after his novel, *A Cry of Absence,* in 1961, which dealt with the destructive effects of white racism, he went through a fallow period because he felt that history had taken away his subject matter. Look back on that period now, what do you think was the total effect of all that ferment on the creative writer?

Gaines: I don't think that it had too great an effect on the subject I wanted to write about. (Pause.) It did add something to what I had in mind that I already wanted to write about. *Catherine Carmier* takes place in sixty-two. Before writing *Catherine,* I never knew

that I wanted to deal with a broad period of time. I never knew
what I was going to deal with, but after that one book, I realized
that I wanted to say something else, and what I wanted to say was
something before 1962. So it was then that I could write *Of Love
and Dust,* and then after writing that book, I realized that I wanted
to go further back. It was then or maybe a little before that I
realized that I wanted to get those stories together. And then I
wrote *Miss Jane Pittman* because I wanted to go further and
further back. During the time I was writing *Miss Jane Pittman,*
between sixty-eight and seventy, so much was going on in California
as well as in the South. That was when Martin Luther King was
killed, that was when Bobby Kennedy was killed, that was when
all the demonstrations were going on on the campuses. All of these
things were going on when I was writing this book. The civil
rights movement, the demands by blacks, all these things added
something to the black experience which I was trying to capture.
It brought it up to the present. I could go as far back as 1862 in *Miss
Jane* and bring the story up to 1962, but I can go beyond that
now, because by the time I finished *Miss Jane,* other things were
happening. So I could just continue to go on. Someone asked me why
Miss Jane ended in 1962, I said, well, I didn't want to get involved
with JFK's assassination—Miss Jane would have died just before
that—but other stories could be affected by it. *In My Father's
House* is post Martin Luther King, and I could write that book
only because those things had happened during that time. It was
really only a continuation of what I was trying to do all that time. I'm
still talking about the plantation life, the old lady who lives out in
the field, the small town, the racism in the small town in "The
Sky is Gray," as another element in the civil rights movement. The
little boy in "The Sky is Gray" cannot go into this place to have
a glass of milk; this is what Phillip Martin is fighting for in *In My
Father's House.* It's just a continuation, a broadening, it did not
change my philosophy.

WP: How did you get into teaching?

Gaines: My books were not supporting me. I was being invited to
give readings—I've read everywhere in this country—different institutions would ask me, would you like to come over for three weeks or
something like that? For example, Denison University back in Gran-

ville, Ohio, asked, would you like to come by for six weeks, and I said sure, and eight or nine years later, they gave me an honorary doctorate. In May I'm going to pick up an honorary doctorate at Whittier, Nixon's old college; I taught there a quarter. I was at the University of Arkansas at Fayetteville for a week. I've been everywhere. I made absolutely nothing on *In My Father's House* except for the advance they gave me. Well, I made a few bucks, but nothing that could pay me for the seven years I spent writing it. During one of those dry periods right after I published the book, I got a special delivery letter from the University of Southwestern Louisiana here in Lafayette asking if I would like to teach for one semester or four semesters, for a half year or two years, and I didn't want to. I said, I don't mind leaving San Francisco for a short period of time, I don't mind going out and giving a reading, but I don't want to leave for any long period of time. But I was as broke as I could possibly be, I was there with some buddies and my lady friend, and she said, well, I would try it if I were you, and they convinced me to do it, and I got in touch with the English department. I came down, and we met in Baton Rouge at the Hilton, and we talked and talked, and they told me what I would have and what they would pay and what they wanted me to do, and I agreed.

I came down in eighty-one and spent a year, and they asked me if I would like to come back every year for one semester, and I said okay. At that same time, the University of Houston asked me to do the same thing, to teach one semester on alternate years, and I thought I could teach one semester at Houston on one year and one semester at USL on the next. I could write the rest of the time. In eighty-three, when I came here to teach my second year at USL, they gave me the key to this house. They said, this will be your home if you would like to have it, and we're offering you tenure. Good Lord, now, I have to call the people in Houston and tell them that I'm not coming back to Texas. This is how I got into teaching. I teach three hours and I have four hours for office hours. Usually, I spend more time in my office talking with students than I do in the classroom.

WP: I realize that you haven't been teaching that long, but have you had any outstanding students?

Gaines: Well, I've had students who have already published a few things. One student my first year had I think two stories published in *The Southern Review*. That was Jude Roy. He writes about Cajun life. I've had other students who've had things published. One young lady has had poetry published. I don't do poetry, and I don't know anything about it at all. I have students who have potential, but I tell them I had potential too, but it took me ten years after I left college in order to get something going. Well, I published *Catherine Carmier* seven years after I got out of college. However, in 1964 no one had heard of it. I think they printed fifteen-hundred copies and probably sold one-thousand, and five-hundred went on remainder.

WP: What did you do during those seven years?

Gaines: I worked. I worked in the post office. I worked as a printer's helper. I washed dishes. I did all kinds of things. It was all part of my life.

WP: That kind of background was I think more typical of an earlier period than of now.

Gaines: Oh, yes, at that time I was offered a little teaching job, but I said no. I was staying away. I wanted to write and teaching would take everything that I have. I had heard enough about people trying to write and to teach at the same time. I had had teachers at San Francisco State who were writers, and of course Wallace Stegner at Stanford was a writer who wrote some good books while he was teaching, but all the awards that he received, the Pulitzer awards and the other awards, have been in the last ten years after leaving Stanford.

WP: What sort of reading do you like to do in your spare time?

Gaines: I like to go back to the old things. I can read Hemingway and Faulkner at any time. I pick up Tolstoy, the romantic poets.

WP: Of the people I've talked to, Dostoevsky seems to be the particular favorite.

Gaines: I don't know. People think that I should like Dostoevsky, and I've never liked Dostoevsky. (Laughs.) I think I got enough Dostoevsky when I read *Crime and Punishment* and *The Brothers Karamozov*. Dostoevsky took over, and he wore me out. I've always known what I wanted to say, and I wanted someone to show me how to say it, and Turgenev always showed me much more

than Dostoevsky ever could. Turgenev's *Fathers and Children* or
Fathers and Sons showed me more than any book of Dostoevsky.
Dostoevsky wrote so much of hunger, of deprivation and pain that
people said, you've gone through that sort of thing, you should
like Dostoevsky. He had a big influence on Richard Wright, on
Ellison, and on the early black writers, but I've never ever
thought of him as being a teacher. I was much more influenced by
Flaubert, Maupassant, and especially Turgenev. *Fathers and
Children* was a bible to me when I was writing *Catherine Carmier*.
I read that book every day. For example, when Charlotte meets
Jackson, it was the same as when Bazarov meets his parents. I
didn't know how an older person could meet a young person. I
didn't know what a young person would do during the time he was
thinking about leaving, what he would do during that time he was
not with a girl. But then I read how Bazarov went through the fields
with a switch knocking the leaves off the weeds and popping
tassels off flowers. So I made Jackson walk down to my favorite
river and take these rocks and skim them across the water. This
was the kind of thing I learned. When I mention Turgenev, I've
been told that Turgenev was an aristocrat and wrote about the
aristocracy, but I'm talking about form. James and Flaubert thought
a hell of a lot of Turgenev, and form is what I'm interested in.

WP: What current novelists are you interested in? Walker Percy
seems to be the top dog now among Southern novelists, most of
whom have a kind of love-hate relationship with him because he's
so famous.

Gaines: I really don't have any favorite writer. I met Walker for
the first time at the Southern Review Literary Conference. He
read, I read, Eudora Welty read, Robert Penn Warren read. I really
don't know his works that well. I don't read contemporary novels
except when someone sends me one. If it's a collection of stories,
I'll read some of them and put it down.

WP: James Baldwin is an interesting writer, but it seems to me
that his fiction has been crippled by his feelings of hatred. I'm not
talking about his essays, which are brilliant.

Gaines: I agree with you.

WP: In spite of the fact that his books have sold a lot, I don't
think he's an important writer of fiction.

Gaines: I agree with you. I think probably his best book was his first book, *Go Tell It on the Mountain*. *Giovanni's Room* was okay. In *Another Country* you begin to see that the form is falling apart. I haven't read anything since *Another Country*. That was the last of the fiction I read of his.

WP: There is a good analysis of his fiction in an old book, *The Negro Novel in America,* by Robert Bone.

Gaines: That's another book that was really criticized by a lot of the black critics. They thought that Bone had decided which were the good black novels and which were not.

WP: Is he black or white?

Gaines: He's white. I met Bone in sixty-four at a conference just outside of Monterey, California. A red-headed guy who taught at Columbia, or the City College of New York, someplace like that. I saw him again at the Library of Congress, I think it was, in seventy-four, after *Miss Jane* was made into a film. After doing *The Negro Novel in America,* he also did *The Negro Short Story in America.* I admire his work. I think he's a damn good critic. I think he knows what he's talking about. He's dogmatic, but I think he's bright. He said, these are the books: Jean Toomer's *Cane,* Ellison's *Invisible Man,* Wright's *Native Son,* and a few others. And he said why he thought that these books were better than others.

WP: The writers that I've talked to have all had a love-hate relationship with teaching. They liked it for supporting them, but they felt that it cut into their time too deeply and took too much of their energy.

Gaines: It does, it takes a lot of time and energy, but I've done seven books, if you consider the children's book *A Long Day in November* as one of them, and I think now, if I concentrate for the six or seven months away from my teaching—I'm not teaching this semester—I teach every fall—I think I should be able to get something done. I still try to write well when I write and I still would like to write six or seven more books—I don't think it's possible—but I would like to do it, I don't feel now that I have to put in those eight hours or those five hours five days a week twelve months of the year. I don't care about doing that any more. If I had a lot of money and absolutely nothing to do except write, I might put in three hours a day and work ten or eleven months out of the year.

WP: Basically you write totally about Louisiana, although I realize that there are occasional excursions off to California or elsewhere. Is there any feeling that you wanted to come back to Louisiana to be closer to your subject matter?

Gaines: No, no. I could write just as well in San Francisco about Louisiana as I can here in Lafayette. Everything I've had published has been written in San Francisco on a little table. Well, *A Gathering of Old Men* was written on a big table, but all the other books were written on a small table facing a wall. I would come to Louisiana and spend a week or two a couple times a year, and that was what I was doing, and I would see what I want to see. What I was writing about all this time was no longer here. That sharecropping place, the store, the houses, are not there. The river is there, but the banks are all built up now. I can see the past sitting in a place in San Francisco just as well as I can see it sitting in a place in Louisiana. I can see it better there because I don't have the distractions.

WP: How do you write? You said that you typed *Catherine?*

Gaines: That was before I really knew what I was going to do. I really had written it out in long-hand and then I was picking it out on the typewriter. I still write in longhand.

WP: Do you type it or have someone else type it?

Gaines: Oh, no, I type it myself because I'm constantly changing. I'm constantly changing, especially dialogue. Descriptive passages are difficult for me to do, so I'm constantly changing them from time to time.

WP: I think of you as an intensely dramatic writer. Have you thought about writing plays?

Gaines: In Louisiana, the people moved westward; they went to California, to Los Angeles, San Francisco, that general area. Eastward of Louisiana—Mississippi, Georgia, Alabama—people moved eastward, to Chicago, New York, Philly, in that direction—now, I think if I had gone east, I would have ended up as a playwright. I probably would have ended up in a big city where you don't have all the space you have out West. It would have been much more intense, and I think I would have ended up as a playwright, I

think because of my use of dialogue, not because I like to describe
big city feelings. I love outdoor space, places to run and play and
do all kinds of things, and the West is the place for open spaces and
the novel.

I think if the movement of my people had been eastward, I would
have become a playwright, and I think that, without false mod-
esty, I could have been a pretty good one. I think I could have been
a better playwright than I am a novelist, really. I think I would
have concentrated on dialogue even more than I do now, and I think
I would have concentrated more on keeping characters at a
certain point after I had mastered technique. I did a little of it in
college. I studied language arts with an emphasis toward creative
writing. My minor was English lit, but my major was language art.
You have some playwriting and direction, speech, journalism, a
little of all the language arts. I liked doing it, I liked writing
little skits.

WP: Most writers today are published by several different publishers, but you've only been published by two, Dial and Knopf.

Gaines: Well, Dial and Knopf, but the first one, *Catherine,* was
published by Atheneum. It took me so long to write that book
that they were not interested in me afterwards. Dial was. Dial was
one of those publishing houses that would take a chance. They
would not pay you very much money. About the only person they
paid money to at that time was Norman Mailer. Baldwin and
Mailer were Dial writers at that time.

WP: How did you arrive at Knopf?

Gaines: My agent, Dorothea Oppenheimer, felt that after *Miss
Jane Pittman,* Dial was not doing enough, the company was breaking
up, Doctorow had gone, Bill Decker, who was my editor, had gone,
I think the publisher had gone. The whole business was breaking
up. Dorothea felt that *Miss Jane* should have been one of the top
books, it should have won the Pulitzer or the National Book Award if
there had been enough support and enough pressure. Quite a few
people felt *Miss Jane* would win the Pulitzer. As a matter of fact,
Wally Stegner beat me out with his book. He thought that I would
win. Others thought I would win the National Book Award, but it
went to Flannery O'Connor for her *Collected Stories,* posthumously

of course. So my teacher beat me out for the Pulitzer and a dead woman beat me out for the National Book Award.

We could have gone to Farrar, Straus and Giroux, but they had turned us down originally, and we could not forgive them for that. But I'm very happy with Knopf, with my editor, Ash Greene and the rest of the people there.

WP: How many of your books are in print?

Gaines: All of them, except *Catherine,* and the children's version of *A Long Day in November.* North Point still has copies of *Catherine* around, but they're not printing any more copies. *Bloodline, Of Love and Dust* and *In My Father's House* are all published by Norton library. *Miss Jane* is still printed by Bantam, and *A Gathering of Old Men* is printed by Vintage.

WP: How many translations have you had?

Gaines: When we go back over to the conference room, I can show you the different translations. They've been translated into Japanese, into Chinese, German, Norwegian, Russian, Swiss . . .

WP: Did you get any money from the Russians?

Gaines: No, I haven't gotten any money from the Russians yet. (Laughs.) I've got money from a lot of the others, but not from the Russians yet.

WP: I wonder how they handled the dialect.

Gaines: I don't know how any of them handled the dialect. People who have read the German version say that they handled it pretty well. But I've had books published in about eight or nine different foreign countries. I think *A Gathering* is coming out in Portugal. Amazingly, none of the books have been translated into French yet. I know some people at the Sorbonne, but as of now nothing has been done.

WP: What is the relationship between intelligence in general and the ability to write novels?

Gaines: Well, I think Joyce was the brightest guy around and I don't think he was the greatest novelist. What he did with language and style changed the world. I think Hemingway was a hell of a short story writer, but I don't think he was the greatest novelist during his time. You don't have to be the brightest person in the world. I don't think Faulkner could have dared touch Joyce as far as intelligence goes, but good Lord, compare what he has written. No, it's something else that makes that writer.

WP: Madison Jones said that Faulkner seemed to have a genius. He simply didn't seem aware of what he was doing.

Gaines: Absolutely, I would agree. I think Faulkner the genius writer and Faulkner the man are two different people. He was not the brightest man in the world or he probably would not have said some of the things that he said in his interviews. When he sat down with that pencil and that little handwriting that he had when he wrote these things, he was possessed by demons who had taken over. I think he said that the characters always take over on page one-fourteen, or something. Hemingway criticized Faulkner for not rewriting carefully enough, but I think Faulkner did the best he could according to the way he rewrote. His handwriting showed that he was very patient, but if he had been a much more educated man, I think that he would have written in a different way. But it wouldn't necessarily have been better.

WP: A lot of twentieth-century writers have written a lot of criticism. Have you written any?

Gaines: I can't. I could not give you a lecture on writing. I could not give you a lecture on my writing. I've never written an essay. I've written a couple little things, but they're pretty bad. As far as really deep analytical theories about my own stuff, let alone on Ellison or Baldwin or on the others, I can talk with someone who knows Baldwin, or Ellison, or Joyce, or Turgenev. I can sit around and talk with them at a party or in a classroom, but for me to stand up there and give an hour talk on these people or on my own stuff, there is no way that I can do it. I know Faulkner appeared at Virginia and several other universities, but I don't know that he ever lectured. Anthony Burgess and I were at Chapel Hill in 1969, and I got up and talked for fifteen or twenty minutes, and I sat down, and he got up, and put a hand in this coat pocket and a hand in this coat pocket, and he talked for about an hour and a half. (Laughs.) He started with Shakespeare and came down to this character who wrote something last month. Good Lord, I could never do that sort of thing.

WP: Could you say anything about your current project?

Gaines: I don't usually talk about it. This is where you get all the

ohs and the ahs when you're trying to say something about
something that you really don't understand yet. The time of the
novel would be when the executions were taking place in the parish
seat in which the crime was committed. That would be until about
the mid-fifties. The reason why I wanted that particular time was
because I wanted the community in some way to be involved. A
teacher who is on vacation has been asked by the prisoner's
grandmother to visit this boy, this young man, on death row, and to
make him know something about himself and life before he dies.
The reason why she wants that is that, when the public defender
who was trying to get him off appealed to the jury, he said that his
man has no more intelligence than an animal. As a matter of fact,
putting this "boy"—he uses the word "boy" all the time throughout
his defense—in the electric chair would be like putting a hog in the
electric chair. "None of you all around here would like to execute
a hog, now would you." Still, he has an all white male jury, and he
is sentenced to die. The godmother, or the grandmother—I haven't
decided which she is going to be—says, okay, if he has to die, I
don't want him to die as an animal. I want him to die as a man.
She approaches the teacher, and the teacher says, "I don't want to
have anything to do with it." He is the kind of teacher who
existed up until the last twenty years when the only profession that
blacks could get in the Southern part of the United States was
teaching. And he is a guy who would rather not be here. He would
rather be an artist or a writer or a playwright. He would like to be
someone else in New York or Los Angeles or somewhere where he
could study that and not teach, but he has an older person there that
he is attached to, and he feels that he owes something to her, and
that's the only reason why he's hanging around. He doesn't want
to teach, he doesn't want to do anything, and teaching this class in
this church school is just a way to earn a living so that he can get
away some day. He's just running in place. When this old lady
approaches him about teaching this guy to be a human being, a
man, at first he says no, but somehow she convinces him to do it,
to accept the challenge of his life, to teach this guy who could die in a
month or two, or six months. The reason I haven't decided how
long is that I haven't talked to enough lawyers yet to know how
long the process would be.

As a matter of fact, on Monday, I'm supposed to meet an older sheriff. Although he did not witness an execution, he said through someone else that he could have someone there with him who had gone through this sort of thing. I want to know exactly what the prison cells looked like in the forties and fifties. I want to know what kind of clothes the prisoners wore, what kind of food they ate, what kind of exercise they took. I want to know if there were windows, I want to know all these sort of things. I talked to a former DA a couple of months ago, and he gave me some information I could use, but far from all the information I need. There are people here who are getting me contacts with people who know these things. In this story, I want the approach that Shaw uses in *Pygmalion,* also the Elephant Man type thing. Not physically, of course, but there is a kind of mask over the brain. The brain has not had the chance to get the light that would make him aware of all the things a man should possibly be aware of. What is a beach like? What is it like to have a vacation? What is it like to know a poem? What is it like to have a birthday, a day all your own with all the trimmings? What is the Constitution, and what is the Bill of Rights all about? Who was Frederick Douglass, or who was so-and-so? He never experienced any of that in his lifetime.

I'll be perfectly honest, as of right now, I don't know what that teacher is going to say when he walks into that room. (Laughs.) I have no idea at all. I do have questions: how far would a guard stand away from them while the teacher is there? How did the blacks communicate with each other while the guards were around? How can you make this young man here a true human being? Is it right to do that, knowing that he could die a week after he realizes what a poem is all about. This is what I'll have to work out.

WP: Have you ever considered writing a novel set in San Francisco or some other place?

Gaines: Yes, I've tried three San Francisco novels. I've even tried my army experience, but nothing worked out. I've got to get all that Louisiana experience out of me first, and I don't know how long that's going to take. I may never be able to do it.

An Interview with Ernest J. Gaines

Marcia Gaudet and Carl Wooton / 1986

From *New Orleans Review* 14 (Winter 1987): 62–70. Used by permission.

Ernest J. Gaines—a native of Oscar, Louisiana, in Pointe Coupee Parish—grew up on a plantation as part of a rural, black, bilingual, oral culture. At sixteen, Gaines left Louisiana to join his mother and stepfather in Vallejo, California. Gaines graduated from San Francisco State College and received a creative writing fellowship from Stanford University. He is the author of a collection of short stories, *Bloodline* (1968), and the novels *Catherine Carmier* (1964), *Of Love and Dust* (1967), *A Long Day in November* (1971), *The Autobiography of Miss Jane Pittman* (1971), *In My Father's House* (1978), and *A Gathering of Old Men* (1983). South Louisiana is the setting for all of Gaines's fiction, and the town of Bayonne in his writing is based on New Roads, Louisiana. Though a resident of San Francisco for much of his life, Gaines visited Louisiana often and maintained close ties with the people. He returned in 1981 as a Visiting Professor at the University of Southwestern Louisiana Lafayette, where he has been Writer-in-Residence since 1984. He spends his summers in San Francisco to avoid the Louisiana heat.

After watching the movie version of A Gathering of Old Men, *what's your general response to what they did with the movie in relation to your book?*

Well, I think they did a pretty good job. The biggest change is the ending. When they came to Louisiana to shoot the film, the director told me they had changed it. He said, "I think it's for the best, and I think you'll like it."

Did you?

I don't know if I like it or not. I never argue with what they do in Hollywood. They have their own way of communicating with an audience, and I don't argue with it. Most people remember the film version of *The Autobiography of Miss Jane Pittman* by the ending—Miss Jane walking to the fountain—which I did not write. With *A Gathering of Old Men,* I was trying to prove a point— showing the old men standing. They brought guns, and I believe in the Old Chekhovian idea that if you bring a gun into the play, the gun must go off by the drop of the curtain. I don't know if there is any difference in the point made in the movie. They just didn't think they had to stick too close to Chekhov.

I think if this film had been made for the theater, they could have done it better. Since it was done for television, maybe they didn't want a black and white shoot-out. I heard from some of the New York press that people were disappointed with the ending of the movie. They wanted to see the ending as I had written it.

How much of the filming of A Gathering of Old Men *did you get to watch?*

I went down to Thibodaux three weekends. I went on Saturdays and watched the shooting. Out of all the shooting, which took about a month, I saw about six days of it. There are lots of things you can criticize anytime someone makes something else out of your work. I'm sure Shakespeare could have criticized productions of his work, Tolstoy or Faulkner, you know, God with the Bible. Somebody is going to have to pay for it when they get up there with Him. They're going to have to pay for what they did. They'll line up and they'll have to pay Faulkner and Hemingway and Shakespeare for what they've done to their works.

It's a different medium. There's a story about Brahms. He saw one of his concertos being conducted by some crazy gypsy. This guy was just bouncing and jumping in the air directing the orchestra, and Brahms just sat there. At the end, someone asked him, "Herr Brahms, what do you think?" And Brahms said, "So, it can be done like that, too." And really, this is what you do. You say, "So, well, it can be done like that. I didn't know that." There are quite a few things they did that I didn't care about. They took liberties with dialogue, and they used their own dialects.

They changed names of characters. Instead of thirteen, or whatever number of old men I have speaking in the book, there are about six or seven speaking. They combined characters, taking the dialogue from two or three characters and giving it to one. They changed the clothes. They changed the size of the characters. In *A Gathering of Old Men,* the character Mapes is big. Richard Widmark [who plays Mapes in the film] is thin.

Fortunately before we started shooting the film, the director [Volker Schlondorff] asked me to take him to the place where I had grown up. I showed him the house there so he could have an idea what the house looked like. I think he really recreated it. The house that they have in the film is just like the one that I showed him. The road is quite a bit like the real road. The scenery is quite authentic. It was the dialogue which they tried to change a lot when they started combining things. When they started taking a few lines from here and a few lines from there and putting them together into one speech, and adding their own terms to it—that's when they took liberties I did not approve of. But as I said, I'm not part of it. I'm not in the filmmaking business.

Do you think they maintained the humor and the comic aspects?

That is one of the things I'm afraid does not really come through. Sometimes they don't speak the lines exactly the way I wrote them. For example, Widmark is supposed to say something that is very funny, but he does not say it funny. I told Volker, "I didn't hear any laughter," and he said, "Well, you can't hear laughter here because it was not meant for those people to laugh." And he said, "You'll hear laughter from the audience." And I said, "Ohhhh." I said, "I'm the audience now, and I didn't laugh, so I don't know whether or not I'll laugh later at the television screen."

I talked to a newspaper guy from Florida, and he questioned having a German director for the film. He said, "But does he know American humor? Does he know American mood?" You can't just bring in anybody and make this thing funny. You can make it dramatic, but you must know the subtleties to bring off the humor. The humor just didn't come off as it could have come off. Humor depends on that sense of pausing and understanding how the language is used. I don't think the director could handle this. He doesn't know the South. He did a better job with the drama. What went well was when he went into Fix's house. Stocker Fontelieu, who is from New Orleans, plays Fix. Oh, he was good at that. When he comes on the scene he knows what to do.

One thing that everyone seems pleased with was that Lou Gossett, Jr. would play Mathu. How did you feel about it when you saw it being filmed?

I saw Gossett in a couple of scenes which were fantastic. One was the scene before Charlie returns and the old men gather in Mathu's house and he's telling them that they should go home. He's going to take responsibility. Gossett really speaks that scene very, very well. My main criticism is that at the very end he is supposed to have a long speech, and this is really minimized.

When I was told that he was in the film, I couldn't really imagine his being Mathu because Gossett is, I think, fifty and, what you could say, good-looking. But then Cicely [Tyson] was much younger when she played Miss Jane. Cicely was still in her thirties when she played someone who was 110. As soon as I saw Gossett in the makeup I knew he could do it because he had all the mannerisms of someone seventy years old. When Gower Frost, the producer, told me that Richard Widmark was playing Mapes, I thought, "Good Lord!" But then when you see it done, you can see that these guys are very good at it.

We were discussing characters one day before they started shooting. Gower Frost and I were talking about Charlie, and I was trying to show him how important it was that Charlie be big, so that when Charlie comes back, this huge guy comes back and people look up to him. And Volker—Volker's very short—said, "People can look at a short man the same way." and I said, "Well, I like bulk. Charlie should be bulk." And they did get someone like that: Walter Breaux. He is big. I have a picture of me standing between Walter and the guy playing Beau Boutan, the murder victim. These guys both weigh over three hundred pounds. I weigh 225, and I look small. These are huge men.

In the film made from "The Sky Is Gray," they used a corn field instead of a cane field, and the sky never was gray in the film. Do those kinds of changes bother you?

No, they don't bother me because by the time you make a film of a book, the writer—unless he's a one book writer—has just about forgotten that book and he's gone to something else. And it's a different medium altogether. You just feel like, okay, let them do what

they want to do. You know, take the money and buy something.
Invest the money if it's enough. If not, pay off the bills and hope
that they'll make a decent film and the people will watch it and go
out and buy the book. You're much more interested in selling the
book than you are the film. Whether it's a good film or a bad film,
people will go out and get that book. *Miss Jane Pittman* is a very
good example. Before the filming, I think we'd had only about three
printings in hardback and three or four printings in paperback.
Since then, we've had, say, twelve printings in hardback and about
twenty-two, twenty-three printings in paperback. Because of that
film many colleges and high schools and universities have used that
book. Even a bad film will get people interested in the book.

*Were you pleased with the film versions of "The Sky Is Gray"
and* Miss Jane Pittman?

Let's say *Miss Jane Pittman* was maybe a five on a scale of one
to ten and then "The Sky Is Gray" about the same. With *Miss
Jane Pittman,* you could not get the entire story of a hundred years
in two hours. You had to choose points, pieces, and then try to
mold that into a whole. In "The Sky Is Gray," the main character
is a little boy about eight years old, and they could not find a little boy
eight years old to carry the story. So they had to get a larger boy
about thirteen years old, and that makes a difference on the effect
of the story.

*The novel about Miss Jane uses the first person point of view. It's
very difficult for the camera to look at the character and through
the eyes of the character at the same time.*

Something was said about the filming of Flaubert's *Madame
Bovary.* In the book you can smell the cabbage cooking. In the film
you never could smell the cabbage. There are certain things that you
do capture, things that you do put on the screen. There are certain
things in the book that you cannot put on the screen—many things.
You can put action on the screen, but I don't know that you can put
thoughts on the screen and dreams on the screen and really the
depth of the personality on the screen. I don't know that you can
put that on the screen, flash it on the screen.

*You have said over and over again that you see yourself as a
storyteller and that you came from a place that was oral, where*

*people talked the stories. One of the things we see in your work is
that you've taken an oral tradition of storytelling and you've
transformed it into a literary medium.*

Right, I try to do that. That's one of the hardest things in the
world to do. You can go to any place, any bar on the corner out
there and find people who can tell the greatest stories in the
world—they can tell you some stories—but if you give one of
them a pen and some paper and say, "Okay, write this stuff down,"
he'll run. He'll drop those things and start running. It's a tough
thing to do, to try to recapture these things. But I try to do that, yes.

*How do you make the leap from the oral storytelling tradition to
the literary medium?*

Well, I think it's a combination of things. I think Joyce does it. I
think he does it in *Finnegans Wake,* and nobody can understand
what the hell is going on there. I think he also did it in other stories.
A good example would be "Ivy Day in the Committee Room." It's
the old tradition of these old guys telling the story about the great
fighter, the Irish patriot, Parnell, and Joyce can put this in literature
because Joyce had such a great literary background. Faulkner does
the same thing. "Spotted Horses" is nothing but a guy telling a
story about some wild horses beating up on somebody, cutting
people up and running people all over the place, and Twain does
the same thing. Twain and Faulkner are the fathers of this, this
combination of that oral tradition and then integrating it into a
literary tradition. So it's something that I inherited from having that
kind of background and then having studied literature.

*Do you think it's possible for a writer to be able to do this if he's
not, first of all, a part of that oral tradition?*

I think a writer writes about what he is part of. He has to. I don't
know that he could do it if he does not have this kind of
background. I don't know that Faulkner could have written what he
wrote if he had not come from that kind of background where
people squatted around the place, around the stores or the courthouse square or wherever they did, and then did their work like
that. I don't know if Twain could have done it had he not been part
of that traditional Mississippi River storytelling crowd, and then

knowing literature. And I don't know if you don't have that kind of tradition if you can do the same thing.

What you and Faulkner do is to add to the writing something to compensate for not having the audience and the sound and the performance there.

And then you leave off things, too. You leave out some of the things that they do tell you in order to make it in that literary form. You're transferring from the oral thing, a guy sitting there telling you a story. You have to take what he's telling you and use those twenty-six letters over here to put this thing down accurately. You try to put it down very accurately. But then you know you cannot do it because you cannot use all the gestures; you cannot use all the sounds of his voice, his improper syntax, whatever he does. That does not convey to the reader because the reader cannot understand what you're talking about.

For example, let's say we get someone who is a great Cajun storyteller. He can tell the greatest story in the world. You cannot write that! You better not try to write it. Nobody's going to read it. Nobody can understand it. Even someone who knows what he's talking about can't understand a thing, so you don't write it that way.

You can take what he told you and you say, I'm going halfway with what he told me, and I'm going to get what I've learned from all these years of reading. Then I'm going to use proper syntax; I'm going to use proper spelling; I'm going to do all those other little things. I'm going to take from what he gave me and I'm going to use from my background; I'm going to use something from over here that I have, and then I'm going to combine these things and then I'm going to put it out there and pray that someone will understand. I have to do something that can be recognized. I have to write the proper kind of dialogue that you can understand. I try to write in short sentences so you can grasp the dialogue. I try to make things as clear as possible. An actor or performer can make gestures or throw his voice out and cry and weep and do all sorts of things like that. What I have to do is use those twenty-six letters that tell you these things, so I can build up my scenes in that way.

You've talked before about models that you emulated, in the manner that Hemingway says he did Twain, and Norris did Zola.

You do emulate, you do, when you start out. I started out in the libraries, and I was just reading everything in my late teens in libraries. But I was fortunate when I came out of the army that I had some very good teachers who were just coming into San Francisco at that time. They were eager to help, and they were just coming out from the Korean War. At that same time we had the Beat Scene going on in San Francisco, so we were reading a lot of books. Once my teachers saw what I wanted to write about—and that was about rural Louisiana, and this was in the mid-fifties, fifty-five, fifty-six—they encouraged me and recommended writers and stories to read.

I also discovered how music can help, and as Hemingway suggested, paintings can help, just by going to a museum or art gallery. Just look at paintings and see how you can describe a beautiful room with only two or three things, without having to go through everything in the room. Right now I'm thinking of Van Gogh's painting called "Vincent's Room"—it's the room where he used to live and sleep—and how he could do it so well with only two or three things or pieces of things.

I've also learned from the discipline of great athletes by just watching them. I ran a lot of track myself. I was the worst football player ever put a helmet on his head, but I was pretty good at track in college. I know about the discipline of athletes, and I know that same discipline must pertain to the writer, to the artist. He must be disciplined. He must do things over and over and over and over and over. And these kinds of things are also a great influence. The grace under pressure thing I think I learned from Hemingway. I've always said to students, especially black students, that somehow I feel that Hemingway was writing more about blacks than he was really about whites when he was using the grace under pressure theme. I see that Hemingway usually put his people in a moment where they must have grace under pressure, and I've often looked at black life, not only as a moment, but more as something constant, everyday. This is what my characters must come through.

I also learned how to understate things from Hemingway, and I learned from his structure of paragraphs, his structure of sentences, and his dialogue. Hemingway can repeat the lighting of a cigarette, the length or shortness of the cigarette, or the ash

hanging, to show how time moves. He repeats little things throughout a scene to make you know the movement of time. Hemingway's
importance to me is a combination of the language and that particular theme of grace under pressure. Of course there are also his
drinking well and eating well. I like to do that, too.

I learned much about dialogue from Faulkner, especially when
we're dealing with our Southern dialects. I learned rhythms from
Gertrude Stein, learned to put a complete story in a day from
Joyce's *Ulysses* or Tolstoy's "The Death of Ivan Ilych."

*You have spoken before about how Russian writers influenced
you.*

Yes, I started out with form from Ivan Turgenev. I was very much
impressed, not only with form but with their use of peasantry. I
think serfs are used much more humanely in their fiction than, say,
the slaves were used, or the blacks were used, by many of the
Southern writers. I remember Tolstoy says, "You just watch a serf,
just watch him. He'll never tell you the truth." He says, now if
you watch closely, you'll figure out the truth, but boy he's going to
lead you all through the swamps, all through the woods, and then
you get it. Then you get the truth out of him, and I learned that
from just listening to these guys tell a story.

*Many writers claim that one of the things they're trying to do is
to create order out of all the chaos and disorder in the world. Do you
have a sense of doing that?*

I try. I think art is order. I think art must be order, no matter
what you do with it. I don't care what Picasso did with twisted
faces and bodies—all of that sort of thing. I think there has to be a
form of order there or it's not art. The novel to me is art. The
short story is art. And there must be order. I don't care what the
chaos is. You must put it in some kind of decent form. When you
leave this thing, you say you've gone through war, you've gone
through hell, but this is not hell. This is a piece of art. This is
work. This is a picture of hell. After reading this, you felt something
very—not good about hell—something good about this piece of
work. This is all it takes.

*You said earlier that music also helped. How do you think that
music helped you as a writer?*

During the time I was writing *The Autobiography of Miss Jane Pittman,* I was playing Mussorgsky's "Pictures at an Exhibition." It's about someone going to a museum or art gallery and looking at pictures against the wall. There are different kinds of pictures: dramatic pictures, comic pictures, different colors, all depicted in sound. There is a common motif going through the whole thing. At one time when I was writing *The Autobiography of Miss Jane Pittman,* I was thinking about sketches of a plantation because I had been listening to that so much. I was thinking sketches, sketches, sketches, and then I ceased thinking of sketches, for the autobiography.

Another thing about music: I think some of the best descriptions, especially dealing with blacks, some of the best descriptions of the big flood of '27, which most southern writers have written about, have been described better in music, especially by great blues signers like Bessie Smith, Josh White, Leadbelly, and many others. The whites did the newspaper things of that time, but when it came down to the more intimate things, I think the black blues singers gave us better descriptions even than the black writers did. Another thing especially in jazz music is repetition—repeating and repeating to get the point over—which I try to do in dialogue. I learned from music something that Hemingway also does and that is understatement. Certain musicians, like Lester Young, one of the greatest jazz saxophonists, could play around a note. For example, he didn't have to go through the old beat after beat of "Stardust." He could give you a feeling of "Stardust" by playing around the note. I tried to explain that in one interview when we did "The Sky Is Gray" for the film. In "The Sky Is Gray" the mother and her child must go to town to get the tooth pulled. They must sit in an all black waiting room. They can't have any food or drink or anything "uptown." They must go "back of town" in order to eat or drink. Now if I had wanted to hit the nail on the head, I could have put them in a white restaurant and had them thrown out, but by the fact that they have to go back of town, you know that they would not have been accepted uptown. So, I'm not saying, "Go in here and get thrown out," but instead I'm saying, "Go back of town to eat." This is what they would have had to do. The only whites they come in contact with are people who are kind to them—the old lady who gives them food at the very end, and others at the place where she can go in and pretend to buy an axe handle so the kid can warm himself. It's not hitting the nail on the head, but playing around it. I think this is much more effective.

You have a large collection of jazz albums and have commented before that you usually play music when you're writing. Do you still do that?

Oh, yes. Whether I'm playing jazz or classical music, or just the radio, I usually have music in the background, but soft, so it does not disturb me. I have to keep music. It relaxes me, and at the same time it gives me a sense of rhythm, of beat.

Do you think maybe it tells you the atmosphere or the kind of feeling you want?

I don't know that it sets a mood or anything like that. I think I have to sort of build myself to the mood before I begin to write. Yet at times, it can. It's possible that when I was writing *The Autobiography of Miss Jane Pittman,* because I played "Pictures at an Exhibition" just about everyday while I was writing it—two years I guess—maybe I needed that to get started. But sometimes I play music just for the background—but soft in the background. I don't play Beethoven's Fifth because that's too disturbing. I play some sort of soft music—violin or cello, or whatever—as sort of the background. It's just like you need water or coffee around the place, you know. You have some music in the background to keep you going that day, I guess.

How was music present in your world as you were growing up?

Well, of course, I came from a plantation. There was a church not very far from our house; I could hear the people singing all the time. I had to go to Sunday school and church as a child, and, of course, the people sang. I could never carry a tune myself, but the old ones did. And my mother sang, and my aunt. I didn't hear classical music or anything like that. I don't think the radio worked half the time, but there was always music, somebody doing something.

So far you've described the indirect importance music has had in your writing. Do you ever see it creeping in more directly, through musical language or musical references?

Oh, no. I don't think I ever use music really like that. In *Of Love and Dust*, Jim has a guitar. I think in "The Sky Is Gray," the young kid, James, thinks back on the old man who plays a guitar around the house. When I was a small child we did have a man like that who played the guitar around the place. But I don't know anything about music. I can't read music at all. I remember when I had to do the reading of the "Portrait of Lincoln" with the University of Southwestern Louisiana orchestra, I explained to the conductor, "I don't know one note of music, so whenever you want me to start reading, you must nod your head." We had a record of Carl Sandburg reading it so I could figure out the rhythm and speed, the way the thing should be read. But I couldn't follow the notes on paper. I don't know a thing about music.

What do you mean by a writer's "work" when you talk to students?

Well, I think if we're dealing with time, physical work is getting up and working at the desk. But I would think that a writer never stops working as long as he is conscious; as long as he is awake, he is thinking about his work. And then he sits down four or five hours, six hours, whatever he does a day and does his work there. Work means having your antennae out, too, that you're tuned in. And as Hemingway once said—I have a lot of Hemingway quotes—a writer must have a built-in s—detector. He must know when someone is bulls—ting him. He must know fact from fiction. He must know when someone's pulling his leg; he must know when someone is touching him on the back, whether it's a good handshake, things like this. So the writer is always working. But maybe in work, I mean discipline and sitting down at that desk.

A writer is always observing people.

He is. Well, it's not observing people. He's being. People used to ask me, "Say, why do you go back to Louisiana from California?" And I'd say I'd go back to Louisiana just to be. I never did come back here with a microscope and say, put your hand under here; I want to see skin color and all that sort of thing. I never did just stare at people and say there's a man over there and he's five feet eight, nine inches tall. But when I'd come back, I'd come back just to be back, and then if I went to a cafe to eat, something would come into me. I don't have to look at the place and say this is a little thing I'm going to put down. But if I'm there, something will happen: the color of the oil cloth on the table—you know those checkered oil cloths?—whether blue and white or red and white or red and black, something would happen, and unconsciously I'd become aware of it. I'd become aware of the taste of the food. All this sort of thing because your antennae are out. You're not staring at things, but you're . . .

You're sort of absorbing it . . .
You're absorbing it, yes.

Do you ever get so involved with the fictional world that you're creating that you sometimes have difficulty telling the difference between that one and the one you're walking around in?
No, I don't. But when I was writing *Catherine Carmier*—and I think *Of Love and Dust*—I used to pray to God to turn it off sometime because I would be so involved that I could not rest. And I didn't care for anything else. And I would just say, "Listen, I'd rather be just a poor writer. If I have to be a good writer to go through this hell, please turn it off. I just can't take anymore of this stuff. I'd rather be just poor and ordinary, just one of the other guys, you know, but just turn it off." But I don't think I've ever reached the point where I was unaware of my surroundings. I've never been in the place that I was writing about.

Humor is very much a part of your writing. Do you feel that your vision is an essentially comic, optimistic one?
I don't really know that I'm very optimistic. I think in much black folklore and blues that even when things are at their worst there's often something humorous that comes through. Even with tough, hard men, whose lives are really rough, something funny at times can happen. I don't know that I'm pessimistic about life, but I don't know that I'm terribly optimistic either. I see lots of things as being humorous, even if it's in a ridiculous way. When people take advantage of people, or when people hurt other people, it's often just ridiculous and the humor comes through. My characters are not usually one hundred percent bitter, not hardened to the point that they cannot feel and give and change. Humor and joking are part of

change. I don't know that it is a sign of optimism in my work. I don't go that far.

You've maintained that you wrote what you wanted to write about and that you wouldn't change your writing just to appeal to an audience or to sell your books. But you've also acknowledged making changes suggested by your editor in A Gathering of Old Men. *How do you see the relationship between writer and editor and what kind of relationships have you had with your editors?*

The most important relationship has been not with an editor but with my agent, Dorothea Oppenheimer. She would suggest things, and it was her opinion I appreciated more than anyone else's. I dealt primarily with her. Yet, at the same time, the editor did make these suggestions for *A Gathering*. He was right. I could understand how right he was. It was a matter of expediency. What I was trying to do originally was show how all these people lived before that moment, what they did with their lives before that moment that brought them all together. I had the guy sitting on his porch, or I had the guy sitting at the river fishing, or I had the guy doing something else before he arrives at Mathu's house. The editor said to have him come to Mathu's house while thinking back or have him speak with one of the other characters on the scene and then, in turn, tell what he was doing. That's what editors learn from television and movies. You always see the car arriving, especially on television. You don't know where he's coming from, but suddenly he arrives at a certain place like this. And through dialogue they explain where he had come from.

Now, when writing *The Autobiography of Miss Jane Pittman,* my editor, who was Bill Decker at Dial, told me from the beginning that the story should be told from the autobiographical point of view, and I couldn't understand what the hell he was talking about. He said to let Miss Jane tell the story. I was telling it from several characters just as I do in *A Gathering of Old Men.* The original title was *A Short Biography of Miss Jane Pittman.* Well, once it was "Sketches of a Plantation," then it was "A Short Biography of Miss Jane Pittman," when everyone else tells the story after she's dead. And he said that isn't working, but I couldn't understand what the hell he was talking about for a year.

And then I realized, "Damn, it isn't working. It isn't going to
work." That's what a good editor can do. A good agent, too, who
reads carefully. Dorothea has suggested more than any editor.
She was an editor before she became an agent. They can make
damned good suggestions. Not always. Lot of times they make
suggestions that you cannot accept. I remember that Bob Gottlieb
made suggestions about *In My Father's House* that I could not
accept at all. So I just said, "Well, no, I disagree with you." Bill
made some good suggestions for *The Autobiography of Miss Jane
Pittman,* just as Ed Doctorow made excellent suggestions for *Of
Love and Dust.* He was my editor-in-chief at Dial at that particular
time before he became a famous writer. For example, when he first
saw *Of Love and Dust,* he said, "Ernie, I really like the first part
of that novel, and I really like the last part of that novel, but the
first part of that novel and the last part of that novel have nothing
to do with each other." And he said you have to do one or the other
with this novel, which I did. I sent it back to him in about three
months, and he said it was a hundred percent improved, and he said
he wanted me to run it through the typewriter just one more time.
Do whatever I want, just run it through one more time. I did and he
published it.

In an article in The Southern Review *(October 1974), Jerry Bryant
refers to a version in which Marcus and Louise escape.*
They escaped, but it was not working out. See, the first part was
tragic. That's what Doctorow was saying: the first part was tragic,
but the second part was humorous. Marcus was saying I'm getting
out of this goddamned place. I'm going to show you guys how to
do it. So he started bribing people and getting wine or whiskey or
whatever at the grocery store. He knew they weren't going to kill
him, so he went and got things on credit at the grocery store and he
started selling it to the people in the quarters. They'd just take
the bottle and turn it up, you know, for twenty-five cents or fifty
cents, so he's accumulating money all the time. He was something
like Snopes in "Spotted Horses." He was playing all kinds of tricks
on people. He'd do anything since he knew that the guy would
not kill him because he's supposed to work his way out of there. So
he could do anything he wanted to do. After doing all these

things, after pulling all kinds of deals on all kinds of people, he
escapes. And Doctorow says, "No, Ernie, no, no, no. We don't
have any poetic justice here. This guy's a killer. He's going to kill
her one day, and something has to work out here. If you want to
make it a comic novel, make it a comic novel."

*What Bryant says is that it wouldn't have been an acceptable
ending to have the black man leave with the white woman at that
time, implying that's why you changed it.*

That was not Doctorow's criticism of it. He said I made it comic
at the end. He said that the first part was tragic and the second
part was comic. He didn't say he shouldn't escape with her. He
said it does not follow that the first part of the book is tragic and
you expect doom, you expect something to happen, something very
terrible to happen, and then in the second part of the book he
becomes a comic character and I'm having all kinds of fun with
him. I told Doctorow, "Why the hell should he pay for it? The
hell with it. Let the man get away." He was talking about balance.
He was talking about form. He wasn't talking about the theme,
the social thing. He wasn't worried about the ethics of it.

I didn't change it because of the social issue. I would never have
changed it because of that. And that's one of the things I was
saying a few minutes ago. Editors show me technique and how to
do things, but don't ever tell me what to write. No, I did not
change it because in the forties the black was not supposed to get
away or anything like that.

You wouldn't change your writing to make people buy it.

No way! No way will I change, no! People have asked me quite
often, who do you write for? I say I don't write for any particular
group. But if there's a gun put to my head and someone says,
"Okay, name somebody you write for," I'd say, I write for the
black youth of the South. And if there are two groups, I'd say I
write for the black and white youth of the South. Those are the
people I would write for.

Number one, I would want the black youth to say, "Hey, I am
somebody," and I'd want the white youth to say, "Hey, that is
part of me out there, and I can only understand myself truly if I can
understand my neighbor, if I can understand the person around me."

That's the only way one can understand himself, if he can understand other things around him. You know Donne's "No man is an island" and "Don't ask for whom the bell tolls"—every little piece of things around us makes us a little bit whole. I mean we can go through the world being half people, and most of us do that most of our lives. But in order to understand more about ourselves and the world, we must understand what's around. So that's what I'd want: the white kids to understand what the black kid is, and the black kid to understand who he is.

Writer Draws on Pointe Coupee Childhood

Steve Culpepper and Mary Broussard / 1988

From the *Baton Rouge Sunday Advocate* 4 December 1988. Used by permission.

Much of this flat, rural part of the world is wrapped in a thick green carpet of sugarcane, notched at the edges here and there with tiny camps of cabins and gardens and clotheslines.

Plantations still control much of the agricultural land near False River. Black people still do much of the work.

It was that way before the Civil War; it was that way before the second world war.

That's how novelist Ernest Gaines remembers the first 15 years of his life in Pointe Coupee Parish: as a time of poverty and hard work, of generations of black people stuck on the plantation, getting nowhere, kept down.

"By the '30s, when I was born, conditions were not too much different from the times of slavery. We were attached to the place," he said, recalling the plantation his family lived on when he was a child.

"You couldn't move around and do whatever you wanted to do. During the time I grew up, I understood much of what has been written in books about slavery and the reconstruction period, farm life and plantation life. I could have never written *The Autobiography of Miss Jane Pittman* or *A Gathering of Old Men* had I not lived it. But I would not wish it on any other child. I went into the fields when I was eight years old. I went into the swamps at 12."

Gaines considers himself lucky to have gotten out of the parish, which, until the early 1950s, had no high school for blacks.

"Not all kids had the chances I had. It was luck," Gaines said. "Those who stayed here, most ended up with very little education, not going to high school at all. Some were luckier. Some could go

217

to high school and some went on to Southern University or to a university in New Orleans."

In 1948, at 15, Gaines moved from Pointe Coupee Parish to San Francisco, where his stepfather and mother had work.

"My mother and stepfather had gone there during the war. My stepfather was in the merchant marines. My mother was working in military plants there and I would follow them later. I was left with an aunt on False River. The reason I was left—I could still go to St. Augustine. I went there for three years and then went to California to further my education, because there was no high school there for me."

Gaines could not even exercise his love of reading at the parish library, which did not allow blacks. Today, the library contains an autographed copy of one of Gaines's books.

St. Augustine was a black Catholic school in New Roads which has since shut down. It educated children through the seventh grade. Before St. Augustine, Gaines was schooled at church.

Education for blacks in those days was haphazard. Elementary schools for black children were set up in the little churches scattered around the parish. Salaries of the teachers were paid by the white School Board, but the salaries were fractions of the salaries paid white teachers.

"I went to school in a church. We didn't have a school. You would sit on benches or pews and your desk was your lap. You had your book on your lap; off your knee. Or you turned around and got down on your knees and used your pew as your desk," he said.

"School was taught in the church. On Sundays, it was a church. Five days during the week, it was a school. The (white public school) superintendent, once or twice a year, would come by and talk for a few minutes and leave. That's probably all the visits we ever got from public school authorities.

"I was on this plantation, River Lake Plantation, and I went to school there myself. We were supposed to have six months of school, but of course we didn't. You were lucky if you had five months. School didn't start until late October and you were out in early April."

The school year for black children coincided with growing seasons: "We had cotton until the first of October. Then, by middle of April, we began to plant and harvest other things, potatoes and whatever you had in the field. And children whose fathers were sharecroppers had to go into the fields."

Gaines remembers the little church school. "There was no such thing as inside toilets. We hauled water from the well to drink. We hauled wood for heat. Real rural."

In California, Gaines got his high school diploma, and unlike most of the friends he left back in Pointe Coupee, got a college education.

"My other brothers and sisters, the ones born in California, graduated high school, many went to college. All their children went to school. Whereas, the ones left here, not all went to school or finished school."

An education is meaningful in more than one way, for more than the person getting it. "If you have a group who go to school, they tend to send their children to school. Outside of school, in the day-to-day, 'life was real hard,' " Gaines remembers. The school bus wouldn't go the extra distance to pick up Gaines and his friends. "I remember standing on the riverbanks to hitchhike rides or catch a ride on the little country bus that passed by. So, these are things you had to do."

Gaines disputes the notion that a hard life is good. "I don't know that living a hard life is good for anybody. It gave me food for writing."

The hard life, the unfair treatment of blacks, those were part of the way of life and it was accepted, Gaines said.

"I hope it never happens again to anyone. Even when I was growing up there I never thought it was the worst sort of life because everybody else around me was the same way. Everybody was poor. Everybody wore the same clothes, ate the same food, went to school five months, did the same work. That was life. But the older people always thought it was something else and wanted me to do other things."

Gaines might well not have become a writer of international reputation had he stayed in Pointe Coupee Parish. He might not have even gone to school.

"I don't know if I would've even gone to school or not," Gaines said. "We had others who did go to high school. I'm pretty sure the talent I had was average. I knew kids there who were athletic, who would have been great baseball players or fighters or actors or maybe writers or stand-up comedians. Or singers. They never got a chance living in a place like that."

Gaines, who divides his time between Lafayette and San Francisco, keeps up with some of his old friends from Pointe Coupee.

"I know several people still there. A good friend is in New Roads. He taught at Rosenwald High School. I see him once every other month or so. We get together. I have a brother in Port Allen, another living in Bueche in West Baton Rouge Parish. I have a couple of friends in Baton Rouge. Many, many have died violent deaths or heart attacks or strokes. Quite a few have gone past in their 30s and 40s."

Gaines said that poverty in the parish wasn't just the problem of blacks. "Not only blacks, but if you have no education, I don't know what you can do for the next generation. What can you do?"

Talking with Ernest Gaines
Marcia Gaudet and Carl Wooton / 1988

From *Callaloo* 11.2 (1985): 229–57. Used by permission.

Gaudet: Do you want to talk about your current project?

Gaines: Oh, I don't want to talk about it.

Wooton: You've talked a great deal about Hemingway, Twain, Faulkner, and the Russian writers who have had a very great influence on you. You also said that when you became a writer, one of the things that influenced you was that you couldn't find stories by and about black people. Which black writers do you think had some influence on you?

Gaines: No black writer had influence on me. I went to California when I was fifteen years old. Of course, I had not read any books here in Louisiana. If there were books there in the libraries, I would not have been allowed to go there, but I doubt that there were books by blacks at that time in the libraries around New Roads. When I went to California, I went to a small town. I went to Vallejo instead of San Francisco, but even there there were not too many books by black writers. All of my reading—even if I wanted to read about peasant life—turned out to be by white writers. When I went to college, I studied white writers. We're talking about the early fifties. Richard Wright was probably the most well-known black writer at that time, but his novel, *Native Son,* was not taught. Passages would be brought up in the class, why-Bigger-does-what-he-does type of stuff, why he is angry, and all this sort of thing. *Invisible Man* had just come out, but it was not in the curriculum yet. You did not read *Invisible Man* as a part of American literature at that time. At a place like San Francisco State at that time, you were still reading Hemingway, reading Faulkner. You were not reading the black writers then as you would be ten years later. When I was developing as a writer, the books were not there. They were not being taught in the classroom, and only a few of them were there. As I said, *Native Son* and *Black Boy* were there, and *Invisible Man* had just come out. Baldwin's essays were just being read, but they were not being taught. They were just there. At that particular time I was so far behind the average kid I had to go to school with because I had not read anything. I was still catching up, so I did not have time to go out and read anything other than what I was assigned to read. They'd say read "Dry September" this week for this class; read "Dry September" and read Twain's *Huckleberry Finn*. When the black novels were not taught, I didn't have the chance to read them, even if I could have found them. So black writers had no influence on me at all. One book—and I've said this many times before—one book by a black writer that would have had as much influence on me as any other book would be *Cane* by Jean Toomer. What he does in those short chapters are things that I wish I could do today, those little short chapters, those little songs, the poetry between the chapters. That is still my favorite novel of any black writer.

Gaudet: You've said many times that Louisiana is your area. Do you think maybe Toomer would have influenced you because he was writing about the same kinds of things and about this southern area?

Gaines: I think it may have been subject matter as well as structure. I like that kind of structure, putting the short chapters together to make a novel. Of course I try to do that in the *Bloodline* stories, getting all these things together to make a novel, like Faulkner did in *Go Down, Moses*. It would be theme and structure in *Cane*, but especially structure. One of the good things that happened when I was studying writing at San Francisco State, as well as at Stanford, was they taught me technique, not telling me what to write, but how to write it and how to write it better. I was not pushed with a lot of political ideas. I was not pushed with demands to write about race or anything else. They said write what you want to write about, bring it in and we'll discuss it. And they discussed it more from a technical point of view. I try to teach now from a technical point of view. My students can write about anything they want. I don't care what they write about, born-again Christian, Klansman, or anything you want to write about, as long as you write well. If you don't write well, then I have to criticize it. And fortunately, that was what I needed at the time. I always knew what I wanted to do. I had to find a way in which to do it. For example, before I wrote "The Sky Is Gray," I had to read Eudora Welty. I was assigned once to read "A Worn Path," and I thought this is a great story. I read "A Worn Path" at least ten years before I wrote "The Sky Is Gray." When I went to write "The Sky Is Gray," I knew a model, just as I did in "A Long Day in November," with the first part of Faulkner's *The Sound and the Fury*. These are the kinds of things I learned, and these are the kinds of things they were helping me with, Wallace Stegner at Stanford, and Stanley Anderson and Mark Harris at San Francisco State. They were telling me to read these things. I don't know that any black writer could have helped me any more technically.

Wooton: It seems like an almost incredible working of chance to consider the differences between your work and the works of many other black writers that resulted from the fact that when you left the South, you went west and the others went north. You went to San Francisco, and they went to Chicago and Detroit and New York, so that you evidence a totally different sense of what it was leaving the South and going to something very different from what the others went to.

Gaines: Well, I went to a small town, too, Vallejo. Say if I had gone to Los Angeles and gone to Watts, it would have been a different thing altogether. A big city where there was a total black ghetto could have been a different thing altogether. But I went to a small town in northern California, and the people who were in this town—the blacks, Latinos, Orientals—had just been moving in after the war, in '48. So I went to a place where you had all these races. I mean my teammates, my playmates were Japanese, Chinese, Filipinos, whites, other blacks, the Latinos. I went to a place where you constantly heard different languages, kids going home to eat different kinds of dishes, talking about different things in school together. If I had been sent to Watts where you had a total black ghetto, maybe the other thing could have happened to me. If I had gone to Harlem, it could have happened. If I had gone to the south side of Chicago, it could have happened. But I was lucky. Then after that I went into the army and when I came back, I came back to metropolitan San Francisco, a completely integrated society. At the time I started writing, really getting serious about writing, it was the Beat era. All the races again shared all kinds of ideas. You'd go into these nightclubs and hear all these different readings of poetry and prose with jazz in the background. You ran into all these different things. Not that I was influenced by the Beat stuff, the Kerouacs and all these kinds of guys. I thought they were all crazy in the first place. But I didn't mind being there to see what they were doing. I sat back and watched it. To get back to the black influence, many of the young black writers, even my age and younger ones, were influenced by the most successful of black novels and that was Richard Wright's *Native Son*. They all tried to imitate this kind of urban thing. I was not urban. I tried to play that urban stuff for about two years after I went to California. If anybody asked me where I came from, I'd say, "Oh, I came from New Orleans." When they'd say name the street you lived on, I'd say, "Canal Street?" Everybody knew it was a damned lie. Finally I realized, hey man, you gotta be what you are. So, I thought, well, this is what I am. This is all I am. *Native Son* would not have had an influence on me, had I read it. It's urban, Chicago. It was not a part of my experience. I didn't know a thing about urban life. If I had come from New Orleans, if I had been there and seen the violence, seen the [French] Quarter, seen that kind of background, maybe I could have tried to write that. But I came from a place where people sat around and chewed sugar cane and roasted sweet potatoes and peanuts in the ashes and sat on ditch banks and told tales and sat on porches and went into the swamps and went into the fields—that's what I came from.

Gaudet: The big city was New Roads.

Gaines: New Roads was the big city. I'd go there to see—I don't think there was a stop light there—just to see a light. All that made a big difference. I think if I'd gone to the eastern part of the country, I probably would have gone into playwriting. My earlier teachers said I had that sense of place, using small areas and then a lot of dialogue and that my whole scenes were place and then dialogue, place and dialogue. My movement was limited when I was a kid growing up. I mean I had the fields and things like that, but we were limited to the quarters as our living place. Just about everything we did was limited to the quarters. We went to the big city of New Roads every so often on Friday nights to see cowboy movies, but everything else was limited to that small area.

Gaudet: One of the things we've mentioned but haven't directly talked about is the image of aging in your works. There are a number of old women characters who play prominent roles in your fiction. There's the mother-in-law in "A Long Day in November," who is an aggressive kind of older woman, and you have the older women and how they are dealing with mortality and aging in "Just Like a Tree," which may be where you do the most with the idea of aging. These older women seem to be much more in control of their world than do, say, the older men in *A Gathering of Old Men,* at least up to the time the story starts. Do you see the process of aging, the effects of aging, as different for women from what it is for men?

Gaines: The only way I can answer this is by saying I was raised by older women as a child. My stepfather who raised me was not often at home; he was in the merchant marine. I was the oldest child around the place, and you must remember that I left Louisiana when I was fifteen years old, so until that time I was around the house a lot. Of course I went into the fields and into the swamp, where the men worked, but the relationships with the men were quite tenuous. I worked around them, but I went back home. I came in contact with them, meeting them in the quarters, or riding in a car or a wagon with them, talking to them, and working in the fields around there, but it was not as strong a relationship as the one at the house with my aunt and the people who visited her. I was around older women much more than I was around the men who came around the place where I lived. Yet, there were times when men did talk, and I think I became closer to older men when I started coming back to the South and wanted to write about things. And it seemed the older men were the ones who were there, the ones who had survived, so in *A Gathering of Old Men,* I could bring them into the story much better than I could earlier because when I lived in the South earlier they were not as close to me as were the older women. All that shows the impact the older women had on my young life, and maybe that is the reason the older men did not come in as strong figures in the earlier books and stories.

Gaudet: The point is not to say that one group was in fact strong and the other one was not, but instead that for whatever reasons the women seem to feel more secure than the men do.

Gaines: I can see that, too, because the women in their work did not come in conflict with the outer world as much as the men did in their work. The men competed with the white man and there could be conflicts there. The black man competed with the white man as sharecropper and when he went into town, whereas the black woman very seldom competed. She was just a worker there. She was a worker in the big house, and she was a worker in the field. She did not have to—as I have in *A Gathering of Old Men*—compete with racing to the derrick to unload the sugar cane or go into the cotton gin to unload the cotton. In my world it was not a competitive thing between the black woman and that outer world. She just did what she was supposed to do.

Gaudet: So she had the sense that this place in the quarters was hers. She could operate there fairly securely.

Gaines: I don't know how secure her position was. I guess she had to suffer and work.

Wooton: Obviously we're talking about security here in relative terms, but your talking about this makes me think of *Catherine Carmier*. Raoul is competing with the white sharecroppers, but while Della will be affected by that competition, she is not engaged in it in the same way. She also has not had the sense of defeat that the men have had, or the frustration. And in *A Gathering of Old Men*, it's finally that frustration and sense of defeat all coming together to the point at which they're not going to do that anymore.

Gaines: Well they've reached a point in old age at seventy years where it doesn't make any difference anymore. Raoul is a man maybe in his fifties. Now when these other men were fifty they would not compete like this. That's what Mapes keeps telling them, saying, "Hey, you would not have done that thirty years ago." So at seventy, seventy-five, and eighty, they say, "Well, what the hell am I going to live for? So I die today, what is that?" But they would not say that at fifty, not as a group. As one, yes, maybe, but they would never have come together like that.

Gaudet: This all seems connected to how you portray men and women in general, and to how you show the black man in relation

to women and how other black writers, for example Alice Walker
and Ntozake Shange, show that relationship. There is such a
contrast, in fact, between your portrayal of these man-woman
relationships and the way we see them in other black writers' works,
that there is a question about which portrayal is an accurate one.
Some people say you are too kind to the black male character.

Gaines: Those same kind of people have said I'm too kind to
white characters, and others have said I make my black heroes
too nice, too. But I've lived with and seen the actions of these men.
I think I know more about the black male, because I'm male
myself. I know something about his dreams. I listened to them
when I was a kid growing up; I've drunk with him, and I've been
in the army and in athletics. I know what men dream about. All
men dream about certain things. All men have hopes, and all men
brutalize other things near them, at home, when they cannot fulfill
those hopes. I read Joyce's Dublin stories, and I see the same sort of
thing. I read this story "The Informer" that was made into a great
film, about how these men are afraid of the Black and Tan, the
British, and how they treated other people around them. You'll find
that among men, the more brutalized they are, the more they brutalize
other people. I remember reading Faulkner's "Dry September,"
where they come from this lynch mob and this guy comes home
to his wife. His wife says something to him, and he wants to beat
her up. It's just continual brutalization of one thing after another.
The lynching was not even enough for him to get rid of all the
aggressiveness or hatred or whatever it was that drove him to
participate in the lynching. He comes back to the house and he
continues it at home. But then there's the other side of things as
well. It's not only one side. I never look at things just one way. In
my writing about black males, I've known the cowards, I've
known the men who would take chances, men who, if they were
given the equal chance, would be as brave as any man. We can see
that in athletics. We can see that in reading about soldiers, guys
fighting in Viet Nam or the Second World War, that a man, given
an equal chance, will say, "Okay, I'm a man," and he does his job
as well as anyone else does. This is complicated stuff.

Gaudet: There's a lot of violence in some of your stories, for
example the fight at the house party in *Of Love and Dust*. But it

seems to be more directed toward other men, and not toward the women. Do you think the others have a false image, that they're showing too much of that violence of men toward women?

Gaines: I don't know, because I think if they did not have the violence there, they'd have the violence someplace else. If the violence were not exercised at that particular party, it would have been exercised somewhere else. But what brought on this violence? What brought on this thing at that particular time at the house party? Number one, it's hot. Number two, the beer is warm. Number three, there's nothing else to do. Number four, Marcus is there and he's looking for a fight because he couldn't get with this woman he wants. The woman cannot be with him because of other reasons. She's told him, "Get away from me," because she belongs to Sydney Bonbon. It's not just a guy going out there and beating up on a woman, or beating up on somebody else because of nothing else. You have to look at what causes these things. You can't say a guy beating up on a person out there is just beating up on someone. What brought him to beat up on that person, or to act the way he's doing? This is the kind of thing that I try to figure out.

Gaudet: Do you think that the South Louisiana setting, with that unique mixture of French and Cajun and black makes your writing different from that of other southern writers? Or do you see yourself basically as a southern writer or a Louisiana writer?

Gaines: I see myself as a writer, and I happen to have been born here. I was born black. I was born on a plantation. I've lived in that interracial, or ethnic, mixture of the Cajun, and the big house owned by the Creoles—not Cajuns, but Creoles—and the blacks. I was associated very early with the Baptist Church; I was christened as a Baptist. But I went to Catholic school, a little school in New Roads, my last three years in Louisiana. I had to go through their kind of discipline. I had to go to Mass. I didn't go to confession or anything like that. I didn't take the Holy Sacrament. I had to go through all these kinds of things. My aunt who raised me and who was crippled spoke Creole. Some of the old ladies on the plantation and some of the old men spoke Creole. I traveled around with another aunt of mine who sold the little cosmetic things all over Point Coupee and West Baton Rouge parishes, and I met

all these people who put these things on their faces and made
themselves smell sweet, and they spoke French because my aunt
spoke Creole. I am a different writer from, say, Faulkner, and I'm
a different writer from a lot of black writers. A writer from North
Louisiana would not have had the same experiences I had in South
Louisiana. One who came from Mississippi or Alabama or Georgia or Texas would not have had the same experience. I never think
of myself as number one a black writer, quote black, or Louisiana
black, but as a writer who happens to draw from his environment
what his life is, what is heritage is. I try to put that down on paper. I
think my work is unique in that I think I come from a place that is
quite unique, certainly very different from all the rest of the southern
states. Louisiana has a tremendous Romantic history about it, the
Spanish and the French, and all those things. We're just a different
group, and we have problems maybe others don't have or don't pay
so much attention to. I think we have a big problem among the darker
skinned and the fairer skinned black people in this state, more than
in any other state in the union. I see it all the time, and I live it. I
saw it in New Orleans just this last week, and I've seen it in areas
around Lafayette and Baton Rouge. I've experienced that.

Gaudet: That's the kind of thing you handle in *Catherine Carmier*.
Raoul has an identity problem because obviously he has not
identified himself as white, either.

Gaines: Right. That's one of the things about Lillian. Lillian says,
"Hey, listen, wait awhile. I cannot live in this middle-of-the-road
kind of situation. I cannot cross this fence anymore. I'm white
enough to go over there, and I'm going to make this choice. I'm going
over there because I can't live across this fence anymore the way
I've been trained to do." And I saw a lot of people at the museum
in New Orleans the other night who could have gone one way or the
other. And yet they're saying they are black, but they don't feel
that way—they don't feel that they are.

Gaudet: In Louisiana it's always been something more like an
ethnic identity, linked to the idea of the Creole of Color. The
group of fair-skinned racially mixed people was at one time, if not
almost a separate race, at least a separate ethnic group, who
prided themselves on being neither black nor white.

Gaines: That's what all the Creole stuff is about right now,

230 Conversations with Ernest Gaines

because if you think about it, there's no such thing as a Creole with mixed blood. There's no such thing as a Creole with African ancestry. But that is the one identity they could use: "I'm not black, I'm not white, I'm Creole." That is a falseness in itself because the Creoles were either French or Spanish.

Gaudet: Of course, today Creole is usually used to mean mixed blood.

Gaines: Well, this is what I mean. You can easily say that I'm not black, but I'm Creole, and most of them hide behind this until it becomes necessary, in politics or whatever, in order to get what you need to accomplish. Then you can say "I'm black." But I think that deep down inside they know they haven't paid their dues. Too many black people got murdered and bled to change this thing in the South while these people hung back. Yet because they were closer in their features to the Caucasians, closer to the whites in power, they were the ones who could get in much easier than the black ones who had to die for it. They were not black when they had to go out there and die in the streets and suffer in the streets as the blacks had to do. In a class I was visiting, this kid sat in the back—a dark-skinned kid, almost as dark as I am—and he said that he never heard of anything like that in his family. I didn't want to call the kid a liar. He said that his ancestry were those people that I talked about. I cannot imagine a family made up of a mixture of darker people and fairer people who have not had these problems. I had it in my family.

Wooton: The first-person point of view is very important to you, but you have different kinds of first-person points of view. How do you search for and find the voice you have to have to tell the particular story?

Gaines: In *Of Love and Dust,* which is the first of the first-person point of view novels, I knew Marcus could not tell the story. He was too much involved in it. I had to find someone believable. He has to be acceptable. Even if he has to use tricks, he has to be able to communicate. Huckleberry Finn used all kinds of little tricks to communicate with all kinds of people and find out little things he needs to find out about. Nick Carraway in *The Great Gatsby* has to be someone who can communicate with Gatsby and the super-rich Daisy and her husband and their crowd. You search for a

character who's believable, who is somewhat likeable—he can be
a rascal but he's believable—and who can communicate with different levels. And if he can't, he must find someone else to help him
communicate to the audience. He must find that person. He must
run into someone, he must create someone. I mean that writer
has to create someone. Character A cannot possibly reach Character C, so you must create a Character B to communicate from
Character C to Character A. Then Character A can take it back to
the reader. You must do that. Now, I don't do things like this is
Character A, this is Character B, this is Character C. Once I get
involved in it, I'm just like a Shakespearean messenger. I get
messages out there. Somebody's going to bring a letter on the stage
right now to get this stage clear for the next act. Somebody must
come and do this for me.

Wooton: Obviously in *Of Love and Dust,* you set yourself up with
what might appear to some an impossible problem. How in the
world can Jim know what's going on in that bedroom? Or how can
he know how Marcus gets Louise to come down to the fence to
talk to him? He doesn't have any way of knowing.

Gaines: Of course! These are the kinds of things that you must
invent something believable for. Number one, you believe in Jim.
You believe in Jim as a decent guy who is coming to you and telling
you what is going on. Jim gets along with everybody else. He gets
along with Marcus very, very well. He's got to get along with
Marcus because that's the only way he's going to tell Marcus's
story. To create Jim, he has to be a believable person. He has to be
a kind of guy that you can say, well, he can be weak or something
like that—I don't like him all the time—but I believe this guy. I
believe what this guy is telling me. So, Aunt Margaret has to tell him
about things, and Aunt Margaret tells things from sound. Margaret
doesn't see a thing in that bedroom. That's one of the techniques.
Another technique that I've learned is from radio where you can
only hear things and they tell you what's going on. You know, all
the old, fifties radio stories—"This is happening on the fiftieth floor
of the Fairmont Hotel and it's foggy out there"—you don't do things
like that but I mean the guy had to build up the atmosphere and
build up everything for you to see what was going on in their stories.
And when it came to writing it down, I learned a lot from listening

to radio. But, you create a believable character. You must create that believable character to communicate to your reader. And once you do that, you can use tricks. Every writer uses some sort of tricks or another, every damned writer. Shakespeare uses them. Faulkner uses them. Anybody who uses the first-person point of view has to use tricks because the limitation of the first-person point of view is that that person can't be there all the time. And you say, okay, he can't be there at all times, so how am I going to get this message to my reader? Now I must create an incident that's believable. It can't be too ridiculous. It can be just little bits brought into my story. But I must get that information and bring it to my reader.

Wooton: Can you elaborate a little bit on tricks?

Gaines: Well, the trick is that Aunt Margaret must hear it for Jim to tell it. Without Aunt Margaret being there, Jim can't tell the story. Without Sun Brown coming down the quarters at that particular time, he can't see Marcus and Louise at the fence. I have to create Sun Brown. These are the little tricks. But the tricks must be subtle, too. We can't just write, "Big, thick trick," you know.

Wooton: The scene that's only being heard also gives the opportunity for humor because she has to interpret it to Jim. It's funny just thinking about all that's going on in the bedroom and her sitting out there and having to listen to it. And she has to explain it to Jim and tell the child something the child will accept without telling her what's really going on.

Gaines: Of course, and she can't possibly tell Jim all that's going on. Jim has to interpolate what she's saying. She's saying, "You know what I heard," and Jim's saying, "Oh, she heard noises and all like that." She's not telling him everything. She's not giving him all the little, explicit details. Jim's watching her gestures; he's watching her face. But we take all that out. Jim is seeing beyond what she's saying. Jim is reading between the lines. This is an old woman. This old woman is not going to explain these explicit sex sounds and all that kind of stuff. Jim has to read between all the things that she says and then he gives it to you.

Wooton: One of the amazing things about how this technique works is that when you take these two voices and combine them, it becomes almost like an omniscient voice, almost like a third-person kind of thing. We've been talking about where your narrator is

in order to tell the story, but that leads to speculation about where
you are as a writer, what your sense of this narrating character is
and how this is happening.

Gaines: I don't think I'm there at all. One of the things Jim says
as he's driving his tractor is God doesn't care anymore. He's up
there playing cards. He's playing Solitaire by himself and saying
now you guys do anything you want down there. I've done all I
can do. You people are gonna do it anyhow, so just do what you
want to do and include me out!

Wooton: Then you do not see yourself as Thackeray saw himself,
as a puppeteer constantly pulling the strings?

Gaines: No, no, no, no. I try not to do that. I try to avoid it. One
of the things that I've always criticized about Ellison's *Invisible
Man* is that Ellison is always the puppeteer. He's always there. You
never lose him. And that is not the way, especially in this
picaresque novel. That thing is supposed to take over and you're
not supposed to sense that writer ever again. That thing's supposed to just take over and go! You stay away from those people
and let those people do. Unless they just become ridiculous and
then you say, okay, now you don't do that.

Wooton: We talked before about listening to an old man sitting on
the porch and telling stories about his past. He told us everything he
could about sixty years of politics in Louisiana in terms of how it
affected him. We didn't care whether or not he got all the dates right.
We were just as interested in the way he was telling it as we were in
what he was telling us. That's often true when we're listening to
somebody or watching somebody tell a story. You've said before
that you write for your stories to be read aloud, that you more or
less think your stories are being told in that kind of way. Do you
have some sense of yourself as both storyteller and performer the
way the old man was when he was sitting on that porch talking to us?

Gaines: Well, I must bring in some kind of reality to what he's
talking about. For example, if he is telling me a story and I want
to repeat something he said, I have to do some research. If he's
going to talk about the event of Huey Long's death—for example,
I had to bring that in in *The Autobiography of Miss Jane Pittman*—I
cannot just write what he says because I'm not absolutely sure about
what he says. So what I do is I go back and read something on this

Conversations with Ernest Gaines

stuff. I've been listening to blacks talk about Long's death all my life, but I don't want to look like a damned fool by putting down what they said in a book. They might be telling me anything. This is a very important thing when you write about Louisiana. You can mess up on Long's death because everybody has messed up on Long's death. I can talk to everybody around here and they're all going to tell me a different story about Long's death, why he died and how he died and all that sort of thing. After listening to everything these people had to say, I thought when I got ready to write that chapter I better do some research. So I read T. Harry Williams' biography and I read Robert Penn Warren's book, *All the King's Men,* and Long's book, *Every Man a King.* I read newspaper clippings. I did all kinds of things. Then I went to the Louisiana room at the LSU library and I went through page after page, manila folder after manila folder of things. Then I said, okay, I've got all this information and now I must go back and give it to this little old lady back here, Miss Jane. I've got to give her all this information, but I can't give her this information as I got it. I can't give her this information as a trained historian. I must in some way—and that's how we come back to the voice thing—give her all this information and let her tell this thing the way she would tell it, as an illiterate black woman a hundred years old talking about these things. I must let her do it. It's like getting pork and putting it in the machine and grinding it up and grinding it up and grinding it up and letting it come out a different way from what it was when it was obtained. This is what you do, and you give it to her like that. At the same time that I give her that information, I hope that I'm not being a puppeteer feeding this to this person. I have to keep her in character. I cannot just give her hunks of history and throw them to her and have her describe, it was Sunday at seven o'clock and he was going from New Orleans to such and such a place and Weiss comes from behind this pillar and shoots him. I don't need all that because she never would have spoken that way. I would have been the one speaking that way. The historian would have been the one speaking that way. But I have to give her that information as if she were just holding a regular conversation with her friends sitting out on the porch. She doesn't know. She has heard from third or fourth or fifth persons. She's heard this information. She's never read it in a

book or a newspaper. She has just heard about it, and this is what
she talks about. My character is going to say what I want my
character to say, but she's going to say it in the way that you
think she would've said it. She's a character and she has to do what
I want her to do, give you the information I want her to give you.

Wooton: The old man on the porch is telling a story, but he also
is obviously conscious of us sitting there listening to him. Do you
have that kind of consciousness?

Gaines: Oh! No, no. See, the old man is telling the story orally.
I'm using letters to put this thing down. I'm using a different thing.
I'm using letters to say "The man did this, and this is what the man
did." I'm not using the gestures. I'm saying what he's saying, but
I'm not talking to an audience. I'm putting it down. I'm writing it
down. It's like a man writing things down in his diary: Dear
Diary, this is what I did today. Thoreau writing in *Walden,* this is
what it looks like. I'm not writing to any kind of a group of
people. I'm not writing to anybody. I'm writing to my diary. I'm
putting down my feelings, my observations, and things like this
into this diary.

Wooton: Are you also trying to disappear?

Gaines: I'm disappearing if I am writing from that first-person
point of view. I'm totally disappearing because I must put everything into that character. That character has to be the entire person.

Wooton: What about in *Catherine Carmier* and *In My Father's
House?* Were you trying to get the same kind of distance? Is the
third-person voice as clear and separate, as distinct from you as a
first-person voice is?

Gaines: I don't know that it is. I don't think that it is and that's
why it's much more difficult for me to do. And I think it's much
more difficult for American writers. I was saying earlier that what
we've done with the first person is as great in literature as
anything else we have done, any of our characters that we have
created, any of the stories we have told, or anything else. I know that
I'm not nearly as in control in the third-person omniscient as I am
in the first-person. If I get a character too close to me, I can't
work with him. I'm having to deal with a character in this book I'm
working on now. He's too damned close to me, and I'm having
all kinds of problems. He's one of the reasons I'm not working as

fast. He's too much like me. He's cynical at times. He hates things. He wants to say, "Goddamnit all. The hell with this stuff."

Gaudet: Is he the narrator?

Gaines: He's the narrator. If I get a guy who just could go, I'm with him. I can say you take it. I don't want the ball anymore, so you carry the ball.

Wooton: Are you having trouble making the distinction between the character and the writer?

Gaines: It's not between the character and the writer. It's the voice, not the person himself, but the voice. He speaks too much like me. You know you shouldn't let yourself think too much. It's good to just go on and do the work and stop all the damned thinking. When I come to the omniscient point of view and I create a character, a narrator who's much like myself, I do too much thinking. I don't have the freedom. That's one of the things I criticize *Invisible Man* about. There's too much thinking going on all the time. There's thinking in every Goddamned sentence. You don't think. Let the thing flow. Let it go.

Gaudet: Can you say anything more about your work-in-progress?

Gaines: I can say that it deals with a teacher who visits a guy on death row. That has been said in the opening chapter, when the defense is trying to get something less than the death penalty for him. This guy is going into a bar. He's as broke as anything. He doesn't have any money and he's going into this bar, and it's probably cold weather. Two guys come along and say, hey, man, do you want a ride? He says, all right. So he gets into the car with them, and these guys don't have any money. And he says I don't have a penny on me. These guys start talking about how they need some booze, saying let's go over to the old man. We've spent our money there all the time, and he should be able to let us have a pint until grinding, until the sugar cane cutting time. When they go into the store, the old man's there all by himself and this guy, this third guy, goes along in that store with them. The old man knows them and speaks to them the way he does all the time, saying hello and how's your family and all that kind of stuff. One of them speaks to him and he says we want a bottle of wine. The old man says, okay, give me your money. When they put the money on the counter, he knows there's not enough money. He says no, no, no,

you bring your money, then you'll get your bottle. They say,
come on, you know we're good for it. The old man says no, no, so
one of the guys starts going around the counter. He's going to
take it. The old man says, hey, don't come back here. I told you
already, you must bring the money. The guy is walking toward
him, so the old man breaks toward his cash register where he has a
gun. This guy standing back doesn't know what the hell is going
on around him. All of a sudden, there is shooting all around. When
he realizes what has happened, the old man is dying, and these
two guys are dead. And then he doesn't know what to do. He hears
this voice calling him and calling him, and he doesn't know what
to do. Finally he goes around the counter. The old man is dying,
and the guy feels, God, he knows I was here and now he's going
to blame me for all this. He's going to tell. He doesn't know what
he's doing. He just grabs a bottle and he starts drinking. He's
looking at this man and drinking and drinking and drinking like this.
And as he turns he sees the cash register is open from when the old
man grabbed the revolver, and he grabs the money. He says I need
money. By now the old man has died. This is told from a teacher's
point of view who knows nothing about any of this. I get all of this
later. As he starts out, two men come into the place. Now you
see this kind of action during the trial. This happens in the forties.
That's why I wanted to see the local prisons where the executions
went on at that time. The trial goes on. The jury is made up of
twelve white men, and this kid is sentenced to death, although he
says he had nothing to do with it. But the prosecutor says, wait
awhile. He went there with those guys. He's telling us he had
nothing to do with it. We don't know that. We know that everybody's dead except him, and he came out of the place with a
bottle and money in his pocket. So, he convinces the jury and the
young man is sentenced to die. The court-appointed defense attorney
tries to get him off by saying this is not a man. This is a fool. You
wouldn't call him a man. This boy has no idea what size his
clothes are. He doesn't know Christmas from Fourth of July. He
doesn't know a thing about Keats. He doesn't know Byron, or
the Bill of Rights. He can't plan any murder or robbery. He didn't
do any of this. Finally he says I'd just as soon tie down some kind
of animal in the electric chair, a hog or something like that. Never-

theless, he's sentenced to die for this crime. Now, his grandmother, or his Nanane or his auntie, or whoever she is, approaches
this school teacher. She tells him, I don't know how much time
he has left, I don't know whether it's a year, several months,
several weeks, whatever, but I want you to approach him and
bring him to the level of a man. Then let him die as a man. That's
what I want. And this is where I am now. This teacher is sort of
like I am. I don't want to have a damned thing to do with any of
this. That's what I want. And this is where I am now. This teacher
is sort of like I am. I don't want to have a damned thing to do with
any of this. That's what he's saying at first. I don't want to have
anything to do with this. The crime is there. It's over with. He's a
school teacher on this plantation. He says my job is to keep other
kids from going that way. I want nothing to do with any of this. So,
this is what the story is about. I've reached the point now, chapter
six, that he's deciding whether or not he will go to the courthouse
to visit this guy. I still don't know what the hell he's going to say to
this guy. I have no idea what the guard's going to say. I know he
has a little car, a '46 Ford he drives around. I don't know where
he's going to get gas from, where he's going to fill the tank. I've no
idea of anything, nothing. But as the thing will move along, it will
come out. These are the problems I'm having with this. And this is
what I wanted to see, what a jail looks like, how does this guy
sleep. Those are small details. I have a twofold problem here.
Number one, I can create the jail. That's easy for me to do. But
to get that character to tell that damned story in a way that makes
it flow smoothly . . . I don't know what the teacher wants, you
see. I know the teacher doesn't want to be there, but I know
damned well he's going to be there. This is the kind of conflict
I'm having there. I have to get that personality together and make
him do what I want him to do without controlling him. Like
winding him up and saying, Goddamnit, you ought to give these
people the information. These people are out there waiting for
you to give him that information now. I'm not going to gee-haw on
you every time I want you to go left or right. You've got to do
what I want you to do for me. And I haven't got him there, but I've
got him to a certain point where he's doing some of the things. I
haven't got him to the point where he's going to do most of it. I

think I've got a pretty good start. I was working on that today.
Anyway, that's what this story is about. I think it's going to be very
good once I get it. I can tell it better than I can write it now, because
I've been trying to write it for the last couple of years or so.

Wooton: How old is the boy?

Gaines: About twenty-one. He's as illiterate as someone can be.
I want him on that level—not an idiot; he knows how to work; he
knows how to follow orders. The defense attorney says, now,
listen, he can plow, he can load sacks and pick cotton and all that
sort of stuff. But we're talking about what a man is. What is a man?
This is one of the things that the teacher must find out. And
another conflict is in the question, Why should we make this man a
man if he's going to die tomorrow? Why do this? The old lady
says I want it done. The sheriff's against it because all you can do
is aggravate things. Let it go. But I've got to create something
that happens in the past. The little old lady says I want it done and
your wife owes me something. I don't know what she has on the
guy's wife. These are the little tricks. I said something about tricks
a moment ago. I must find some reason to convince that sheriff
through this old lady and the sheriff's wife that the teacher will
come to the jail twice a week. That's what I call little tricks. You
pull all these little deals and you throw them all in there. It's just
like making gumbo. If you mix it well, you don't notice the tricks.

Gaudet: We don't want you to tell us, but do you know whether
or not he's going to be executed?

Gaines: I don't know. But I know one thing. I'm going to have
him give a very good speech before it happens, if it happens. He
has to stand up as a strong man and give this talk. It's almost like in
The Confessions of Nat Turner, that there's a guy who is interested in
what this guy has to say because he's followed this whole thing. It's
a pygmalion type thing, the Elephant Man type thing. I want all
of that. The Helen Keller thing, you know. And there's a guy who's
been following this. I don't know who this guy's going to be,
whether he's going to be a newspaper guy or his defense attorney
or someone else, but he's going to be there. He's going to follow
everything that's going down, and he's going to make notes. The
day before this guy's supposed to be executed, if the guy will be
executed or not—I really don't know, to be honest with you—this

guy's going to talk to him. He's going to say, tell me things, tell me what it is. And the guy's going to tell him—he's going to stand up real tall—and tell him what he thinks manliness is and citizenship and what life is about and then he's just going to say, okay, let them do what they want. The teacher is cynical—I mean he hates teaching, says I hate the whole goddamned thing—but hearing what he has done for this man who was condemned will bring something out of him. And he will go back to these kids, these small kids he has around him, and he will realize he has a duty to perform. And that duty is not to run away to the north as he wanted to, to get the hell away from all of these things. But, okay, I'll just give my life here and this is it. But this other person, this condemned man must be the one to convert him to this, to give his life. That's what the whole thing is about. He in one way makes the condemned boy, who is like an animal, a man, and the condemned one makes him a man so that he can go back to develop something. That's what this is about. If I ever get it done.

Interview with Ernest Gaines

Elsa Saeta and Izora Skinner / 1991

From *Texas College English* 23.2 (1991): 1–6. Used by permission.

Ernest Gaines' novels and short stories have earned him a niche among major contemporary American writers. His two best known novels, *The Autobiography of Miss Jane Pittman* (1971) and *A Gathering of Old Men* (1983), have been made into television movies. His short story, "The Sky is Gray," is one of the selections for the American Short Story Series filmed by the National Endowment for the Humanities for public television. Other works include the novels *Catherine Carmier* (1964), *Of Love and Dust* (1967), and *In My Father's House* (1978), and the short story collection *Bloodline* (1968).

Gaines is presently a writer in residence at the University of Southwestern Louisiana, Lafayette.

The author granted the following interview on March 27, 1991, while visiting the University of Texas—Pan American as a guest of the school's Living Author Series Program. The interview was conducted by Elsa Saeta and Izora Skinner.

Q: Since your subject matter is often rather grim, how do you account for the humor in your work?

A: I didn't know that my subject matter was grim. I don't know how to tell a story without some humor. No matter what the problem is, what the story is about, I can't tell it without humor because in daily life there is not only the grimness around us but there is humor as well. I don't go consciously to writing humor, it just evolves—it just comes into the writing. It comes in through certain characters in the story. Just as I said in "The Sky is Gray," the world is neither black nor white but there's a grayness there, so no matter how dark things seem, there's humor always somewhere around.

Q: A number of your characters talk about manhood, but their

concern goes beyond its literal meaning. Is manhood a kind of
metaphor in your work?

A: I think what I try to do in my fiction is to show that there
comes a time in one's life—in everybody's life—not only in my
character's but in your life and mine and everyone else's—when
dignity demands that you act. What do you do when you're
confronted with a problem or with an obstacle—whether it's with
your health, or whether you're seeing a child slapped or a woman
being hurt, or whether you're witnessing an accident or an insult by
someone, what do you do at that moment? This is the kind of
manhood that I try to show in my work. Quite often for my
characters this can mean death or it can mean imprisonment or it
can mean bodily harm, but it's the thing that makes life worthwhile
in that you stand up at the time.

Good examples are in *A Gathering of Old Men,* of course, when
the old men stand. They have not stood before but one day they
do stand. They try to make up for the past which they cannot do,
but at least they stood that day. You find the same thing with Miss
Jane Pittman because she would not let anything get in the way of
whatever she wanted—whatever she thought that she should do
from raising the kid [Ned] to going to the fountain at the end of
the story.

You use the word "manhood" because you associate it with most
of my male characters rather than with the female characters, but
it's that moment in life when you stand. Manliness is that moment
when it is necessary to be human—it's that moment when you
refuse to back down. Your conscience will not allow you to back
down whether it's to help a child, to help a drunk, or whatever it
is; dignity demands that you act. That's the kind of manliness I try
to reach for.

Q: It seems somewhat similar to what Hemingway called "grace
under pressure. . . ."

A: Yes, I've said that. I've spoken about that many, many times.
How well you come through. What do you do when you have to
do the right thing? Hemingway's grace under pressure is doing it
right . . . doing it right but under pressure. Mine is doing
it—making an effort to do it and even if it's not as pure as what
Hemingway would want it to be—you did make the effort to do it.

Q: In a couple of your novels, you use third person point of view; in the other three, you use first person point of view. Do you feel more comfortable with first person point of view?

A: I do feel more comfortable with the first person point of view as well as the multiple point of view as in *A Gathering*. Omniscient—in the omniscient, I become too conscious of my work, of myself, rather than letting the characters take over. I, as writer, really can't do it myself, but I can get into the persona of some other character and let him carry the story. For example, *The Autobiography of Miss Jane Pittman,* once I got the voice of Miss Jane the story was very easy to write. I've been asked how I write so well about this female character . . . I think I've mentioned this incident before. When they were reviewing the book, *Newsweek* asked for a picture to accompany the review. They called and asked for a picture and when I said there was no picture because the book was a novel, I could hear the woman on the other end of the line saying "Oh my God. . . ." they had the review written and were just waiting for the picture. How do I write so well about this female character? Well, I just caught the voice—a voice that is much more imaginative than mine.

In the case of *A Gathering of Old Men,* I started originally not from the omniscient point of view, not from the third person point of view, but from the single point of view. Lou Dimes tells the whole thing. But I found that he could not tell the story itself like I wanted it told because he could not see the little boy running down the street banging his butt and he couldn't see Janey inside the house talking to herself and he couldn't see many of the other characters. He could not reveal their inner thinking to the audience as they could themselves. I went from his single point of view to the multiple point of view because I didn't want to go back to the omniscient. I feel trapped in the omniscient. I've written two novels—*In My Father's House* and *Catherine Carmier*—from that point of view, but I feel much freer and I think my narratives flow more smoothly with the first person or the multiple point of view.

Q: What particular writers would you say influenced you the most?

A: I had to read all—just about everybody in college. I can start with the American writers—Twain, Faulkner and Hemingway. I

can go to the French writers—de Maupassant and Flaubert. Joyce
in Ireland, Chekhov and Turgenev in Russia. I had to study
Shakespeare, so I learned from reading the great tragedies *Othello*
and *Lear*. I suppose I got something out of reading *Don Quixote*.
So there are writers who influenced me, but also books. For
example, a book like *Gatsby* is one of the best constructed little
novels in modern literature. I could learn from there how to put
together a small novel—how well he developed each paragraph
beginning with a block and building into a pyramid. I get something
from all writers.

Of course, writers were influential because I use the same tools
that they use. It is common to ask the writer what writers influenced
him, and these writers did. I learned from Hemingway's limited use
of dialogue and his paragraph structure. At the same time I got a
lot from Faulkner's humor. Reading the way he described things
and the way he wrote about things helped me. From someone like
Joyce—with Joyce and Greek tragedy—I got the idea of the one
day thing: how can you put everything together in a day? For
example, *A Gathering* takes place in a day and most of my stories
usually take place in a day or overnight. For example, "The Sky
is Gray" takes place in only a few hours . . . "Just Like a Tree,"
the very last story in the *Bloodline* stories, takes place within a
few hours. . . . "Bloodline," the title story, takes place within a
few hours. How do you get all of this together and get your point
across within a few hours? By reading Joyce, by reading Greek
tragedy, by reading these different writers, I learned these things.
Someone once said that if you steal from one guy that's plagiarism,
but if you steal from all, you're a genius . . . so I steal from everybody
I can. I've learned from them all.

Someone once asked Hemingway that question about what writer
had influenced him and he mentioned several writers but then he
started mentioning painters, and bullfighters, and hunters, and
fishermen, and all this sort of thing because not only do writers
influence you but people influence you. Great athletes have always
influenced me in that I like watching them doing what they do so well
and realizing that this is due to work . . . to work and plain
discipline. The writer must be disciplined and I don't think
anybody's more disciplined than the professional athlete. I like

watching them work out. They use their body moves to get what
they want, we—the writers—use words, the great musicians use
sound, the painters use color or form. You get something from all
of them. You get something from watching someone sweep a yard.
I was watching a lady sweep a yard yesterday. She was so
particular about the way she was doing it. She got on the sidewalk
and made sure she got all the dust off the sidewalk. She raked the
leaves and made sure she got them out of the corner. A speck of
dust on the walk or leaves on the lawn as she gathered them all
up . . . she was very conscious about everything. And I was just
watching her realizing that you do the thing right. She was doing
everything right. So I like watching people who are good at what
they do.

I've learned especially from my own people, maybe not in literature but from music. I listen to the great blues singers, especially
the rural blues singers and how they in their own way describe the
hard life out there. Maybe that's where the grimness comes from
. . . but I listen to everybody. I like listening . . . so I've learned
from them all.

Q: I think I recall your saying that you modeled "The Sky is
Gray" on Welty's "A Worn Path." Would you elaborate on this?

A: Not modeled on it, but I don't know that I would have been
able to write "Sky" had I not read Eudora Welty's "A Worn Path."
The journey is the thing: the journey of the old woman going to the
doctor, going to town to get medicine for the kid. This is what I
was going for—the journey. What does the journey mean besides
going to town and coming back?

The short story ["The Sky is Gray"] has been approached in all
kinds of ways. It's a woman's story according to the feminists who
say this is the story of a proud woman. Others will see it as the
story of a young man's initiation into manhood. Others say that it
is a story about poverty and pride . . . I guess a little bit of all of it
is there.

Q: Would you agree that the structure and theme of *Bloodline*
parallel that of Faulkner's *Go Down Moses?*

A: Yes, that was my intention. My intention was to write a series
of stories. After it was published, someone said it was an episodic
novel. I didn't know about that when I was writing the stories

because I didn't write the stories in the sequence in which they were published. But I knew I wanted to write certain stories about different age groups of the Black male in the rural South during the thirties and forties. I wanted to write a series of stories about that and that's what the bloodline is all about. The bloodline is not that they are all bloodline related—that they're connected by blood—they're connected by experience. It's a common experience that they all share.

Before Faulkner's *Go Down Moses,* I'd read Sherwood Anderson's *Winesburg, Ohio* and, of course, I'd read Joyce's *Dubliners.* That's what I was trying to do . . . I knew I wanted to write a series of stories; I didn't have any idea that they'd form an episodic novel.

Q: What did you learn from creative writing classes?

A: Well, I may regret saying this, I don't think writers can be made unless a writer comes into a class with something. I think you have to bring something into that creative writing class and you have to bring more than just paper and a pencil and you have to bring more than "I want to learn to write today." You have to bring the past—you have to bring something of the past with you. I was talking to a friend of mine just the other day and she said, "You would not be able to write the things you have written had you not come up the way you did. You had to go into the fields, you had to work hard, you were around the old people a lot and you listened to them and you wrote letters for them and read papers for them—all kinds of things like that and this is the kind of thing that you brought into the classroom when you said, 'I want to write the short story . . . I want to write the novel.' " My teachers at San Francisco State and later at Stanford saw this and said, "You want to write those things—then write, but these are the books we recommend that can help you understand what literature is. Read—not only Faulkner and Hemingway—but read everybody else—read Twain, read Chekhov, read Joyce, read everybody." Reading to see how these authors [Cather, Hemingway, Faulkner] put their stories together helped me develop my characters, plot, use of dialogue, and use of humor.

Practically, what I got out of the class was that my teachers read my stories and they took the old red pencil and they just went

down and said—"good here . . . build here . . . take all this out here
. . . you're becoming too Faulknerian here . . . too much like
Hemingway over here . . . you need to find and use your own voice
. . . you have it in you but you have to do it yourself and you can
only do it by rewriting the work . . . you have to go over it and go
over it and go over it again." That's what I got out of class. You
have to bring something into the class in order to get something out
of it. You have to want to be a writer—you have to have something
to say. The instructor helps you bring it out if it's there. I think
that's what I got out of my experience.

Q: You teach creative writing. What can you teach a student
about writing fiction?

A: First they bring something in to me. I teach graduate students
and I select my own students. I select them on the basis of what
they have written. They're already writing when they come to me.
I usually teach one night a week for three hours and we—there's
usually 12 to 15 of us—sit at a round table and the writer reads his
work to us. Everyone else has a copy of the work and has already
written his criticism of it. After the writer reads his work in front of
the group, we sit around and discuss it. You have the opinion of
13–14 people who are at the same level as the student plus mine as
someone who knows something about writing, someone who has
been at the work for a while, someone who's done a lot of reading,
someone who's read all kinds of manuscripts. I've been reading
manuscripts for I don't know how many years and so I have a
feeling for what a story should be like. But I always tell the writer
"you have to take it all with a grain of salt—you must be your
harshest critic—you must do it." I help them with their craft. I
try to stay away from philosophies and what their symbols are
supposed to symbolize. I stay away from those sorts of things and
help them with the craft. I have students in my classes whom I
think I've helped . . . they've had things published and I think
I've had something to do with it.

Q: You've created a number of unique characters. Do you have a
personal favorite?

A: Oh no, no . . . that's like asking a father "who is your favorite
child?" I dare not get into that. I don't have any favorites—I like
all my characters—I like even the bad ones. I know most people

think Miss Jane is the favorite because she's probably the most famous of the characters, but I like them all because I feel they're all different. I like them all—I don't have a favorite.

Q: What about the novels; did any one of the novels cause you greater pain than the others?

A: *In My Father's House* caused me the greatest pain. It took me about 7 years to write that book. I used every approach in the world to write that book. I just couldn't do it. I think of all the books I've written this is the least successful because I was just tired by the end of that book. The easiest book to write was *Of Love and Dust*—I wrote that book in about 8 months. But *In My Father's House* took 7 years, I just didn't know how—it was a combination of theme and character development—just about everything. But, it was also a book I felt I had to write. It's a father/son thing and that's one of the themes in most of my novels. The black father looking for the son or the son looking for the father . . .

Q: In this particular book, the father does finally acknowledge the son . . .

A: Well yes, but I think it's a bit late at the time—at least the son feels that it's a little late.

Q: Has your perception of any of your characters or works changed over time?

A: I just came to the conclusion the other day that Miss Jane is not about Miss Jane; it's about the four men in her life. I don't know why I thought of that just the other day. There are these four men—Ned whom she raises, Joe Pittman whom she marries, Tee Bob, who is really very important in the book, is the young white guy who falls in love with the octaroon teacher, and Jimmy who leads the civil rights movement. . . . Although it affects her, I think the book—especially the latter half or three quarters of the book—is really about those men much more than it is about her. The book is a panoramic thing and spans four eras, each of which is represented by one of these four male characters. For example, Ned as a little boy fits into the war years, Joe Pittman is the settling down, the Reconstruction or peasant years, Tee Bob represents the plantation system, and Jimmy, who goes back to the quarters, to the people, to the church, is the civil rights years. It's the lives of those four men really.

While I was working on *The Autobiography,* I kept Gertrude
Stein's *The Autobiography of Alice B. Toklas* in mind because I liked
the rhythm of the title *The Autobiography of Alice B. Toklas . . .
The Autobiography of Miss Jane Pittman. The Autobiography of
Alice B. Toklas* is about everybody but Alice B. Toklas, so I felt I
could do the same with Miss Jane. I could start with this central
character, and then, of course, as she gets older the book moves
further and further away from her being directly involved in the
action of the novel. That's why the other characters take over much
more than she. From the time Joe Pittman comes on the scene
with the horse, the male characters begin taking over. She's involved, but she's not the center of the action; she's the one telling
what's going on. That book came out in 1971, so 20 years later I
realize what I've done. . . .

Q: Our students who read the novel *A Gathering of Old Men* and
then watched the TV film of the novel were very critical of the
TV version. How do you feel about the TV production?

A: I've said to others—and I hope the producers never hear what
I've said about the film—I've said that I didn't like the beginning,
the middle, or the ending. I didn't like the opening scene because
it's supposed to be a mystery. You don't even know that he
[Beau] came up in the yard with a gun—you don't know anything—
you're not supposed to know anything—the only thing you know
is that there was a shot and the next thing you see is this guy [Beau]
is dead. That's all you're supposed to know. I also thought the scenes
in the yard were too relaxed. When you're waiting for a lynch
mob—if you're expecting a lynch mob—you don't go around
playing baseball or you don't go around cracking pecans with a
loaded gun or you don't play checkers. Every little sound causes
your nerves to stand. If you believe there's a mob coming, you're
waiting—you're just waiting. It's [the film] too relaxed. I don't
care for the ending either . . . there's so many things. Then they
combined characters: they made Yank and Dirty Red the same
guy and they're two opposite people.

There's lots of things that they did that were improper—that were
wrong. The film puts everything on Beau. Most of the old men
don't even know Beau, they're too old to know Beau. By the time
Beau becomes the farmer there, these old men are all retired. The old

men remember Fix, Beau's father. This is a Southern problem. We live in the past so much—we live so much in the past. The old men live in the past—they're trying to make up for the past that day. Mapes lives in the past; he thinks he can still come in and slap people around. Candy more than anybody else lives in the past. The sense of this dwelling on the past is minimized in the film. But once you sell the rights to the film, you've sold the rights to it and you just can't do anything about it.

Q: While reading *A Gathering of Old Men,* many of our students were shocked to discover that as late as the 1970s this type of prejudice and discrimination was still occurring. Is that idea in the back of your mind—the fact that we take progress for granted and assume that we've moved beyond all that. . . .

A: I feel that anything can happen at any time. Since I wrote that book, you know what has happened in lots of places: you see what happened in Los Angeles recently, the same thing is happening in New York. A lynch mob is a lynch mob—you don't have to wear a sheet or live in East Texas or Mississippi or Louisiana or Alabama—you can live in New York, you can be in police blues, or you can be a gang of kids and have someone accidentally go into the wrong neighborhood at the wrong time. This is what I think I was trying to say; anything can happen at almost any time.

Another one of the themes running around this story is the idea of working together. The football players are very important in the novel. The only way you can really do things and the only way we are going to be Americans is that we have to work together. While many of the other characters in the novel are trapped in the past, the only ones who live in the present are Salt and Pepper. They're the ones living in the present and they're the ones who must make this America work. We've got to block for each other and do all kinds of things to get to the goal. The football players are a symbol for how we must do this together.

Q: Can you account for how you chose writing as a profession?

A: When I went to California, I was 15 years old and I ended up at the library reading and reading and reading. And eventually I decided I wanted to write. I wanted to see something about my own people and there were no such books in that library. I'd read books about peasant life no matter who wrote it: Steinbeck writing about

the Mexicans in the Salinas Valley, Cather writing about the
peasants in Nebraska, Chekhov writing about peasants in Russia,
de Maupassant . . . I'd just read them because they wrote about
people of the earth.

An interviewer once asked me what book influenced me to write
the most. I thought, and I thought, and I thought, and I finally
said—"I don't know." He said "Maybe it was the book that was
not there and you felt that you needed to put it there." And I've
always felt that since then . . . my reason for writing was trying to
put that book there that was not there. I think all writers do
that—Goethe has said that everything's been said, but it needs
saying again.

Q: In what sense, if any, does the novelist have a moral obligation
to his audience?

A: Writing is a very difficult thing and writing well is more
difficult. The only moral obligation the writer has is to write well and
never ever do any work that he cannot feel proud of. He owes that
to his art and not to anyone else but to that work . . . not to an
audience . . . not to himself. He doesn't owe anybody anything . . .
but the work itself. The work itself is the only thing.

Q: Most of your work seems to be very life affirming. You've said
in another interview that part of your goal is to help the reader
and yourself develop character.

A: Yes, that's right. I think if one writes, one expects to be read.
What you expect to get out of that writing . . . what you want
your reader to get out of the writing is something about himself.
What you get out of it is that you learn something about yourself—so
it is character building. That is why I hesitated when you asked
which were my favorite characters. As a writer, you go deep
inside of you to bring out a character who can show that thing that
you wish you could do or you wish someone else could do—that is
the one who goes just a little bit farther and will not accept anything
but justice. I suppose I did say that the object of my writing is the
building of character—my character through the characters I build
in the book and whoever reads it can find something that will help
improve his/her character as well.

Many years ago, I was asked what group I wrote for. I said I
write for the black youth of the South so that maybe he can find

out something about himself . . . and the white youth of the South
because only when he knows something about his neighbor will
he know something about himself. So this is what I suppose I mean
by character building. As I have said before, my aim in literature
is to develop character so that if you pick up the book, you will see
something you feel is true, something not seen before, that will
develop your character from that day forward.

Writing about Race in Difficult Times: An Interview with Ernest J. Gaines

Michael Sartisky / 1993

This interview was conducted by Michael Sartisky, Ph.D., President of the Louisiana Endowment for the Humanities, at the Tennessee Williams Literary Festival, New Orleans, on March 26, 1993. Copyright 1994 Michael Sartisky.

MS: Good Morning. I'm Michael Sartisky, and this is a gentleman who needs far less introduction. This is Ernest J. Gaines, author of *The Autobiography of Miss Jane Pittman,* and another half dozen works that, for those of you acquainted with them, are just wonderful pieces. This is totally unrehearsed, unprecedented.

EG: That's right, we have no idea what we're going to do.

MS: We have no idea and he's as nervous as a cat on a tin roof, not being sure of what I'm going to ask him. Ernie and I have been chatting about some of these subjects for about ten years. We've asked this morning to talk about writing about race in difficult times. I thought I'd begin like this:

Ernie talks, Ernie thinks in terms of his literature. He sees himself as being very much in the novelistic tradition. It should be acknowledged that people in every moment in history think that difficult times refers to their time. We know that race is an issue in this country today: the Rodney King trial is ongoing. But race, of course, in this country's history has been ever-present. I'd like to start off with the novelistic tradition to get us into the conversation, just very briefly.

Ralph Ellison, who wrote *Invisible Man* prior to what we now call the Civil Rights Movement, begins with an epilogue in which he quotes yet another American novel. There's a tradition here which moves back. He's quoting Herman Melville's short novel

Benito Cereno, which you may recall involves a slave revolt, a
revolt actually not of slaves but of Africans on a slave ship being
brought over to this country to be slaves. The Spaniards who own
the ship have been captured by the Africans and eventually are
rescued. The question of who is the victim and who is rescued is a
little complex in this story. But towards the end of the novel,
when they've already been rescued, this is said, " 'You are saved',"
cried Captain Delano, more and more astonished and pained.
"You are saved. What has cast such a shadow upon you?" He's
talking to the Spanish captain. And Ellison just stops there. He
doesn't answer the question. It kind of resounds; if you go back to
Herman, the answer is very simply, the negro.

The negro, the Black, the African-American, casts a shadow
across American culture, across American literature. The question of
race, of slavery itself, ultimately of relations between people of
different races, is what informs the literature. Ernie Gaines,
perhaps as well as anyone, has written about that very difficult
subject.

So, if you'll forgive me, since I know the questions and you
don't, the first one I want to toss at you is: Considering American
history—and as I just said—the American literary tradition, would
you agree that for you and your work, race is, in fact, one of the
central themes or questions?

EG: I don't know if you can write at all, seriously, without
invoking race, especially Southerners. Of course, people like
Melville did look into that subject as well. But it's almost impossible
for us to write seriously without bringing in race. From Twain's
Huckleberry Finn to all of Faulkner's stuff, the best of that stuff,
the best of, I would say, Southern literature would have race involved.
I would think that the rest of the country would too. If there were
as many blacks there as here in the South, they would be much
more concerned about bringing race into it. But even they don't
escape it. You find it in Fitzgerald, in *Gatsby,* and probably
Hemingway. Hemingway can't escape this, in so much of his work
race is always involved. It has to be there.

MS: At the risk of pursuing the obvious, you said for us as
Southerners, particularly here in the South, slavery ended—I'll
play devil's advocate here a little bit—slavery ended legally one

hundred thirty-odd years ago. Why is it still so much ever-present in our literature, in our culture today?

EG: Well, you know Faulkner said that the past isn't past, it isn't even dead, so we just can't escape it. You can't go into any white middle class home and not hear about the Civil War. You can't go into a Southern university and not be aware of southern literature and southern history, and southern history before the war . . . especially before the war and during the war. So it's present; it's always here. We still see the result of it among my own people. The effects and the legacy of slavery, it's always there: those cast-down eyes when standing up. It's still there.

MS: When thinking about the topic for this session, "Writing About Racism in Difficult Times," the first thing that comes to mind is racial conflict—conflict between blacks and whites—but your novels and short stories do far more than that.

I want to suggest this as the framework, the order in which I'm going to pursue the questions. Writing about race can simply mean writing about the African-American experience itself, giving voice to a people who perhaps did not have a voice. Writing about race can also mean—as Ernie's novels reflect—the way in which, as he just mentioned, race becomes a present factor, not just between blacks and whites. Race is also something that affects the black community internal to itself, does it not? Ultimately, in the course of this discussion this morning, I want to come back to the question of the actual conflict between the black community and the white community.

To give a little bit of illustration about the African-American experience as it is perceived by that community and not by the white community, I wonder if you'd be willing to read a passage from *A Gathering of Old Men*? It's an exchange between two of the characters. Just to set the scene very briefly for you: a Cajun has been killed and is lying dead in the field and it is not clear who has shot him. A young white woman who has grown up on the plantation and is very intimately involved with the black community says that she shot him. But at the same time, 15 or 20 elderly black men from the community all get the identical shotgun and fire off the identical shot gun shell and they all appear on the porch, on the gallery of the house next to where he's been shot and they *all* claim that they are the one who shot him. The sheriff, whose name is Mapes, comes upon the scene and he's trying to sort out what's going on. In the course of this, they start to explain, among other things, why they're there. The passage begins here and it stops there . . .

EG: Johnny Paul grunted out loud. "No, you don't see."

He wasn't looking at Mapes, he was looking toward the tractor and the trailers of cane out there in the road. But I could tell he wasn't seeing any of that. I couldn't tell what he was thinking until I saw his eyes shifting up the quarters where his mama and papa used to stay. But the old house wasn't there now. It had gone like all the others had gone. Now weeds covered the place where the house used to be. "Y'all look," he said. "Look now. Y'all see anything? What y'all see?"

"I see nothing but weeds, Johnny Paul," Mapes said. "If that's what you're trying to say."

"Yes, sir," Johnny Paul said. He didn't look at Mapes; he was still looking up at the quarters. "Yes, sir, I figured that's all you would see. But what do the rest don't see? What y'all don't see, Rufe?" he asked me. He didn't look at me, still looking up at the quarters. "What y'all don't see, Clatoo? What y'all don't see, Glo? What y'all don't see, Corrine, Rooster, Beulah? What y'all don't see, all the rest of y'all?"

"I don't have time for people telling me what they can't or don't see, Johnny Paul," Mapes said. "I want—"

Johnny Paul turned on him. He was tall as Mapes, but thin, thin. He was the color of Brown Mule chewing tobacco. His eyes gray, gray like Mapes' eyes, but not hard like Mapes' eyes. He looked dead at Mapes.

"You ain't got nothing but time, Sheriff."

"What?" Mapes said.

"I did it," Johnny Paul said.

"I see," Mapes said. "Either I stand here and let you talk about things you don't see, and the things the others don't see, or I take you in? I see."

"Yes, sir," Johnny Paul said. "But you still don't see. Yes, sir, what you see is the weeds, but you don't see what we don't see."

"Do you see it, Johnny Paul?" Mapes asked him.

"Nah, I don't see it," Johnny Paul said. "That's why I kilt him."
"I see," Mapes said.
"No, you don't," Johnny Paul said. "No, you don't. You had to
be here to don't see it now. You can't just come down here every
now and then. You had to live here seventy-seven years to don't see
it now. No, Sheriff, you don't see. You don't even know what I
don't see."

MS: In this unseen presence of this history that is known to one
community and that another, the white, "can't see," even while
seeing it, do you want to play back and forth with that?

EG: What Mapes has seen is only the weeds; he hadn't seen the
flowers when the flowers were there because he doesn't see the
old people when they were there, when they sat around on all the
porches. He doesn't see any of that. All he knows is that there's
been a crime committed, and he feels that he should come there,
solve the crime immediately, and go home. Go fishing, he wants to
go fishing.

MS: And what's really there?

EG: What is there? The people, the history, the soul, and spirit
and everything is there.

MS: You're saying when Mapes comes to it, the crime has just
been committed, and he's focused entirely on the present
moment.

EG: Of course.

MS: This man's dead, who did it? That's the focus.

EG: And he uses the same kind of past methods of trying to solve
it by beating people up and then the old men say, you don't know
what's going on and we have to stop here.

MS: Something has changed?

EG: Something has changed, yes.

MS: Just as when Ellison in using the epigraph from Melville,
asks a question, "What is this that casts this shadow?", but
doesn't answer it, there is that presence of the unseen, the unspo-
ken, the unknown. It's a presence that is so powerful, so perva-
sive, that it's there before those who have partaken of it. You're
saying it's always there?

EG: It's always there, yes. If I can go to another piece of work,
in "The Sky is Gray," I don't do it overtly, I don't show the racism

and prejudice. I don't have to go kicking people out or saying awful things to people. However, during the entire day of "The Sky is Gray," the people can't go into certain places. There's a wall there, they cannot enter the place to have a drink of water or to eat or to even get warm, because they're cold outside. So the thing is there without your having to have all the other overt obstacles there. The thing is there, that wall is there, that law that has been written is still there. So that when you say slavery ended one hundred thirty years ago, that wall is still there, that law is still there, although many things have broken down since the 1940s when "The Sky is Gray" took place, but there are many of those walls that are still there, invisible walls to most people, but they're still there.

MS: There are these different phases, then, in our history. There was the period of slavery itself during which Melville writes *Benito Cereno,* and during that period, you're saying the oppression was overt.

EG: Yes, yes.

MS: It was there, in the whips, the chains, the beatings, the forced labor, the conditions within the living quarters of the African-American community. Where's the next major historical shift?

EG: Well, after the war and when the Jim Crow laws were written was the next period.

MS: So then it becomes the law and it is stripped of the physical apparatus, but the oppression is still tangible in much the same way?

EG: Absolutely, yes.

MS: In your work, what are the historical moments or events that seem to you to be changing the fabric and structure of these relations? For example, in a number of works World War II gets mentioned. Can you talk about that?

EG: Most of my writing, except for *Miss Jane Pittman,* is between the thirties and the forties, so World War II is, of course, always major. *A Gathering of Old Men* takes place in '79 or something like that. So that's the period I write about, that period between say the time I was born and the late sixties into the seventies. It depends on what novel, on what story, I'm involved with. When I wrote

Miss Jane Pittman, I brought in events from the 1860s. Writing *A Gathering of Old Men,* there were references back to many of the past. So I cover that period, I concentrated between the thirties and the late seventies.

There's a certain thing I'm doing: I'm writing about rural Louisiana. I'm not writing about New Orleans; I don't know a thing about New Orleans. I could not write about New Orleans. I might write a little bit about Baton Rouge, more about the New Roads or False River area. So I bring in the kind of thing which could have happened to the people in those areas. I lived in San Francisco about forty-five years and I still can't write about San Francisco, so I write about the little world I know a little bit about.

MS: You just celebrated your 60th birthday.

EG: Yeah, well, you were there.

MS: I was there. I'm glad it was yours and not mine, by the way.

EG: (laughter) You'll get yours.

MS: I'll get mine. (laughter) That remains to be seen, or as Faulkner said, "That ain't been proved yet." You were born in 1933 but your writing, the vast bulk of your work, especially the early work, concentrates on a period when you were very young?

EG: Yes.

MS: But you're writing about the adults of that period?

EG: I've been asked, "How can you write about a child at this age?" I'm writing on children and the governor of Old Miss, when I was a little boy at one time. I was writing about Miss Jane Pittman—well that's another story—I was raised around those kind of people, I was raised by very old people. I heard them talk. I was with them all the time. I was serving them coffee; I was serving them water or whatever, so I was with them all the time. Although I was born in '33, by '40, I was aware of things. And things didn't change too much between those years; things didn't change too much in rural Louisiana. Things were pretty much the same.

Until I went to California in '48, you did the same sort of day labor you probably did as in the time of slavery. There were some tractors, but the majority of the sharecroppers still lifted the cane with their arms. They still literally picked up the sacks of potatoes, the sacks of cotton with their arms; they threw this stuff on a wagon. I went into the swamps as a child. We still pulled the end of a saw—we didn't have motor saws—as they must have done a hundred years earlier. So it was not very hard for me to write about the thirties, because they were doing the same thing they were doing in the turn of the century, so it wasn't very hard to write about it.

MS: The quality of life itself persisted, even if your time changed.

EG: Oh yes, yes.

MS: Change is very slow.

EG: Yes, especially for my people there. Some of the white families began to get tractors by the time I left there in '48. I don't know of any Blacks in that area who had tractors.

MS: The tractors, I noticed, appear over and over. In fact, in *Of Love and Dust,* you refer to James Kelly "watering" the tractor, right?

EG: That's the machine that was going to change the rural South: industrialization. They changed the labor laws and everything else. So the machine was the thing which made it easier for some people, but it meant it pushed other people away from the land, the only thing that they had and it pushed them away.

MS: Coming back to the historical factors that affected race and that appear constantly in your novels as background causes, In *Bloodline,* for example, Copper returns, Christian returns from World War II.

EG: No, no no. He makes that up; there's no such thing as war. He created that whole thing himself. There is no army.

MS: (Laughter) I knew there was no army, I wasn't that unconscious. But I thought that he was a veteran.

EG: He was no veteran. No he's not. But I do bring in the war a lot in most of the things there. I know I did in *A Gathering of Old Men.*

MS: What did World War II change?

EG: That's a good point, because World War II was when many of the young, black men who worked on the land went into military service and they never did come back. Many of the people did as my people did. My mother and my stepfather went to California during that time because they could not work the land anymore, because the land was too poor to give them any kind of a living for us. So they went out, they left. World War II changed

all of that, World War II and the military. But it was the changing,
it was the people moving away from those places and leaving just
the old people. Eventually those tractors that I keep mentioning would
push those old people to a point where they didn't have any kind of
work to do on those places anymore.

MS: The tractors also seem to be frequently associated with
the Cajuns?

EG: Well, the whites were the ones who got the machinery, yes,
and the Cajuns were the sharecroppers from Pointe Coupee Parish
where I come from. They were the sharecroppers there, the blacks
and the Cajuns were the farmers in that area. They farmed
someone else's land, but they were the ones.

MS: Did I glean correctly from a number of the works that what
was going on, one of the sources of the conflict seemed to be an
increasing intrusion, coupled with the tractors, of the Cajuns into
land that had been farmed previously by the Blacks?

EG: Well, they had lived there all their lives; they worked it. My
folks were at the same place for a hundred years. I knew someone
to whom I dedicated *A Gathering of Old Men;* he knew my grandparents' grandparents. They had worked this land over and over
and over for five generations that worked the land. Suddenly there's
another group coming in now, and because they were white they
had more advantages. They had the better land, land nearest the
river where my people had the land back near the swamps where
it was not as good.

Where you are if you have two people who are competing with
one other, you're going to have problems. I don't care who it is.
You know what's going on in the world today; it's nothing different.
It's the same old thing. Wherever you go, you want to go to
Europe, you want to go to the Mid East, anyplace you want to go,
you find the same problems today.

MS: I thought that was an interesting distinction, because the
conflict that was persisting in your work was the racial conflict—
particularly between blacks and Cajuns—between one group of
people who came from people who had been slaves and a group
of people who weren't necessarily slave owners. Right?

EG: Right.

MS: You make a distinction in the work between the Marshalls

who owned the plantation and the Cajuns, so the racial conflict is
not necessarily a vestige of a conflict between those who owned
slaves and those who were slaves, but in fact has been imbedded
in the community on racial lines.

EG: Of course.

MS: In your novels the major conflict is between the Blacks and
the Cajuns.

EG: That's what I just said, about the people who are competing
with people on the same level. You do not compete with the
Marshalls. The Marshalls own the land. The Marshalls own this
land, so they didn't come into the fields to work. They leased the
land to the two different groups and they race their tractors or their
wagons to the derrick to load that sugarcane and send it to the
mill and sometime when those tractors and those wagons were
coming together there were conflicts.

MS: As with Robert Carmier in *Catherine Carmier*?

EG: Yes, in *Catherine Carmier* as well as Silas' brother in *A
Gathering of Old Men*. He talks about the beating that his brother
takes, because his brother tries to race the machine—I was playing
the John Henry bit there—but when you're competing against
anybody there's going to be conflict. I don't care where you are.

MS: You had just mentioned something a little earlier in terms of
growing up in a community first of all in which conditions of life were
still very similar to what they had been back even in slavery times
and knowing people who knew people who had been slaves. Just
recently Ruth Laney completed a documentary film, to my knowledge the first documentary film about you and your work . . .

EG: Well, someone did a smaller short film about twenty years
ago, but it was not nearly what this one is.

MS: In this film by Ruth Laney called *Louisiana Stories*, you
talked about giving voice to this community and you tie it to land
in much the same way. I wonder if you'd be willing to read this first
section from *A Gathering of Old Men*?

EG: "You had to be there then to be able to don't see it and don't
hear it now. But I was here then, and I don't see it now, and that's
why I did it. I did it for them back there under them trees. I did it
'cause that tractor is getting closer and closer to that graveyard, and I
was scared if I didn't do it, one day that tractor was gon' come in

there and plow up them graves, getting rid of all proof that we
ever was. Like now they trying to get rid of all proof that black
people ever farmed this land with plows and mules—like if they
had nothing from the start but motor machines. Sure one day they
will get rid of the proof that we ever was, but they ain't gon' do it
while I'm still here. Mama and Papa worked too hard in these fields.
They Mama and they Papa worked too hard in these same fields.
They Mama and Papa people worked too hard, too hard to have
that tractor just come in that graveyard and destroy all proof that
we ever was. I'm the last one left. I had to see that the graves stayed
for a little while longer."

MS: I'd like to move on a little bit to another aspect of writing
about race, going back to your first novel, *Catherine Carmier*.

EG: Let me interject something right now. I don't write about
race. I never think of race when I'm writing. I just try to write a
good story—a novel or a short story—and because we live where
we live and in the time in which we live, race then must come into
it. We try to write about conflict, we try to write about love, we try
to write about things that have been written, since Greek tragedies, since Shakespeare. I don't think I've had any lynchings
compared to Faulkner or Erskine Caldwell or so many other Southern
writers or even Mark Twain. I haven't had any of these things. I
don't think they had in mind to write about race.

I don't know that Faulkner had to write about race or maybe he
had to write about something which was bothering him, but I
don't know that if you just said, "Bill, what are you writing about?"
that he would say, "I'm writing about this race thing here." In,
for example, *Intruder in the Dust,* he's writing about a certain time.
In *Huckleberry Finn,* I don't know that Twain said that, "Look,
I'm only going to write about race, I'm going to write about what
happened during the time this story took place." But we have to write
about some thing, and you have to fill those three hundred pages so
the things that we are aware about, the things that we are experi-
encing come into that book. But I don't know if you can write
seriously and not include the problem, but that is not the first thing
that comes into your mind.

MS: I understand the distinction you are making. In fact, that is
why I tried to start this off by first saying, let's talk about race in the

sense of talking about the African-American experience rather than as if writing about race could or in any way should be reduced to the conflict between black and white.

EG: I would hate to see or think that we would not bring back race into the work. I think a lot of people would like to not see it. I've had that both from white students as well as black students. I've had a letter from a teacher in Mississippi, she said that she can't teach *Miss Jane Pittman* because her white students don't want to read it and her black students don't want to read it. So she said, "What should I do?" I didn't answer the letter. She said, her white students don't want to read it because I make white people mean in *The Autobiography of Miss Jane Pittman* and the black students don't want to read it because I said "nigger" in it. People have always said that, but a lot of people have been mean in Mississippi, and in Louisiana as well. So you put that in there and they don't want to hear it anymore. They don't want to know about the history of the world. I don't say that we should live in the past, but I think that we should be aware of the past and that's all I've tried to do.

MS: Let's go to the first time that you wrote about the life and people and the community that you knew. Your first novel was *Catherine Carmier,* published I believe in 1964, a novel I strongly recommend, one which has not received as much notice as, for example, *Miss Jane,* but an extraordinary work. There the Cajuns are present. In fact, from the first page, but they're there in the background and in fact they never come really into the foreground in the entire novel. It is a novel that is focussed entirely on the black community. What motivated you to write that novel first? Why did you choose that story? And particularly since in telling the story ultimately of Catherine Carmier, you first start with Robert Carmier. Why then don't you tell us something about the conflicts from your own life which inform your writing?

EG: First I tried a book when I was about sixteen years old. I tried to write a novel; I sent this thing to New York and I was the only person who thought I suppose that it was a novel. They certainly didn't think it was a novel.

MS: This was the one where you typed it on both sides of the pages, cut as if it were a book?

EG: Yes, I didn't know a thing about it, so I got that regular sized

page and cut it in half and I tried to type with one finger all over
the place, and I typed on the other side of the page. I typed single
space and I sent that to New York so they sent it back. That was
about '49 or '50 then I was at Stanford in '58–'59 and some New
York editor or agent said that no one makes money—I was writing
short stories in that day—writing short stories, so I just stopped
writing short stories that day. I said I would go back to the novel
and I remembered the novel I had tried to write.

It was a simple love story between a fair-skinned girl and a dark-
skinned guy—he's Protestant; she's Catholic—and the conflict
they had. I went to school and I lived here fifteen and a half years
before going to California. I'd gone my last three years to a
Catholic School in New Roads, St. Augustine, and, of course we
had the mixture of creole, they're fair, and darker people, my
color, darker. There were those conflicts.

I knew a girl I could ride the school bus back from the school and
we could talk until she got within maybe a mile of her house and then
she even moved away from the seat where I was sitting. She would
not dare her parents seeing her sitting beside me talking to her. I think
when I was a little boy, there was a little girl who's maybe not that
fair, but I was much in love with her and her name was Catherine
and I tried to write a love story. The style of this story is based
around Turgenev's *Fathers and Sons*. Someone coming from the
North, coming back to the South, and meeting a beautiful lady,
coming back to the old place, to the old people and just as
Bazarov does, the doctoral student coming back home for a while
to be with his mother and father. Jackson comes back to be with his
Aunt Charlotte. Basically I based it around that structure of Turgenev's novel as I was at that point in my life still influenced by
his style.

MS: The nihilist shows up again in "The Sky is Gray"?

EG: Oh, yes. At that time I was reading not only *Fathers and
Sons;* I was also reading *Crime and Punishment.* I was very much
moved by these nihilists like Bazarov or even Steven Daedelus in
Portrait of the Artist. It was just about that time I was the age of
these people and then I thought this was "the thing" at that time.
You questioned everything: religion, government, parents, and
whatever, though I didn't go as far as Raskolnikov did. I talked

about that, but I didn't go quite that far. I had to pay my tuition. What he does is take a hatchet and go kill somebody so, I didn't want to go that far. That's why I chose this, because I wanted to write a love story that time and I was going back to the South after having been away for a while.

MS: Yet the thing that becomes so interesting to a reader—I'll do nothing more than give my own response—is realizing that the black/white conflict that I expected to find is totally in the distance. You don't ignore that it's there; as I said, on the first page those Cajuns are on the porch. It's always there and then they return at the end as the provocateurs to intensify the conflict within the black community. But the novel concentrates far more, as you say, on telling the love story of those people in that time. But there is the conflict along a spectrum of color.

EG: You know, Malcolm Cowley—he was one of the great critics—he knew all the great people. He knew the Hemingways, the Fitzgeralds, and the Faulkners—and it was he who revived Faulkner because Faulkner was like dead in '47 and it was Malcolm who wrote this introduction to *A Portable Faulkner*.

When Jackson first comes back to the South he shows his aunt how he is turning against his religious teachings. He has a gun in the suitcase and Malcolm Cowley, who read everything in literature, and translated all kind of things, he saw that Chekhov thing, and said, "You've got that gun, you better kill somebody."

MS: If you have a gun in the first act, you better use it by the third . . .

EG: I said, "There's nobody to kill." He says, "Why do you have the gun?" I said, "To let his aunt know he's a different person." He says, "No, no, if you're going to have a gun, you have to use the gun." So, I took the gun out, forget the gun. I put a deck of cards in there, because I know how strongly religious she was. I put the deck of cards so when she sees that she realizes that he'd become a great sinner. But I had the gun. So you're absolutely right when you say that you thought the conflict was going to be between black and white at that time, but it does not. The conflict is a love story between Jackson and Catherine and the conflict is between his aunt and himself as well as Jackson and Raoul for Catherine's love.

MS: There is something in your work that is too consistent to be accidental. It's rare in your work that violence occurs center stage. In *Catherine Carmier,* for example, Robert Carmier, who is a creole, light skinned black, who is a "passe-blanc," who has disdain for the darker blacks. Raoul ultimately intensifies that disdain on the part of that family. But Robert Carmier is a man caught in between, because he also ends up racing a Cajun to the derrick where they get into a verbal conflict. He stands up to the Cajun when the Cajun initiates a conflict and says, "I don't care what you do as long as you come at me from the front." And then Robert Carmier disappears.

EG: My great grandfather was a bit like that. He had a conflict like that.

MS: But you tend to imply in the novel that Robert Carmier is, in fact, killed.

EG: Yes.

MS: But you don't have the killing.

EG: No, no, you don't need it anymore. We've had enough of that. You can go back to Ellison and what has cast the shadow. You don't have to go to that extreme. You don't have to do that anymore. You can write well enough without that. Some English editor reviewed *Catherine Carmier* and said that you don't see these things, you don't *see* these people out there, but you *feel* it, you feel it all the time, you're aware of it. That's what they're trying to do: make you aware of the pain without having to shoot you or cut you or hit you.

When I wrote the massacre scene in the *The Autobiography of Miss Jane Pittman,* and I would read this chapter to students, especially to black students, they would say, "How can you read that and not get angry?" Because I want *you* to get angry. I want to do it so well that if you read it a hundred years from now you'd still get angry. For example, the scene is where these people are trying for their freedom from this plantation. They try to escape, they want to leave this plantation. They are caught in the swamps and they're massacred by patrols. They're in these bushes and what I wanted was the sound of the clubs hitting the bushes, the sound of clubs hitting skulls and busting skulls. I wanted the sun to come down. I wanted the sun to come down and its rays through to the earth to the dust that is being raised by this. I wanted to hear absolute silence except for this massacre. I wanted all the animals to leave, I wanted all the birds to leave. I just wanted that and I wanted to get that down so well that you never see any of this, but you *hear* it because you hear it through Miss Jane's ears, but she doesn't see it either. She's just hiding; she's covering this kid. But you hear it and that's what I try to do. You don't have to see it all the time to be aware of it.

That's what I try to do in everything else. In "The Sky is Gray," when they cannot go to a little restaurant to get something to eat or go to a fountain to get a drink of water. They can't go there and if you don't feel that kind of pain, then I don't know what else to do to make you feel pain, make you feel aware of it.

MS: I think that's where I found the greatest power in your work, because you're documenting the pervasiveness of the oppression. Not the cathartic moments, when the beating or lynching occurs, which would be a simpler way to go to evoke outrage. It's like when a tourist comes here in August. They come and it's a hot day, it's a typical New Orleans day. It's 100 degrees and 100% humidity—what I call the lick of the dying elephant, you know, kind of thick and ropey—and they say, "Gee, this is awful, this is hot." They don't get it. It's not that it's hot on that day. It's that for seven months it's like that. It's the pervasiveness of it.

The horror of the oppression, the insidiousness of the racism is not in the lynching, is not in the beating. It's in that pervasiveness and the way in which it's not only in the social code—because you write about social codes a lot—of not being able to go in the front door of stores, in restricted rooms, patterns of behavior, the deference that's required. You're a wonderful cultural anthropologist. You go through the novels and you describe the rituals of how a hat is supposed to be held. Not just held, but fumbled with as well: all of those signals of deference that are expected.

EG: Hold your hands between your knees as Mathu would do when he would go to the big house. He had his hat between his knees like this. He would never put his hat on his knees and cross his knees. That's why I don't cross my knees. He'd keep his hat in this hand. I know what you are saying.

MS: Even among characters, because in most of the works you introduce a figure who is in contrast to that pervasiveness.

EG: Absolutely.

MS: There's always a figure in every novel and manhood is frequently an issue.

EG: Yes, right, I get what has been perceived as the docile black, for example, in *Of Love and Dust* old Bishop, the old butler. In contrast with Marcus you know he's the one who is going to get everything and very quietly do whatever he has to do. Then you get Marcus, Marcus kicks doors down. Of course, you have it in *Miss Jane Pittman* as well, four men and Miss Jane Pittman. Sometimes I think that book is about men, not about Miss Jane. You have it in Ned, the teacher who is killed because he steps over the line. You have it in Joe Pittman who refuses to work as a farmer but he's going to be this cowboy whether it kills him or not. He steps over a line even with nature and nature says, "Okay, just because the others are doing that, don't come to me and expect me to be so kind all the time." When he goes after the horse eventually he is killed. Of course, you have it in Jimmy, the civil rights leader, and when they all told him to stop he said, "I cannot stop," and you also have it in Tee Bob as well. Tee Bob loves Mary Anne as her father and when he cannot have her he must kill himself.

MS: Take a character in your most recent novel, *A Lesson Before Dying*. You have the teacher, Mr. Wiggins, who is one of those figures who is challenging the prevailing mores but he's not doing it overtly. It's not those high level conflicts that you were just illustrating. When he goes to the big house—they summon him—he goes to the kitchen he's waiting with Inez the cook for two and a half hours and he submits to this.

EG: Well, he has to. If he doesn't, he has to go back down in the quarters and face those old ladies, those old black ladies. He'd rather stand there and wait for those whites keeping him waiting before he can go back there and tell them he failed.

MS: I was underestimating the consequences.

EG: Oh yes.

MS: That crosses racial lines too. Let me come to this then, in writing about such issues as the prevailing codes that define

behavior, the pervasiveness, I noted four different kinds of response
to that South fabric. The first is a kind of servility and deference.
One is endurance. Another is resistance, and finally you have
rebellion. I'm making those distinctions, because I think there are
characters throughout the novels that reflect these differences.

You have characters who, like some of the old men in *A Gathering
of Old Men,* ultimately rebel. That's what's so interesting about
that novel: you take them from a full spectrum of response. Men
who all their lives were utterly deferential and appeasing in their
relation to the white community.

Then you have other figures such as Jim Kelly in *Of Love and
Dust* who are enduring. They are not all that deferential and not that
servile and they are respected because they're not. But they don't
really challenge the codes. He has accepted the system. He's not
the figure—and you don't introduce him as the figure—who is going
to change it, but he endures. He's very wise, he's very clear, he's
a very compelling figure, because he has this enormous wisdom
about how you endure and survive in this world. Then you move
on to figures who intensify the level of response. There's a resistance. They're going along, but they're struggling with it more.

Sometimes it's not all even keel. I'm not suggesting that any one
of your characters is just a cardboard figure who only does one of
these things. They often run a wide range, but that ultimately brings
us to rebellion, though violence, as we said before, rarely occurs over
a conflict in the foreground in your novels and you've explained
why it is not necessary to do so. One thing that has always struck
me has been how throughout your work there has always been at
least a potential for rebellion. There are hints of it throughout.
Even in the early work, Copper, as we mentioned before in *Bloodline,* there you qualify because you make him slightly mad though
there's great insight to his madness. You make him an even more
complex figure because the figure of Copper or Christian in that
short story is born of a mixture of black and white. His father was
the master of the plantation and his mother was one of the
workers on the plantation. And he claims his patrimony; he lays
claim to the fact that he is sired of that family.

EG: Through his madness.

MS: Through his madness, but he also possessed the characteristics. He has the nobility, the natural nobility. *A Gathering of Old Men* has in it something I have never encountered anywhere else in literature, any literature. You have a rebellion by old men. You could look in literature throughout the world and find rebellion and revolt against authority reflected in all kinds of ways. In my more radical years when I made a study of such literature, I read very extensively in literatures of revolt and in American literature there are studies of it. Walter Rideout's *The Radical Novel in the United States,* for example, chronicles all such work. I don't know another work in which old men rebel and I found that extraordinarily significant. Could you talk a bit about why that occurred to you, about why that takes place?

EG: After I wrote *The Autobiography of Miss Jane Pittman,* I always had different people who asked me, "Why did you write about a woman?" Well, I said I was tired of my books being personal and I said and this one would be called *The Autobiography of Miss Jane Pittman* and after I did that I had to write about a woman. I guess the easiest way to explain why I wrote *A Gathering of Old Men,* is now I had to write a book about men because I had written about Miss Jane Pittman.

Everybody, no matter who he is, has regrets about failing. One day he failed, one day she failed. If he could only live a life for that moment where he failed again, it's something to make him live at that moment. That moment when he took an insult and dropped his eyes, lowered his eyes, or that moment when he saw someone hurt that he was too cowardly to help. Or that moment when he had a few dollars more and someone was hungry. If I could just make up for that. If I could make up for that. We all feel that way. Everybody in here feels that way. There's a moment in this past life that he'd like to do over again and make this a little better.

Talking with Mr. Zeno, to whom I dedicated *A Gathering of Old Men,* standing there talking to him, listening to him talk about the different people and what had gone on and what had happened to different people and talking about the strength in people and how strong they were, how manly they were, because they had to lift so much cane or they could chop trees down or split logs longer than anyone else. But whenever I'd see him talking that way, I could watch his eyes and know something else that was not there. He would talk about the strength of these men, but something was missing and that was that thing that really makes man. That is: being able to do that thing that you said you cannot do.

Most of these men, and so had he—but he less than others—had taken all the insults that a black could have taken from the turn of the century until he died. He was born before the twentieth century. He died in '82 I think it was, and he was in his 90's at that time. I used to talk to him and there were other old men who would gather on the porch sometimes and I'd just talk to them all. I had pictures of them. Ruth has some of them all in the film *Louisiana Stories*. I was just talking to these old men and they were all talking about how brave someone else was. They were all talking about how brave their grandfathers were. That was a man then, that was a man then, he had done things. But I doubt that their grandfathers had done anymore than they had done, but they always talked about other men. I thought how could I, how could I make, get something that would bring these men together who really want to do something who wanted their one day in the sun, just one day because *A Gathering of Old Men* takes place in only one day. From noon to about 6:00 - 7:00 - 8:00 o'clock at night, how do you do that? You see, you have to get something that has hurt them all. Hurt them all, not that Fix has hurt them all, but because of the conditions they had been hurt by whites. They had come there to help fight Fix and Mapes explains to them that Fix did not do this. It's something else that did this to you. But they say "Fix isn't the guy, but Fix represents that thing that did this to us."

MS: It's the difference between the external oppression and what's been internalized?

EG: It is, yes, it is. This is what I was aiming at, just to get something that could bring them all together. So I focus on *one* guy, Fix. Let them think this it's all Fix and then they'll have reason to stand up. If you had given them something so broad, they'll say, "Well, no, that didn't happen, that happened because of man, mankind. Mankind is always cruel to mankind. That's what caused it." So they had to focus on a single thing.

MS: You also gave each of them a story to tell as they come forward, they testify.

EG: That's right, because they've all been hurt sometime in their lives, all of them. I think there are fifteen or eighteen of them. I never count these characters. I know other people count them and tell me how many I had, but I never count these things.

MS: It's a very curious kind of testimony. There's a dead body behind them in the field. It becomes a kind of trial about the event. But rather than talking about Beau, the victim—he's just kind of lying there off to the side—and normally in a trial we expect the testimony the evidence to bear on the circumstances about the shooting. As you said before, that's Mapes' orientation; he's there in the present moment, wanting simply to determine who did this, but the real trial is not about this at all.

EG: It's just to bring them there. The thing is what has happened in the past, the thing is what has happened to each of them individually. It's not really about Beau. He is just the thing that brings them there, brings them to Mathu's house. That's all.

MS: He becomes the occasion for the larger testimony.

EG: True, true, yes.

MS: Let me ask you to take us in one final direction. As I looked over the body of your work—and I didn't meet Ernie until about ten years ago when he published *A Gathering of Old Men*—you seem to be growing increasingly angry. You're not an angry man, you're not a Raskolnikov, you don't pick up the ax, but in the literature *Miss Jane* is an angrier work than *Catherine Carmier*. *A Gathering of Old Men* is more overt, you have a rebellion in your work in a way it hasn't been there previously. But I noticed that in *A Lesson Before Dying,* written ten years after *A Gathering of Old Men,* you seemed to have gone back to a quieter stance. You've gone back to focus on questions of individual dignity, both Wiggin's and Jefferson's. Mr. Wiggins and Jefferson are coming to terms with themselves and who they were going to be and how they were going to define themselves in this oppressive society. Did you move—I don't want to necessarily say backwards or forward—I don't mean to imply it's a regression of your part, what I'm really wondering is: is your novel in response to what you've seen as changes, deep seated changes in our cultural fabric in the last ten years?

Miss Jane was written during a period that was much more angry: in America in the seventies. *A Gathering of Old Men,* written in the early eighties, was still close, things were more intense. In the ten years since, until very recently, because of the incidents like the Rodney King incident, the tensions have heightened again. But was it anything in America that changed in the ten years?

EG: I don't know that this book has changed that much. Because what has happened in the book is that a man could possibly be innocent, could possibly be innocent and sentenced to death. I don't know if you could get more cruel than that. If you follow Grant Wiggins until the very end, he says, "I cannot believe, I will not believe. I will neither believe in your government neither will I believe in your religion. I don't believe in anything." You can't get more angry than that. But he says, too, in the next line that "I want them to believe. I want them to believe because only if you believe can you be free. Only if you believe in something can you be free." And he says, "That's why I'm still a slave. That's why I want to do all the little things they want me to do. I'll do the reading, writing, and arithmetic and I don't want you to have to do that." That's why he goes to Jefferson and says, "Listen, you can save me. I can't, I can't, you can do much more for me than I can could ever, ever do for you. You can make me aware of, you can show me the direction in which to go." So, Grant's a pretty angry person. All Grant wants to do is leave. We're talking about the forties, too, remember, this story takes place in the forties.

MS: During which time options were very much circumscribed?

EG: Yes, right. All he could do as an educated black man was to teach and although we produced many great teachers, we produced many great teachers, but I've known people who were pushed into teaching who did not want to teach and they were not great teachers. They were not good teachers. They were not even mediocre teachers. They were very poor teachers, because they wanted to do other things and they could not do other things. And Grant wants to leave, just wants to get away from it all and yet when he does, he has to come back again. There's that thing that keeps pulling him back. There's that thing that keeps Catherine Carmier from going. There's that thing that keeps Miss Jane from being able to reach Ohio. There's something else that keeps bringing them back and I can't even identify it myself.

MS: I was just going to say, this from a man who still lives away from here half the year.

EG: But I come back though. I go to San Francisco, but I cannot stay away from here.

Bard from the Bayou

Ruth Laney / 1993

From *The World and I* 8.10 (1993): 304–09. Copyright © 1993 Ruth Laney.

Mention Ernest J. Gaines, and most people frown as though trying to place the name. Add the qualifier "the man who wrote *The Autobiography of Miss Jane Pittman*," and a smile of recognition breaks through.

That book and its title character—later made world famous through a television movie—are household words. So much so that Gaines has instructed his family *not* to mention Miss Jane on his tombstone. "I don't want to be remembered *only* as her creator," he says.

Indeed, he is much more. In six novels and a book of short stories, Gaines has created a complex world of human relationships— black, white, and Creole—set in the plantation country of southern Louisiana. He began publishing his work in the 1960s, when many black writers used their books as soapboxes.

But Gaines was made of sterner stuff, and he had the soul of an artist. "If I can't move you with the story I tell, I don't want to do it through rhetoric," he once said. While the battle for civil rights raged, he closeted himself in a tiny rented room and wrote about Miss Jane, whose life spans 110 years from slavery to the movement. He was intensely aware of the war going on but chose to fight it his own way. "When Bull Conner turned the hoses on the marchers, I just said to myself, 'Write a better paragraph,' " he says.

Most of his work is set in the past—the 1940s through '70s. He treats all his characters—even the most loathsome redneck—with compassion, and he writes and rewrites to give his prose the clean beauty of the classics. "I want to create something I can be proud of years later," he has said.

During his thirty-year career, Gaines gave up all semblance of what most people call normal life, choosing not to marry and have a family so that he could devote himself to his work. Often living hand to mouth, he wrote for up to twelve hours a day. But he never became a household word, even when *Miss Jane* and *A Gathering of Old Men* were seen by millions on television. Nominated for the Pulitzer Prize and the National Book Award, *Miss Jane* won neither.

Gaines won his share of awards and plaudits, but other black writers such as Toni Morrison and his friend Alice Walker excited far more attention. His was a quieter kind of fame, largely centered around *Miss Jane,* which has been translated into a dozen languages and is taught on numerous college campuses. But peak success eluded him until this year.

Gaines turned sixty on January 15, and then he embarked on an exhilarating roller coaster of events:

• In February, the documentary *Ernest J. Gaines: Louisiana Stories* premiered on Louisiana Public Broadcasting; it went on to air on PBS stations around the country. The one-hour program explores the plantation culture in which Gaines grew up and details his years of struggle as a writer.

• In April, Knopf released *A Lesson before Dying,* the story of a black man condemned to the electric chair for a murder he didn't commit. Many critics have pronounced it Gaines' best novel. The book is in its third printing, and a sale to television is in the works.

• In May, Gaines, a lifelong bachelor, married Dianne Saulney, a Louisiana native who is an assistant district attorney in Miami.

• In June, he was relaxing at the condominium he shares with his wife in Miami when the MacArthur Foundation called to say he had won an award popularly known as a "genius grant." Nobody applies for the grants; the foundation finds recipients and gives them up to $375,000, depending on age. Gaines was awarded $355,000.

All this, and the year was only half over!

With so much good news crammed into a few months, Gaines says his luck frightens him a bit. "Whenever too much good happens, I'm afraid," he says. "I hate to be pessimistic, but I think that life is balance. A lot of people are saying, 'You deserve this; you've never received this kind of recognition before.' But I'm getting so much now. And some kind of way, the Old Man balances."

He admits that his recent good fortune may be "the Old Man's" way of making up for years of hardship. Born in 1933 to a family of sharecroppers in Pointe Coupee Parish, Louisiana, Gaines spent the first fifteen years of his life in a two-room cabin with no running water or inside toilet. He and his family lived at River Lake Plantation in workers' quarters, a dirt road lined on either side with cabins built by slaves. Five months out of the year, when they could be spared from fieldwork, the children of Cherie Quarters went to school in the little white church at the head of the lane. At the other end of the lane was the graveyard, where five generations of Gaines' family are buried. It is here that he hopes to be laid to rest someday.

Gaines' mother was only sixteen when he was born, and she returned to the fields within a week. The oldest of twelve children, Ernest James Gaines—known as E.J.—was raised by his great-aunt, Augusteen Jefferson, the person who inspired Miss Jane. Although crippled from birth, "Aunt Teen" cooked for E.J. and his brothers and sister, sewed their clothes on a treadle machine, grew vegetables in a small garden, and even disciplined the children, making them cut switches and bring them to her.

As the oldest child, E.J. was expected to set an example for the younger children. From the time he was eight years old, he was working—pulling corn, digging potatoes, chopping or hauling sugarcane, cutting trees for firewood. But he also liked school and quickly mastered reading and writing. While still a child, he outdistanced most of his elders and often wrote letters for them or read to them. His creativity showed itself early, in the little plays he wrote and staged in the church to entertain the people of the quarter.

Life in Pointe Coupee Parish centered around False River, an oxbow formed when part of the Mississippi was cut off by a change in the river's direction. The people of Cherie Quarters fished and bathed in the river, and E.J. was baptized there at the age of twelve. Although he was raised Baptist, he was sent to St. Augustine Catholic School in the nearby town of New Roads from age thirteen to fifteen. When he graduated from the eighth grade, his education was finished as far as the parish (county) was concerned. There was no other school for black youths.

By then, his mother and stepfather had moved to Vallejo, California. One by one, they sent for the children, starting with E.J. At fifteen, he bade a painful good-bye to his beloved Aunt Teen and set off for California by bus and train.

With him he took enough memories to last a lifetime—and to endlessly supply him with subject matter. "It's not hard for me to re-create that life [in fiction]," he says. "I can sit at my desk in San Francisco or Miami and see it clearly. I lived there for fifteen and a half years. Had I left five years earlier, I would not have had enough experiences. Had I stayed five years longer, I would have been broken—in prison, dead, insane. So many of my friends died in their twenties and thirties. I left at the very best time to leave. I knew the quarter and the plantation and the small town. I knew the Catholics, the Baptists, the Creoles, the mulattoes, the problems between black and white."

At Vallejo High School, Gaines went to class with non-blacks for the first time, not only whites but Japanese, Chinese, Filipinos, Mexicans, and Native Americans. For a while he just soaked all of it up, hanging out with his newfound friends. But his stepfather, a member of the merchant marine, suggested that E.J. could find better things to do than hang out on street corners and steered him to the public library.

It was the first time he had ever stepped inside a library—in Louisiana, they were for whites only. Dazzled by the rows and rows of books, E.J. picked up one, read a few lines, and grabbed another, drunk with the new sensation. Soon he settled down and began reading books about the South, trying to quell his homesick-ness. He plowed through Willa Cather, John Steinbeck, Tolstoy, Turgenev—"anything with a dirt road, trees, and water," he says.

"But I could not find the people I was looking for," he says. "The black people in these books were not like my aunt, my brothers, my sister. I decided to write my own book."

At sixteen, while tending his baby brother, E.J. lay on the floor of his family's apartment and wrote a novel about Louisiana. He persuaded his mother to rent a typewriter, cut typing paper in half to make it book size, and typed his story on both sides of the paper—like a book. He wrapped the novel in brown paper and mailed it to a New York publishing house, dreaming of riches and glory. "I'm sure they thought it was a bomb," says Gaines with a chuckle. "They sent it back to me, and I threw it in the incinerator."

Gaines attended junior college, then spent two years in the Army. With money from the G.I. Bill, he enrolled at San Francisco State College and did graduate work at Stanford University.

In the late 1950s and early '60s, San Francisco was home to the Beats, who haunted coffeehouses and jazz clubs. "You couldn't throw a rock out of a window without hitting a writer," says Gaines, who was nonetheless determined to be a writer.

His chosen subject was the place and people he had left behind. Casting about for ideas, he remembered the book he had written at sixteen, about a black man, a Creole woman, and the strict barriers between their two cultures.

While he struggled to write *Catherine Carmier,* his first novel, Gaines took a series of jobs to pay the rent—washing dishes, working in a post office. He stayed in a one-room apartment with a Murphy bed that folded into the wall, subsisting on hot dogs and pork and beans. "Here I was, the first male in my family to go to college, and I was living like a bum," he says.

With *The Autobiography of Miss Jane Pittman* in 1971, Gaines began to have some success. To write the book, he returned to Louisiana several times, combing libraries for information about slavery, the Civil War, Reconstruction, the reign of Huey Long. Originally planning to tell the story from multiple points of view, he changed his mind, he says, when "I fell in love with my little character." Instead he told the story in the voice of Jane Pittman, who is 10 years old when freedom comes to her Louisiana plantation and lives to be 110 and a civil rights demonstrator.

Gaines struggled for seven years to write his next book, *In My Father's House,* about the gulf between black fathers and sons. It was published in 1978 to mixed reviews. His finances were strained when he injured his knee in a fall and needed surgery.

That's when the University of Southwestern Louisiana threw him a lifeline. Located in Lafayette in the heart of Cajun country, USL offered him a professorship of creative writing and the lifetime use of a three-bedroom house near the campus. Gaines has taught at the school since 1983 and says his newfound riches from the MacArthur won't change the arrangement. "But writing is not the

most important thing to me anymore. My life with Dianne is much
more important now than anything else."

Gaines met his wife in 1988 when he appeared on a panel at the
Miami International Book Fair. Dianne was in the audience and later
bought one of Gaines' books and had him autograph it. They
corresponded but did not see each other again for eighteen
months. Their first "date" was spent at her sister's house in New
Orleans, watching videotapes of a family wedding. "Everybody
liked him," recalls Dianne. "Later we went out for coffee and
beignets and walked around the French Quarter. It was just so
comfortable."

Gaines glows when he speaks of his wife. "We have a very close
relationship," he says. "I keep telling Dianne we've been married for
thirty-three years, because this relationship is the one I dreamed of
when I was writing *Catherine Carmier*."

For many years, Gaines devoted himself single-mindedly to writing. "Many of the kids I went to school with at State, or at
Stanford, couldn't take it," he says of his years of struggle. "They
got married, had families, started teaching, started businesses. But
maybe, at the same time, they didn't have a damned thing to write
about in the first place. Because I think if you have something to
write about and really want to do it, you'll give up everything. If
you want to be a writer, you don't love anybody else but your
writing. You're married to it. You have to have that kind of ego, to
believe that you have something to say that no one else can say. You
will not let anything in the world get in the way of it.

"I had lots of regrets when I went to spend Christmas with my
brothers and sisters and their children—regrets that I didn't have
a little child there of my own. But I knew darned well I had to be a
writer. I could not afford to have a child around, because I would
not have been able to support that child. I had to write."

The Haunting Voice
of Ernest Gaines

Jason Berry / 1993

From the *Atlanta Journal Constitution* 23 March 1993: M1, M4–5. Used by permission.

"Some were dead, but the ones living could talk about them and did talk about them as though they had simply walked into another room only a few minutes before."

Ernest Gaines, 1978, "Miss Jane and I"

POINTE COUPEE PARISH, LA.—The cemetery lies a few miles behind Riverlake plantation house, a raised 1780s manor on False River in Cajun country. The graves occupy a narrow grove nestled in wintry, listless fields of sugar cane.

Shadowed by pecan trees, surrounded by vine-enmeshed bamboo stalks, some two dozen of the souls buried here are memorialized with headstones. Many more of their kith and kin, who worked as field hands or servants in the big house, have no grave markers. Profusions of yellow wildflowers sprout from these sunken spots where the nameless dead, thanks to Ernest J. Gaines, still have voices to be heard.

In a literary career spanning three decades, Mr. Gaines, 60, has published seven novels and a collection of short stories, all set in Bayonne, the fictional name he chose for Pointe Coupee, the South Louisiana community where he was born and raised.

His latest novel, *A Lesson Before Dying*, to be released by Knopf next month in a 35,000 first printing, is sure to strengthen his stature. It is the haunting story of a man facing execution for a crime he may not have committed and the impact of his final days on the people of Bayonne.

The hold of this terrain on Ernest Gaines's imagination sets him apart from authors such as Toni Morrison, Alice Walker and Charles Johnson, whose novels radiate a more eclectic, often spiritualist sense of African-American cultural memory.

Mr. Gaines's most famous work, *The Autobiography of Miss Jane Pittman* was published in 1971, widely translated and later made into a TV movie starring Cicely Tyson. The novel spans 110 years between the Civil War and civil rights movement as recounted by an indomitable woman who endured it all, right in Bayonne.

That book, his fourth, put Mr. Gaines in the front rank of Southern (and African-American) writers.

In 1983 the University of Southwestern Louisiana in Lafayette, the hub city of Cajun country, hired Mr. Gaines to teach as writer-in-residence, with a handsome house in a manicured neighborhood just off campus. His presence revitalized USL's annual Deep South Writers' Conference, and his courses became a magnet for would-be writers in the region.

San Francisco has been his adopted home since the 1950s. There, amidst baying ship horns, chilly fog and a rainbow of cultures, he disregarded advice of friends who thought his fiction should focus on something other than the deprived life of rural blacks down home.

But Ernie Gaines was fixed on that past. He still spends each summer in a large San Francisco apartment, filled with books, writing by hand, excavating memories of Louisiana.

Mr. Gaines grew up in a world that most black Americans would like to forget—"the quarters" behind Riverlake plantation's big house near the town of New Roads. The estate was owned by the Major family during his formative years. The rows of cabins where field workers lived had no electricity or running water until after World War II.

The eldest of six children, Ernest J. Gaines was born when his mother, Adrienne, was 16. Less than a week later she went back to work in the fields. His maternal aunt, Augusteen Jefferson, was primary caretaker to Mr. Gaines and his younger siblings.

Augusteen Jefferson would serve as the principal role model for Miss Jane Pittman and would share in dedication of the book.

Miss Jefferson was crippled. "She crawled over the floor like a child because that was the only way she could move," Mr. Gaines explains. "She pushed herself over the ground to pick pecans. She washed our clothes and cooked our food."

"Never once," he continues, "did I hear her complain about her condition. I don't know why she was crippled, whether she was born that way or possibly dropped as an infant. That was not spoken about."

Aunt Augusteen could "give orders like an army sergeant," Lois Young, the author's sister, explains in "Ernest J. Gaines: Louisiana Stories," a new documentary produced by Ruth Laney and Rick Smith for Louisiana Public Broadcasting.

Miss Jefferson's tiny house became a magnet for elders who sat on "the garry," as they called the gallery, or porch.

At those gatherings the boy, called EJ, helped his aunt by serving coffee. And he listened, absorbing poetic rhythms of black speech, mentally recording the lore of a people who forged cultural passageways out of hardship and struggle.

Reflecting on oral tradition, Alice Walker, author of *The Color Purple*, explains in the LPB documentary: "If we don't get a really good sense of the past, we lose the only stabilizing force that we have, the very thing that links us to the people who came before us, and how they dealt and coped."

EJ attended classes five months a year in a small church that doubled as schoolhouse. Unlike white children who had nine-month academic years, matriculation for black children stopped for seasonal planting and harvests.

"Many of the men who would be my age met violent deaths," he says. "It's gotten more violent with crack and all the guns, but gangs aren't all that new."

The plantation quarters dispersed in the 1960s, when the Major family sold Riverlake. By then, mechanized farming had eliminated sharecroppers. People scattered to New Roads or points afar such as Houston, Baton Rouge and New Orleans.

Today, the owners of the Baton Rouge plantation Magnolia Mound are dismantling and reassembling three cabins from Riverlake for a permanent historical exhibit. Other cabins have been razed.

Standing in the "old place," as he calls the cemetery, warm in the milky sunlight of a February afternoon, a tall, hefty man in whom amiability and reticence are evenly matched, Mr. Gaines points toward the road leading to False River.

"The privies [outhouses] were all in a row behind those trees. Every house had one on the ditch. My grandmother's house had a faucet on the road, and we'd go draw the water and bring it to the house. Those [faucets] weren't put down till the '40s. Before that it was wells; we'd draw the water in buckets."

He speaks in a soft, rolling cadence, with no trace of rancor. "The old people would wash from False River. That river was both a spiritual as well as physical part of us. We ate from the river—catching fish—and we washed our clothes there, and we washed our souls there, through baptism."

EJ was baptized at age 12. Religious intolerance is a theme in his books; he has not been a churchgoer for many years. "I believe in God, but Christianity, the church—well, we have an understanding." Part of that understanding was his decision not to marry. "I knew it would take years to establish myself, and I could not support a family and pursue my work. I did not want to take on those obligations unless I was financially able."

His significant other is Dianne Saulney, an assistant county attorney, in Dade County, Fla., who has grown children from a previous marriage. They met five years ago when he spoke at the Miami International Book Fair, and today they juggle careers and schedules, spending time together in Florida, Louisiana and San Francisco. In February they visited Martinique, where he lectured at the University of Antillies, Guyana.

It is not surprising that his work has such broad popularity among descendants of Africans. Threats or acts of violence from planters, sheriffs and Cajun yeomen charge Mr. Gaines's stories with tension. Subdominant themes of interracial passion and a search for common values permeate his work with rumblings of the heart.

Arching over these concerns is a more universal theme: what it means to be human, how people claim themselves. His characters' quests for freedom unfold with the knowledge that injustices often go unpunished. Mr. Gaines gives these conflicts nuances and subtlety that avoid cardboard stereotypes of white characters.

In *The Autobiography of Miss Jane Pittman*, this reality is driven home when a charismatic young schoolteacher named Ned, whom Miss Jane raised, is killed by an old Cajun, Cluveau.

Before white planters tell him to eliminate Ned for teaching youngsters too much, Cluveau sits with Miss Jane, fishing and talking, eating on her porch in an ironic friendship, tangled in Old South paternalism. After the killing, Cluveau avoids Miss Jane, who finds him and warns that he will suffer until he hears "the chariots of hell." His last 10 years are a psychic hell.

Following publication of *Miss Jane*, Mr. Gaines met a dowager whose family owned another Pointe Coupee plantation. "I know him of whom you speak," she said, referring to a deceased Cajun who had killed blacks—the model for Cluveau. On the highway that straddles False River lies a marker, next to a black church, commemorating a schoolteacher killed in 1902.

"I was never threatened," Mr. Gaines says. "Didn't know anyone who was lynched. But there was subtle racism every day of your life. One could not come up and speak to you [a white man] unless you spoke to me first. The sidewalk—that old story—I'd have to move so you could walk by. Anything could be said to one's mother or sister by whites. You got that all the time."

And yet, an unmistakable benevolence marks his reminiscences of land and people here. Do good memories outweigh the bad?

"Yeah, right," he nods. "I would agree there. But it was hard and tough being the oldest child. I had to go into the swamps to cut wood for the stove as well as fireplace. When you're a 12-year-old kid trying to pull a saw for half a day, it's about the most cruel thing you can do to somebody."

In spite of the meager schooling and virtual absence of books, young EJ read so well that his mother, who remarried after a divorce, allowed him to attend a Roman Catholic grade school in the nearby town of New Roads. He also had the rare luxury for a black boy during the Depression to ride in a car with another aunt, who sold cosmetics, and see some of the outside world.

In 1948, at age 15, he left the plantation to join his mother and stepfather, who had moved to California following the westward migration for better living conditions. "Had I stayed another five years, I would have been broken, bitter," he later said.

The day he left, old and young people sat on Aunt Augusteen's porch, wishing him well. His aunt, whose majestic stoicism had taught him volumes about life, had tears in her eyes. Two years later she would die, never seeing him again.

A New Star in the Canon

Scott Jaschik / 1994

From the *Chronicle of Higher Education* 11 May 1994: A23–24.
Used by permission.

Ernest J. Gaines grins when he's told that more and more professors
are now analyzing his novels in their classrooms. "They think
they know more about me than I do myself," he says.

His amusement is easy to understand. He knows he is hard
to categorize.

Mr. Gaines has joined the canon of African-American literature,
yet he credits 19th-century Russian writers with inspiring his
work. He is a male writer at a time when the stars of black literature
are women. His fans applaud his empathetic portrayals of black
men, yet Mr. Gaines's best-known creation is a woman, the title
character of *The Autobiography of Miss Jane Pittman*. His novels
unflinchingly portray the viciousness of white racism, yet faculty
members say one reason they teach his works is that white students
identify with the black characters.

Even classifying Mr. Gaines geographically is more difficult than
it should be—considering that all of his fiction takes place in a
county modeled on his birthplace of Pointe Coupee Parish in Louisiana. For although he spends each fall teaching at the nearby
University of Southwestern Louisiana, he has written nearly every
word of his eight books in San Francisco.

"I've been called a Southern writer who happened to live in the
West, a California writer who writes about the South, a black
writer, a Louisiana writer," Mr. Gaines says. "I don't know where
I fit in and I don't give a damn."

Where Mr. Gaines fits in, increasingly, is in the nation's classrooms. Since its publication in 1971, *Miss Jane Pittman* has been
widely taught in history and literature classes alike. Other Gaines
works have also claimed students' and teachers' imaginations, especially *A Gathering of Old Men* and the short stories in *Bloodline*.

Now, however, teaching Gaines may take off.

In the last year, his stock in academe shot up when he won one of the so-called genius awards given by the John D. and Catherine T. MacArthur Foundation. He also won the National Book Critics Circle Award for his latest novel, *A Lesson Before Dying*. When Vintage brings out that book in paperback next month, it is expected to start showing up on course reading lists as well. Selections from Mr. Gaines's work will be included in forthcoming anthologies of African-American literature from both McGraw-Hill and Norton, and he is already included in *The Heath Anthology of American Literature*.

Mr. Gaines's work is taught most often in literature classes, sometimes in survey courses and other times in specialized seminars on black or Southern writing. But other disciplines are also using his novels. John M. Grady, for example, teaches *A Gathering of Old Men* in a sociology class at Wheaton College (Mass.) to examine black-white relations.

Why has interest in teaching Mr. Gaines's work grown so rapidly?

"He is an extraordinary writer, and his compassion for both the victims and the victimizers in his books is outstanding," says Bernard W. Bell, a professor of English at Pennsylvania State University and author of the introduction to Mr. Gaines's writings in the McGraw-Hill anthology.

Mr. Bell says that Mr. Gaines's work is as important as his better-known contemporaries, such as Toni Morrison and Alice Walker. It could rise in public consciousness if more people—and professors—were willing to explore more than just a few black authors, he says.

At a time when racial tensions are simmering on many campuses, professors also say that his novels seem to inspire frank discussion among black and white students.

"My students are overwhelmingly middle-class whites, and sometimes I find that there are cultural reasons that prevent them from assimilating some work," says Cedric Gael Bryant, associate professor of English at Colby College. "But with Gaines there is an immediate identification, because he deals with timeless themes: love and hate and courage."

Lawrence Rodgers, a professor of English at Kansas State University, says the students in his African-American literature

class—about half of whom are black and half are white—always
respond well to *A Gathering of Old Men*. "I almost always teach
that book last, but students who by that time in the semester are
fairly grumpy about everything find that they just can't put
it down."

He says the book affirms "the non-hierarchical traditions" in
which black citizens worked together to help each other. The story
tells how a group of old black men all claim responsibility for the
killing of a cruel white man as a means of protecting the person who
actually did it.

In the style of Faulkner, the story is told through the voices of
those men and others—black and white, heroes and villains—who
view the scene. "Gaines's ability to get inside white Southerners'
heads is nothing short of phenomenal," Mr. Rodgers adds.

In largely black courses, too, faculty members report strong
connections between their students and Mr. Gaines's characters.
Willa G. Lowe is a professor of English at historically black Stillman
College. She says her students focus on "the strong bonds among
families, which are a great part of the African-American tradition."

Mr. Gaines's characters also inspire her students by the way they
handle challenges, she says. "He writes about people who have
been held back for so long, but have to make a positive statement
about themselves before they leave this world."

Mr. Gaines's latest work, *A Lesson Before Dying*, deals with that
issue explicitly. It is the story of Jefferson, a black man in late-
1940's Louisiana who is about to be executed for a crime he didn't
commit. Jefferson's lawyer—pleading unsuccessfully for his cli-
ent's life before an all-white jury—argues that Jefferson is less than
human. "I would just as soon put a hog in the electric chair as this,"
the lawyer says. That comment prompts Jefferson's godmother to
recruit a young, cynical teacher, fresh out of a black college, to
visit Jefferson in jail and teach him enough so that he can face death
as a man.

What it means to be a man is at the heart of much of Mr. Gaines's
work. In the short story "The Sky is Gray," a young boy
describes the day his mother saves up enough money to take him to
town to see a dentist for his toothache. Through the boy's eyes,

the reader sees the mother imparting her values of responsibility and dignity.

The Autobiography of Miss Jane Pittman deals with similar themes as it tracks the treatment of blacks from the end of slavery to the start of the civil-rights movement.

Mr. Gaines says these themes come out of his earliest memories of growing up in Louisiana. Born in 1933, he was raised on a plantation with 11 younger siblings. "We didn't have running water, and my responsibility from the time I was 8 years old was to get the water. By the time I was 11 or 12 I was going out with my father to saw wood."

An aunt, Augusteen Jefferson, helped raise the large family, even though, for reasons nobody knew, she was unable to walk. "What I learned from her was a tremendous amount of discipline. She cooked for us and cleaned for us, even though she couldn't walk," he says. "We would bring her things and she would work at a little table and crawl around."

Mr. Gaines dedicated *The Autobiography of Miss Jane Pittman* to that aunt, who, he wrote, "did not walk a day in her life, but who taught me the importance of standing."

His aunt's disability also helped spur Mr. Gaines's writing. Since she couldn't move, friends would come to their small house and sit on the porch to talk. Hearing those stories, Mr. Gaines says, he picked up on the black oral tradition, which he mines for his novels.

Mr. Gaines picked up still more stories as a youth because he was known for being smart, and illiterate older people had him read and write letters for them.

At 15, he moved with his family to California, where he eventually enrolled at San Francisco State University and decided to become a writer. As he read American literature there in the mid-1950's, he found little that spoke to his experience. "I didn't read a single black author there. The only black character I knew was Othello, and he had been written by a white guy 300 years earlier."

Eventually, he was drawn to the 19th-century Russian writers, especially Dostoyevsky, Tolstoy, and Turgenev. The Russians attracted him because their portrayals of serfs were more realistic than anything he read by American writers about poor or black people.

Hemingway also made a lasting impact. Says Mr. Gaines: "I keep telling black students when I visit schools to read Hemingway to see how he writes about grace under pressure. No one has been under more pressure than blacks and not too many groups have come through as gracefully as we have."

Mr. Gaines says he realizes his views may not be popular with those who criticize the teaching of works by "dead white men." But he says that the push to add non-white writers to the curriculum, which he applauds, becomes foolish when it becomes a battle against everyone who was in the traditional canon.

"I think those dead white men should be read, but live black men and women should be read, too," he says. "I would tell any student to read Tolstoy, to read Twain, to read Hemingway, Shakespeare. I say, 'Read it. It can't hurt you.' "

All of his reading, combined with a writing fellowship in 1958 at Stanford University, started Mr. Gaines on his own career. His first novel, *Catherine Carmier,* was published in 1964 and he has steadily followed that with more work.

While Mr. Gaines always returned to Louisiana for visits, he made it his home base again in 1984, when he became a professor of English at the University of Southwestern Louisiana. The university approached him, he says, with the best deal possible: He teaches writing every fall and has the rest of the year for his novels. His students praise his patience. Some take his seminar many times.

Mr. Gaines says that teaching may slow down his writing, but he thinks that is a plus. He took seven years to write *A Lesson Before Dying.* "I probably would have written it much faster if I hadn't been teaching, but it probably wouldn't have had things that it has now."

Saying that he is "never in a hurry," Mr. Gaines writes his books out longhand and does extensive interviews to supplement his own experiences. For *A Lesson Before Dying,* he interviewed small-town sheriffs about their work and talked to death-row lawyers to learn about the impact of working with someone facing execution.

With the success of that book and his recent MacArthur grant, other universities have come courting, but Mr. Gaines says he is committed to Southwestern Louisiana and hopes to teach there for another 10 years before retiring. For now, he is battling carpal-tunnel syndrome through physical therapy so he can get to work on his next project: three novellas.

Two of the novellas will deal with an issue Mr. Gaines has touched on in previous work, the relationships between lighter- and darker-skinned black people. The third, tentatively titled *The Man Who Whipped Children,* will be about a black man on a plantation to whom parents went for help in disciplining their children.

The key to his success as a writer, he says, and what he hopes college students get from his work, is an appreciation of humanity. "I try to use characters whom people can identify with, and then put those characters in situations where people can think they might act the same way," he says.

"Of course the experience of my characters has been as a result of the color of their skin, but there is something deeper than that inside of us. They are black characters, but I aim at a humanity that makes them much more than the color of their skin."

Southern Sage Savors His Rise to Success

Ruth Laney / 1994

From *Emerge* May 1994: 66–67. Used by permission. Copyright © 1994 Ruth Laney.

About 36 years ago, when Ernest J. Gaines was a struggling writer, he took a part-time job in an insurance office. "I used to sneak into the bathroom and write on paper towels," he recalls. "My boss would kick the door and yell, 'Get back to work!' And I'd say, 'Don't you know there's a genius at work in here?' "

Gaines finally found someone to agree with him. Earlier this year, Gaines was awarded the National Book Critics Circle Award for *A Lesson Before Dying*—his first novel in a decade—hailed as one of the best American books of 1993.

And last summer, the Chicago-based MacArthur Foundation awarded him $355,000, a prize popularly known as a "genius grant." "I knew people who had won the MacArthur, but I never thought I'd win," confesses Gaines, a large man whose somber demeanor is occasionally broken by a radiant smile. "I assumed they were political."

The MacArthur honored a lifetime of achievement for the Louisiana-born writer best known for *The Autobiography of Miss Jane Pittman*. It was the pinnacle of a year crowded with milestones. He married for the first time, at the age of 60, and a television documentary about his life was released. Even his back surgery (to remove bone spurs) went well.

Gaines was born in 1933 to a family of sharecroppers at River Lake Plantation in Pointe Coupee Parish, La. They lived in workers' quarters—built by slave ancestors. Five months out of the year, children of "Cherie Quarters" attended school in the little church up the road.

The primary influence on Gaines' life was his great aunt, Augusteen Jefferson, who tended to him and his brothers and sister while their mother worked in the fields. Although crippled from birth, "Aunt Teen" cooked, sewed on a treadle machine that she worked with her hands, grew vegetables and even disciplined the children. From the time he was 8, Gaines worked in the fields. He did well in school and soon became the official scribe of the quarters, writing letters and reading the newspaper for "the old people."

During World War II, his mother and stepfather moved to Vallejo, Calif. One by one, they sent for the children, starting with Gaines in 1948, when he was 15. He attended Vallejo High School and enjoyed hanging out on street corners with his new classmates. But his stepfather, a member of the merchant marine, sternly suggested that Gaines find something better to do, steering him toward the public library. Gaines had never been inside a library—in Louisiana, they were for Whites only.

He felt instantly at home and soon spent hours reading books about the South, trying to find the place and people he had left behind. "But I could not find what I was looking for," he says. "The Black people in these books were not like my aunt, my brothers, my sister."

At 16, Gaines decided to write his own book. He scrawled it in longhand, then persuaded his mother to rent a typewriter. "I cut the paper in half, because that was the size of a book," he says. "I typed on both sides of the paper, because that's how books were printed. Every mistake you could possibly make, I made." Driven by dreams of fame and wealth, he wrapped up the novel and mailed it to a publisher in New York. "The way that package looked, I'm sure they thought it was a bomb," says Gaines with a reminiscent smile. "They sent it back to me, and I threw it in the incinerator."

After high school and junior college, Gaines was drafted into the Army, where he won several short-story contests. With money from the G.I. Bill, he enrolled at what is now San Francisco State University, then did graduate work in creative writing at Stanford University. Casting about for ideas, he remembered the book he had written at 16, about a Black man, a Creole woman and the strict barriers between their two cultures. In 1964, he published a version of that novel, *Catherine Carmier,* which was followed in 1967

by *Of Love and Dust* and in 1968 by the short-story collection
Bloodline.

Gaines took odd jobs—washing dishes, working in a post office
and delivering mail at the company where he wrote on paper
towels. He lived in a small apartment and ate hot dogs or pork-and-
beans. "Here I was, the first male in my family to go to college,
and I was living like a bum," he has said.

With *The Autobiography of Miss Jane Pittman* in 1971, he finally
tasted popular success. He originally told the story from multiple
points of view. But then, he said, "I fell in love with my little
character." Her narrative voice was so convincing that many
reviewers believed Miss Jane was a real person. Gaines struggled
for seven years to write his next book, *In My Father's House*,
about the gulf between African-American fathers and sons. It was
published in 1978 to mixed reviews. By the time he brought out *A
Gathering of Old Men* in 1983, his finances were strained; a knee
injury and surgery made the picture even bleaker.

That's when the University of Southwestern Louisiana stepped
in, offering him a professorship in creative writing and the lifetime
use of a house near the Lafayette campus, where Gaines has been
the writer in residence since 1984.

"USL came through when I was just about down and out," he
says. "I'd like to keep teaching here another 10 years, if I live
that long." Currently, Gaines is taking a hiatus after surgery to ease
pressure in his wrist, from writing his manuscripts in longhand.
"I still want to write as much as I can," he says. "But writing is
not the most important thing to me anymore."

As a young man, Gaines rejected marriage and children to devote
himself to his work. Now, he says, he wants to spend time with
his new wife, Dianne, a Louisiana native who is an assistant district
attorney in Miami. The couple divides its time among Lafayette,
Miami and San Francisco.

Critics have praised *A Lesson Before Dying*, the story of a young
Black man wrongly condemned to Louisiana's electric chair by a
White jury in 1948 and a teacher who tries to help him meet death.

But Gaines is equally pleased by the letters he gets from readers
all over the country, many from people who had never read a
book. "They all say they cried while reading it," he says. "One

lady said she cried sitting by her swimming pool! Another said she
had never seen so much food in one book. She said the whole time
she was reading it, she was either opening the refrigerator door
or crying."

After his whirlwind year, Gaines was happy to get back to
Louisiana. "I used to think that when I was 60, I'd like to live
near a small university, someplace where I could communicate with
young people who like to write," he says.

"Just sit around and talk to them maybe once or twice a week.
And that was before I ever knew that there would be a woman in
my life, or who that woman would be. And now there's Dianne.
What frightens me is that so many things are falling into place."

An Interview with Ernest Gaines

John Lowe / 1994

On 5 May, 1994, I dismissed my seminar early, and hurried over to Pleasant Hall, the University Hotel at Louisiana State University, to pick up Ernest Gaines. We were en route to a reception for him at the nearby African American Cultural Center. Later, I and the other teachers of African American literature took him out to eat at a Lebanese Restaurant; then it was on to his reading, to a packed house of faculty, students, and townspeople, from his new book, *A Lesson Before Dying*. After the reading, Gaines graciously handed out the University's annual creative writing awards, and posed for pictures with the thrilled recipients. He formally fielded questions at both these events, and informally at a second reception and book signing that followed the reading; some of the discussion in the interview that follows here relate to these events.

Gaines was in an ebullient mood. After a difficult year that involved physical pain and surgery, he was feeling much better. He had won the MacArthur Prize, the National Book Critics' Circle Award, and had been on the short list for the Pulitzer. He was shortly to celebrate his first wedding anniversary as well, and he referred frequently to "my Dianne." The interview that follows was conducted at Louisiana State University on 6 May 1994.

JL: I'd like to ask you about something that's obviously very important in your work, the sense of place. I know, too, that you're an admirer of Eudora Welty as well. She said that "it seems plain that the art that speaks most clearly, explicitly, directly, and passionately from its place of origin will remain the longest understood. It is through place that we put out roots, wherever birth, chance, fate or our traveling selves set us down; but where those roots reach toward—whether in America, England or Tim-

buktu—is the deep and running vein, eternal and consistent and
everywhere purely itself, that feeds and is fed by the human
understanding." I wondered how that would coincide with your
sense of place, and what you might add to that.

EG: Well, my folks have lived in the same place for over a
hundred years in Pointe Coupee Parish in South Central Louisiana. I can't imagine writing about any other place, although everything that I've written has been written in San Francisco, in
different apartments in San Francisco. I've tried to write about my
army experiences; I've tried to write about San Francisco, about
Bohemian life and that sort of thing. But everything comes back to
Louisiana. People have asked me many times, why don't I write
about the other places? I tell them once I get my Louisiana stuff out
of me, I will, but I hope I never do. I must write only about what my
roots are, really, and my roots are there. I don't know if you know
this story, but my wife and friends and I are trying to save the
cemetery where my people are buried; my aunt who raised me and
who most greatly influenced my life, I suppose, as well as others
is buried there in an unmarked grave. I don't know exactly the place
where she's buried—I know she's in a certain area. At the time
she passed, we were in California and just didn't have enough
money—I couldn't come back. It is *that* I cannot escape; I must
keep returning to that place, to that cemetery—we are obsessed by
that place—I suppose even more so than any other section of the
country. Mine was very small—but it was all that we had, and if
you're a writer, an artist, you can find a lot of meaning in a small
place. Just as Faulkner wrote about his small place, and Joyce
about his Dublin, Balzac wrote about his Paris—we can write
about ours as well.

JL: Let me ask you about people who think Louisiana isn't worth
writing about—you were talking about that last night.

EG: There are some people who feel that they are not worth
writing about. I teach at the University of Southwestern Louisiana. One day I needed an extra key to my house. I went over to the
physical plant office to have another key made. There were two
young ladies behind the counter—one was white, one was black—
the white young lady gave me the key, and she had me give her
my autograph. She told the other lady, who hadn't been working

there very long, "Do you know Mr. Gaines? He's a very important writer." And the young black lady said, "If he's so important,
what's he doing here?" And what she said was not meant as an
insult to me, but it was an insult to herself and her place—she saw
herself as a person who was not important, and the University
was not important. What I'm always trying to do is show how this
place and these people *are* important. They may think they're
insignificant, but the great stories have been written about people
who constantly question their significance. I don't think I'd want
to write a story about somebody who thinks he's important. I'd be
bored to death trying to do that. That's why I've always been an
admirer of writers such as Chekhov—who pick up people who seem
insignificant and look at their essence. That's why the European
writers impressed me so much more when I first started writing,
because they dealt with peasants.

JL: I know Turgenev's *Father and Sons* had a great influence on
your work.

EG: Oh yes, that book was my bible when I was writing my first
novel, *Catherine Carmier.* The same thing happens in those two
books; a young man educated in a different part of the country
comes back to be with the old people for a short while, and he
falls in love with a beautiful woman, and of course there's tragedy.
I could not be as poetic as Turgenev was with Bazarov—having
the hero dying, saying those lines—but I could deal with my area
and its people.

JL: Well, you say your work isn't as poetic as Turgenev's, but I
would challenge that and say it's very poetic—

EG: Well, sometimes I'm being facetious when I say things like
that, but when I read lines that Bazarov would say—I'm jumping
ahead here, but when I was dealing with Jefferson in *A Lesson
Before Dying,* I knew that before dying he had to make a great
statement, make it just before he sat in the chair—and then I
realized how phony that would be. That's one of the reasons I
invented the diary, so he could attempt to say something—maybe it
didn't come through, but he would attempt to say something—and
at the very end, of course, the only thing he could say was "Tell
Nannan I walked," and that was the most profound thing he *could*
ever say. But in the diary you would see how much he tried to say

something about people. But I want to go back to what I said
about Bazarov dying; I could not have Jefferson do the same things.

JL: Right—well, you were restricted by the setting. Putting him
in that cell drastically affected what you could have him do—and yet
you achieved such a tremendous effect. Since you have jumped
ahead to that, let me turn to *A Lesson Before Dying,* since many
people are reading it now and you haven't discussed it very much
until now. In terms of the diary, you placed that so strategically, and
in a place where people would not expect it to be—most writers
would have put it at the very end. Was it always clear to you that
you would place it where you did?

EG: Well, I didn't know what was going to come into the diary
when I first started writing the book. I knew I had to have him
say something—then it just so happened that this was the place to
put it—the last time that Grant would see him before Jefferson
died. So I had to have him—the diary—out of the book, and then
have Grant pick up the story after that.

JL: Here you have a kind of quiet explosion in the diary; but I
wondered if you agree with me that in a way the diary doesn't
exactly affect Grant, but still, makes the balance of the book shift
more towards Jefferson.

EG: Well, I had to get into Jefferson. No matter how much Grant
would ask him questions, he was evasive. He was too angry; I
had to go into him somewhere along the line; I didn't know how I
was going to do it. He was, however, saying *some* things to Grant;
for instance, the chapter when he was saying to Grant, "I must take
you across," and that sort of thing. But I could not have had the
diary in there—but I thought that the diary would elevate it to a
certain point, and then I would come back to Grant, who was
more of a direct sort of narration. I needed something to get into
Jefferson's mind, to show you who this was, and what was going
to happen. Who this simple little waterboy, or cottonpicker, or
whatever he was, was; it had to be clear he was the savior of
Grant, so Grant could save the children. The way I could get that
over to the reader was to let Jefferson make those little attempts
to explain himself. The diary was there for the reader to see who he
was. That's why you find no punctuation marks, no capitalizing
of the beginnings of sentences, his thoughts just run and run and

run, and I thought I was going to have difficulty with people reading
that. As a matter of fact, my editors wanted to cut part of it, and I
said "Cut what? Cut where? I can't cut it." I tried to keep it
short because I didn't want people to get bored or tired of dialect.
But I didn't know what to cut at all. It wasn't needed for *me* to
try to make you really see who he was—oh, he gave Grant some
answers—those answers were from him, yes, but they were not
his way of speaking all of his true self, and he could do that when
he was alone.

JL: You say you were nervous as to how readers would respond
to this different kind of writing. Is this related to your feeling
about the use of dialect? You spoke yesterday about how dialect
usage can be a problem.

EG: Yes. I can take a certain amount of dialect; but you should
use it sparingly to make a point. But this was eleven or twelve pages
we were dealing with here, and I was a bit concerned about the
reader, especially with the non-punctuation and that sort of
thing—I thought, "I can't lose them—I can't play the Molly Bloom
thing and go to sixty pages." Joyce was writing an experimental
novel, and people want to read him for that. But in my case they're
going to read the book, the story, as it is.

JL: I wanted to ask you about Jefferson's name too, because I
thought it might be a tribute to your aunt [Augusteen Jefferson].

EG: I really don't know. I never think about that. I used two
Presidents' names, and I don't know how they came up. Jefferson
and Grant—I don't know; maybe the names just sounded good, or
maybe I was thinking about Faulkner subconsciously, his Jefferson.
And about my aunt—I can't say. I wasn't really consciously aware
of that when I was thinking about the name—for either one of
them. I don't think I would have called him Grant Wiggins if I had
been thinking about it. I probably would have called him some
kind of Creole name like Beauregarde, or have him call his aunt
Callou or something like that. The names were not the point at
the time.

JL: I guess I also thought that when you named him Grant you
were thinking about the man we see in the McFeeley biography
of the general, as a misunderstood man of great endurance and
stoicism, who forced himself to write his memoirs even as he was

dying of cancer, so as to provide some support for his family. I thought that might have something to do with your Grant staying on the plantation and teaching, and saving the children.

EG: No, it just seemed like a name that would stick. I know, however, that after I had named Vivian I wished I had named her something else. There's a little girl at the school named Gloria Hebert, and I think that's such a beautiful name, and I thought, if I had come up with that earlier, I would have named Vivian that. A beautiful name for a beautiful woman. But it was a little too late.

JL: Let me ask you how you conceptualized her role in the book. To me, the love story is absolutely necessary to understand Grant, but I wonder if you thought of it as something more than that.

EG: You know, that Grant and Vivian relationship is almost like the Jackson and Catherine relationship [in *Catherine Carmier*]. And Jackson is told that he must wait thirty years for his Catherine, and it's about thirty years between those two books—the first one came out in 1964. And I found my Dianne and married her thirty years after that! There's a close connection there. Someone met me the other day in Lafayette at the doctor's office, and she said "I'm so exasperated with *Catherine Carmier*! What you do, you leave us hanging there! You have to write a sequel!" And I said "the sequel is that Dianne and I got married!" [Laughter]. No, Vivian is there to keep Grant there I think; without her he probably wouldn't have stayed long enough to really deal with Jefferson. That is his reason for existing. All the years he's been running in place, that's been his reason for existing. You know the Old Man upstairs works it that way—probably He brought Vivian there to keep Grant there long enough so Jefferson could get into the situation he got into in order to help the others down the line. The Old Man has a lot of things that He slips in without our knowing it.

JL: You also give Vivian children in this book. Is that connected with the children that Grant is teaching? She's always so concerned about her kids—she'll never come out to meet Grant unless she has a babysitter, and he's always understanding of that. You didn't have to have her have children.

EG: No, that's absolutely true, I wanted her to be a wife and a mother. See, they're mature people, they're in their thirties now. What would she have done by that age? There must have been a

marriage in her life by now. Grant has been teaching about ten
years, and so he'd have to be about 31 or 32 and she would be
too—she would have had about two children.

JL: Let me ask you something I've noticed about your work. In
Miss Jane Pittman, for instance, Miss Jane is the center of the book,
and its heroine, but at the same time the book could also be said to
be structured around the three tragedies—

EG: The four men. The book is structured around four men.
Right! That is it—that book is structured around Ned, Joe Pittman, Jimmy Aaron, and Tee Bob.

JL: That's right—I left out Tee Bob.

EG: Tee Bob is very important. Tee Bob and Mary Agnes
LeFabre—that's a tragedy there. He's the fourth man—I knew
what I was doing there. The book's about those four men, really, as
much as it is about Miss Jane herself—she tells it. And I got that
idea from reading Gertrude Stein's *The Autobiography of Alice B.
Toklas,* and that's where I got my title. I got the same idea. What
Gertrude Stein does, Alice B. Toklas is very seldom seen or written
about. I thought what I would do with Miss Jane was start out
writing about her, and then bring in all these other things, but she
tells it, and it is her life as well as all the other peoples' lives
around her. But you're absolutely right—it is based around those
three plus Tee Bob and Mary Agnes. And each one is a different
kind of story. For example, the War Years, with Miss Jane and the
little boy Ned traveling through the swamp—that's the adventure
of all these people going and coming, just as Huck and Jim on the
boat—someone has compared it to adventures like that. The second
book—the Reconstruction Period—is the settling down of peasant
life, the way anybody would want to settle down after going to a
different place and try to make a life of their own. The third is the
plantation, the romantic Southern thing: boy, girl, tragedy, suicide, all that sort of thing. Only I mixed it up with a white and an
octoroon in this case. To make it even more Southern (than all
the other romantic stuff without any kind of social meaning to
it)—because who had produced her in the first place? And the
other section, the last one, The Quarters—it was like a diary, and
Miss Jane's keeping a diary and walking with this little boy along
the street—the narration becomes a different thing altogether. And

so you see the progress from an adventure story down to the diary, she's less and less visible. She dominates the first story, the first book of the novel, the War Years. In the Reconstruction Years, she and Joe Pittman almost share that equally. Then in the Plantation section, Tee Bob and Mary Agnes, she's involved somewhat, but she's less and less visible. Then in the last one with Jimmy, The Quarters, she's just sitting there; she's an old lady. So as the book progresses, she gets older and less directly involved, so the whole pace of each book must be different, the storytelling must be different. But to get back to your point, yes, these are four tragedies.

JL: I also wanted to ask you about the kind of character represented by Ned and Jimmy; they are selected by the community to serve as what is termed "the one," a kind of messiah. Let me ask you about how that kind of leadership role emerges in the community, and how you see that functioning in the new book. Because there you get the idea that Grant is being singled out by these women as "the one"; but maybe it's Jefferson who really becomes "the one"?

EG: Well, I think you've explained it to me! [Laughter]. Well, in any family, any family of five or six, the mother and father or the older people pick out a person in that family to do—to carry on the work, in case something happens. In a place like the Quarter where I lived, those old people, without you knowing, will concentrate on you, and they will choose you. And not only one person will choose you, but a second one will choose you to do things. For example, I used to write letters. Now there were a couple of other guys who could have written the letters for them as well, but they wanted me to do it, and I would do it, and they would give me little gifts of cakes and things like that. Not that I was chosen as "the one," but from observing these things, yes, a community as well as a family—or a country!—will choose somebody to represent them.

JL: Maybe that has something to do with the names you chose too, Grant and Jefferson.

EG: Well, that's quite possible, but as I say, it wasn't a conscious thing.

JL: I want to ask you about another aspect of *A Lesson Before Dying,* in terms of being "the one," and having the diary speak so powerfully, because I was thinking about other works in African American literature that do this. One is Toni Morrison's *Beloved,* where the whole book changes at the end when Beloved has this monologue that seems to speak for an entire racial consciousness, this whole memory of the Middle Passage and what that has meant—and of course the whole book displays this in historical terms, but this is a kind of transcendent, metaphysical thing, and it makes you go back and reread the whole book in a new way, and I wonder if you saw Jefferson's diary as working that way. Even though you've gotten a feeling for Jefferson, the diary becomes a revelation in terms of your sense of him.

EG: No, I didn't have that in mind—I just thought it would be an elevation to himself—to show him that he wasn't illiterate—its aim was to show that he had been trying to say something, that he had accepted his position, not being able to express his humanity, and now he was called upon to do so. I think this was what I was aiming at in this diary.

JL: The other book I was thinking of when I read this was *Native Son,* where Bigger is in prison at the end. One of the things I've always thought of as a mistake in that book was Wright's decision to place this eloquent summary of Bigger's life in the mouth of the white attorney. But then Bigger does have a speech at the end that sort of wipes that out, so maybe that was the intention.

EG: I'm glad you brought that up, because in my first version of the very end of the book, when Paul comes back to the Quarters, and says to Grant, "tell them what a man he was—he showed his manhood." Grant says, "why don't you come in here and tell them now what he was"? And they go into the room, and Paul gives a talk. When I sent that draft in, my agent called me and said, "Listen. You can't have Paul saying that—No. That's Grant. You can't have this white guy come through there now. That's Grant's job, to come into those children."

JL: So you agreed with that.

EG: Yes! That's why Grant tells Paul, you come back some other time, and so he goes into the church to do this. But sometimes a writer is so close to his story that he just doesn't see those kind of things. And when Grant goes back in and he sees those kids standing tall with their arms to their sides waiting, all he can do is start crying because he can't say anything—it's been told, I can't say anything.

JL: This book is set in 1948. You said last night that you had originally intended to set it in 1988. I found that intriguing, because in something I've written on you before, which I think you've read, I said that you're not interested in merely glossing history, but that you want history to speak to our own time. Is that what this book is intended to do? To speak to the particular situation, in fact, that we have more young black men in prison than we do in college?

EG: Well, you know I've seen many reviews of the book, and I got a great review from *The Angolite*—the magazine that comes out of Angola Prison [in Louisiana]. That book would have been a totally different book had that book been written in 88 instead of 48. For one thing, Grant would not have had the same problems. In 88 Miss Emma would not have had to gone up to the place to talk to Pichot. They would have gotten an attorney to step in and do all that. Last night I said that I had written to the warden and asked him if it would have been feasible for a teacher, someone who's not kin, someone who's not a minister, not an attorney, to come in and visit someone. At first he said "You can't come—I couldn't protect you." So I wrote another letter and said, well, listen, I didn't want to come visit anyone—I just wanted to know if something like that would be feasible. He never did answer. I think to myself, what do I do now? A friend of mine took me to meet a sheriff in New Iberia [Louisiana, near Lafayette]. While we sat there talking, I asked the same question of him. He said, "It would depend upon the sheriff." He wouldn't say whether he would do it or not. So to get back to what you're asking, that is the reason why when Miss Emma goes up there, I develop this whole thing around what she had given to that family. It's sort of symbolic of what the blacks have given to the South. Hey—you owe me a favor. You owe me one favor. And she keeps telling him over and over—so what I wanted was a sheriff who could not deny her having someone else visit her son. It was all based around that warden who wouldn't answer my second letter, who was saying "forget it." So in this case I created this woman to keep telling us "you *do* know what I've done." And of course the sheriff is unwilling in the beginning, just as the warden had been with me, but then he does decide to, because of history, because of those hundred years that people have served his house, and through his letting Grant come there, Grant converts Jefferson, and Jefferson converts Grant, and the whole thing comes back to probably help us—I should hope so—also, Paul has been changed, and he is going to make some points—I least I hope so.

JL: I wonder why you chose that particular year, because you have other works you've set then too—that seems to be the *annus mirabilus* for you.

EG: Well, that's the year I left [Louisiana for California]. And you know, something had happened about a year or so before that— this young man had been sentenced to the electric chair twice—I think it was in 46 or 47. Because the chair had failed to work properly the first time. And so I was working around those years—I use those years, a lot, the thirties and forties—I didn't want to put it in 47 because I didn't want anyone to compare those two stories. And I have received letters from different people—attorneys and even ministers—who remember that execution in 1947, and they have asked me if I had it in my mind when I was writing the book. What I *did* learn from that incident was that the state had had a portable electric chair that they could run wires through the window for the night before. I wanted to work the story itself into the frame of a semester for black school children of that time, which was about five and a half to six months if you lived out in the country.

JL: Of course the children are very important to the development of the story—they have to be in school for Grant to relate to them as he talks to Jefferson.

EG: Oh yes, we have to have the children there—and Grant has to spend as much energy in one place as he does in the other.

JL: Tell me how you conceptualized that school, because I've seen a picture of you in front of a building just like that.

EG: Well, that's the school I went to, and my folks went there too.

JL: Were any of your teachers in your head when you were writing the book?

EG: Yeah, but I won't name them [laughter]. But I had some teachers—well, we thought they were mean at that time. Maybe they weren't. And that's one of the things that Grant is saying, and that's one of the things the story's all about. I suppose we have produced as many good teachers, percentage-wise, as anyone else has produced in this country, with much more feeling for their students. But many blacks who would have preferred some other position than just being a schoolteacher, may have been poor schoolteachers because they were forced—that was the only thing they could go into—they did it, but they hated it.

JL: I wondered about that, because in the early scenes at the schoolhouse, Grant seems to be a very harsh teacher in many ways. But at the same time, I think that some people might interpret the way he tells them about the graphic violence that lies ahead for Jefferson, as a variety of "tough love," or something like that—you show him changing in his attitude toward the children as he goes along, but I wonder which aspect of him you were showing at that juncture, because he's still in flux then, I think.

EG: No, he meant to hurt when he was telling them that. He's so frustrated with them and with his world, with that plantation, with the old minister, with this place, that he hates the children—well, he doesn't hate them, but he's very impatient and very intolerant.

JL: Let me ask you about the minister, because throughout the book he seems to be in conflict with Grant, so there's a kind of dialogue that goes forward. Do you see that as representative of a kind of impasse that exists in black culture between the academy and the pulpit?

EG: No, I don't think so [laughs], I think it's one of my problems. In most cases, the local school teachers have tremendous respect for the ministers. Everybody lived together at that time. Maybe inside of him he might have felt, well, I can respect him to a certain point, he's doing a pretty good job, he's helping these people. But I was not aware of those kind of conflicts as I wrote it—you know, people who read "The Sky is Gray" are always saying, "you and those ministers!" and I say, well it's not me, it's my characters, and they say, "well, why is it repeated all the time?"

JL: You present it most powerfully in *In My Father's House,* and you have it in *A Gathering of Old Men* too.

EG: Right, he's the only one who falls. I'm glad you brought that up, because when they were making the film, those old guys who were playing the parts refused to let him fall. They said the minister must be strong as anybody else—he may disagree with us, but he shouldn't fall. And so they changed it—and maybe they were right.

JL: That's sort of the community rising up. Isn't that surprising? How your texts take on a new life after you've finished them—not only in the movies, but in the way people insist on reading them?

EG: Well, I've always felt that the artist writes the whole, he writes big—I don't think he knows the little small things, because he sees the large thing, and he puts that down. Then those others come along and say, well, okay, that's made up from this. I don't think God had all those other Adams in mind when he made the universe in six days. People afterwards come along and start dissecting things, and probably His brain had seen all of this, but He saw it as a whole apple—He didn't see the seas and the little hills—He just saw the apple as a world. I've seen quite a few things that He probably shouldn't have invented!

JL: This 1948 thing—because *Of Love and Dust* is set then too, I wonder if that novel wasn't on your mind when you wrote this one. Because there's a sense in which Jefferson is like Marcus, but in a sense he's not—he's much more passive. You could never think of Marcus going into a long silence.

EG: No—I don't know why I thought of 48, except that it was the year that I left. So that year's much more vivid in my mind than any other. There's no reason that what happened to Jefferson couldn't have happened in 49, or what happened to Marcus couldn't have occurred in 52 or 53, because they were still doing that same kind of work. Similarly, you'd have still have had that portable electric chair up until the early 50s.

JL: One of the things I thought when I heard you had originally planned to set *A Lesson* in 88 was that you must have seen the story speaking to 88. I was thinking maybe you were trying to demonstrate to the readers how where we are now came about.

EG: Yes, I would have done that had I set it in 88, but the jail would not have been the same, the sheriff would not have been the same. I probably would not have needed Miss Emma in the same way—if I had done it in 88, Grant would have been in California. His aunt would have gotten in touch with him and wanted him to come back. He came back and got involved in this and didn't want to, like Jackson in *Catherine Carmier,* but he does stay this time, and he meets this beautiful girl and gets involved. And so the whole thing would probably have spoken more to these kids who are in prison now. I have no idea how I would have handled it. It may have been a blessing in disguise that this warden didn't answer my second letter.

JL: My feeling was that you were saying, we still have the same situation today—but we can understand it better by looking at the situation in 1948, because then it was all out in the open, the attitude of the sheriff and the defense attorney saying "he's just a hog"— that's still the attitude, but it's not said so openly.

EG: Right, sure. Things haven't changed. The little powder-faced woman Grant meets when he's going to pick up the radio? Well, this happened to me in New Roads when they were making the film *A Gathering of Old Men.* Schlondorff [the director] and his assistant and I were looking for a place to have coffee. This lady was hanging a dress out on a rack in front of a store, and I approached her, saying "Excuse me madam, can you tell me where we can get some coffee?" She was short and kind of stocky, and her face was very white and powdered; she looked at me and just turned away from me and spoke to Schlondorff, who was standing aside. So it's the same sort of thing. It's the same woman I had in mind when I was writing a scene set in 1948.

JL: Let me ask you about the role of silence in this book, and in all of your books—the way so many characters maintain silence, which is related to stoicism. Jim Kelly—again, in *Love and Dust,* is our narrator, but he's very silent throughout a lot of the book. He is prominent and then not prominent in the narrative—can you comment on this concept of silence in your books? It seems to me people listen a great deal too—to nature, to various kinds of sound—particularly the older women sitting on porches, listening to the crickets or the birds—Aunt Margaret, Aunt Charlotte, Miss Jane—they seem to be great listeners.

EG: Yes—remembering, I suppose, and thinking. And I think that's where wisdom comes from—listening. There's also silence from a glance, a look gives as much meaning as a word or a line. It's when you've lived in that community and the community is very old—you don't have to speak a word. A word is the most

annoying thing in the world at certain points. Just absolute
silence. You understand when these older women, whether they're
black or white, look at you in a certain way, or *don't* look at you in a
certain way. For example, when Grant slams that door hard when
he's taking off to Pichot's house, and he gives a whole feeling,
emotion just by not seeing his aunt look at him, but knowing that
she's looking at him, and at what part of his body she's looking at,
the back of his head, the side of his face! He's been around her so
much that meaning is there in silence with her. There's this joke
about this guy going into a club where they were telling jokes by
numbers. Someone says "13," and they all break out laughing. Then
they say "33," and some guys roll out on the floor laughing. So this
little guy, after a long silence, says "13," and nobody laughs. He
says "33," and nobody laughs. So he asks this guy, "everybody
laughed at 13 and 33 before, why not when I tell it?" and the guy
says, "You didn't say it right!" [Laughter]. He wasn't a part of the
club—not part of the community. When you're part of the community, when there's even the slightest movement of the hand or a
mere look, or *not* looking—it can mean so much. It's communica-
tion—what Mendelssohn calls "Songs Without Words." The com-
munication is there, but the words are not there.

JL: Yes. In Hurston's *Their Eyes Were Watching God,* Janie says
that Tea Cake is a "glance from God," and that says it all without
describing him in detail.

EG: That's right.

JL: I also wanted to ask you about something that occurred to
me when I was reading *A Lesson.* When the defense attorney
says Jefferson is nothing more than a hog, that's very close to the
central metaphor of Ellison's of invisibility, because when you
turn someone into a hog, they're just part of the landscape—they're
not really there. And of course Ellison just died—I know you
admire Ellison, but you also said at one time, "there's too much
talking in Ellison—let the thing flow." Do you have any thoughts
about his work now that he's gone?

EG: No, I feel the same way. In one sentence Ralph says, "I'm
an Oklahoman, and Oklahoma is not the deep South." What he's
saying there and in most of his essays is that he's not from the
South. Later on, his works get accepted by so many Southern

critics. Although he says he's not a Southerner, I think he's moving us more toward a sense of *South-ern*. And I think when he wrote that book, he had only spent two or three years at Tuskegee. I don't know that Ralph really knew Southern life, Southern tradition, the norms. I think he spent a lot of his time on campus at Tuskegee and then he would go back home during the summers. I don't think he really knew the Southern land—the swamps, the bayous, the fields, picking cotton. I think because of that, he just overplayed his hand sometimes. I'm not an intellectual; I'm not one of those scholars who know all the symbolism that Ellison is using in his book, but it seems to me that he leads this boy rather than guiding him. He takes him and pulls him. For example—and I've said this jokingly—well, half-jokingly—I don't know how in the world that boy could ever have gone by Trueblood's house. Any kid, I don't know how naive he is—and this is what Ralph was doing, showing how naive he was—the most naive person in the University wouldn't have done that. But Ralph Ellison needed that. He needed him to go back there, no matter what rules he had to break. Well, you can break certain rules, but you have a Southern character, a Southern boy who knows the South. Ralph is saying, well, he doesn't know it. I can see someone coming from Oklahoma and doing these kinds of things in the deep South, but I don't know that I can see a Southern boy, a boy who raised up there in Alabama or thereabouts doing these things. But Ralph had to pull him along. He grabs him by the arm and said, this is what I want you to do. I find that throughout the book. I said that when he was alive, and I see no reason why I should change now. I'm not saying that to discredit the book, I'm just saying it's one of the things I find—I just wish it flowed more easily for me.

   JL: On this subject, let me ask you about Southern writing and African American literature's central role in that. I teach Southern literature, and I wouldn't think of teaching it without large portions devoted to black writers, but that was not the case before—a lot of people are reconceptualizing Southern writers. What are the enduring similarities between these traditions of Southern writing, and what are the differences?

   EG: What do you mean by African American and Southern? I thought I was Southern.

JL: What I mean is the way those terms were used in the past—I agree with you. But it seems to me that even many black critics continue to separate the two—they don't take into account African American writers' Southernness.

EG: Well, I never listen to critics! [laughter]. I think Southern writers—any Southern writer—they have much more in common than differences, especially if they write about the South, and if they write about the character of the South—the land, the towns, the cities—I think they have much more in common—they have in common a certain point of view as well. Someone asked me when I wrote *The Autobiography of Miss Jane Pittman,* was I thinking about Dilsey in Faulkner's novel *The Sound and the Fury.* And I said, "No, I did not have Dilsey in mind." And by the way, the difference between Dilsey and Miss Jane Pittman is that Faulkner gets Dilsey talking her story from his kitchen; the young schoolteacher in my book gets Miss Jane's story from Miss Jane's kitchen. And it makes a difference. When Miss Jane is talking to a black teacher in her kitchen, it's a quite different thing. Writers, black and white, were interviewing these ex-slaves during the thirties. Certain black writers would get some information. If a white writer went in there and asked the same people the same thing, they'd give him some information, but they would not give him as much that was revealing as to the black who interviewed them. They'd still be talking about the same thing, but the shading is a little different at the time. So the black writer and the white writer have to write about the same thing. Faulkner wrote about the big flood of '27, just as every great blues singer of the South *sang*—from Ma Rainey down to B. B. King and Muddy Waters and all the others who sang about the story of the great flood of '27.

JL: Richard Wright wrote about it too.

EG: Right—and of course I mentioned it in *The Autobiography of Miss Jane Pittman.* We all do it. We all write about that—now we may look at it differently. I'm pretty sure that many of the whites were saved before many of the blacks when the boat came by to pick up the people. What I may be writing about is, this flood happened, there were dead bodies, dead animals on the water, all these things were going on and yet when it came time to rescue people, that group over there was rescued before we were. And

Faulkner would probably agree, that they rescued them first. So we're writing about the same things; no one has demonstrated the brutality in jails towards blacks as much as Faulkner has, or as much as Caldwell did. At the same time, it is different. I just reviewed Walter Mosley's latest book for *The Los Angeles Times*. And Mosley and Faulkner have been compared to both Dashiell Hammett and Raymond Chandler with this private detective thing. But at the same time—they deal with bad guys, they get shot up and cut, get run out of town, the police beat them up—Spade and Marlowe and Easy Rawlins, they all go through the same thing. But Walter Mosley knows that side of South Central L.A. better than Raymond Chandler does because he fits in there much more; that's a black area there. Chandler has Marlowe go into that area, but Marlowe gets out of there soon enough because he can't stay in there too long. So there's some differences, but lots of similarities, and I would not agree with any critic who tries to stand between myself and my being a Southern writer. I may say things that they may not want to hear or may not want to see, but they cannot completely disagree with me. Many of the letters I received about this latest book have come from Southerners, especially white Southerners. They say that it's an important book in their lives—the same thing happened with *The Autobiography of Miss Jane Pittman*. I've gotten many letters and spoken at many high schools and colleges all over the country. But in the South, I always get Southern students saying, this is a side of history I didn't know. Or kids will say, this is the best book I've ever read (maybe they've only read two books!) [laughter]. One guy told me that the best short story he'd ever read was "The Sky is Gray," and that the best novel he'd ever read was *A Lesson Before Dying*. I'm thinking to myself, how many short stories and novels has this guy read? [laughter]. But there are things that may not have been said before by white writers, things that they say, now that they see we are saying them. Because too many are agreeing with me—"I like what you're doing"—and these are Southern critics, and not just the general public who write letters, too.

JL: I went to a talk Gloria Naylor gave in New Orleans a few years ago, and she was asked about her feeling about the South. She said, "I'm an honorary Southerner, because I was conceived

in Mississippi, but then we moved North." She was discussing
the idea that maybe all African American writers are Southern, in a
sense, because of the history. Do you think there's any validity in
that? What you've said about Ellison problematizes that in an
interesting way.

EG: Right—I can agree with that to a point, yes, because one
thing about all African American writing is that you can't ignore
the fact that the majority of us who came to this country came
under slavery, to do manual work in the South. Not all of us have
lived there, but most of us have, or our parents or grandparents
have. So we do have the connections, the roots—but there are
those who lose touch—I don't want to name any names, but some
of them are very important writers—as far as dialogue, the nuances,
the understatement. You find a lot of Northern blacks and Northern
whites who, when they want to talk about racism, or prejudice,
or whatever, they get a little heavy-handed, because they have to
convince themselves that they know what they're talking about,
whereas when you know what you're talking about, as Hemingway
would say, you can leave out every other line and still get your
message over. That's what I try to do. I want to know my subject
so well that I won't have to keep repeating things—there are times
when you want to do that, but not because you're not sure of what
you're talking about.

JL: I was thinking here about profoundly Southern writers, like
you, Richard Wright, Zora Neale Hurston, John O. Killens, as compared to more recent writers like Toni Morrison and Gloria Naylor,
who seem to be coming to terms with the South, even though
they're not from the South—in *Beloved* and *Mama Day*—in order
to understand history, they have to understand the South.

EG: Yes—to understand their history, I suppose you would have
to. Perhaps if I could talk to Gloria Naylor, I could understand
what she's saying. But there's another thing—I think it's rather
popular now to have that Southern connection. To say that yes,
my father or my grandparents did come from there. But there are
many writers who do not write about it and avoid it without even
consciously avoiding it, because they have other subjects to write
about—the Chicago scene, the Detroit or New York scenes—you
can write about those things.

JL: I'm interested in the problem of representation, and the idea that there are things that a black writer is supposed to write about. Those are two issues, so let me take the second one first, the choice of subject matter. As a Hurston scholar, I've been concerned by some of the attacks that have been made on her. For instance, it's been said, here is the black woman writer, sitting in Harlem during the twenties, with urban poverty all around her. Why is she writing about these peasants in Florida? Why doesn't she write, in other words, like Richard Wright? So I wonder what your thoughts are about expected subject matter?

EG: Well, I was attacked like that too. But before I answer that question, I'd like to say this: no one gives a damn about a writer until he becomes *known*. A writer doesn't choose a profession—he *has* to do it, but not because of community, but because of something even bigger than that. The Old Man upstairs has to get someone to help him carry the load; he gets writers and artists to help him do the work. And we do it—and we do it on our own for a long, long time, and some of us get recognized, and get some aid from the MacArthurs or the Guggenheims or the Rockefellers. Most of us don't get anything, but we must continue to do that work. And I think that the writer has all the right to see the world as he or she wants to look at it. And that is right, whatever he or she feels is important to write. But what I would say is the writer shouldn't waste his talent writing trash. As long as he's writing truth as well as he sees truth, and understands truth. I think he should write whatever he likes. I started writing *The Autobiography of Miss Jane Pittman* in 1968. During that time, there were all kinds of demonstrations going on at San Francisco State, for Black Studies, for instance. We had Hayakawa as President of the University at that time, and he was bringing cops onto the campus, and they were busting heads. He was not going to let these demonstrators disturb his college. And here I am, locked up in my little small one-bedroom apartment, writing about a hundred and ten year old woman in Louisiana. Of course San Francisco State was my alma mater. I would see these people, or they would call me on the telephone or write me letters. "What in the hell are you doing?" "Well, I'm writing about a hundred and ten year old woman." "Who wants to hear about a hundred and ten year old woman

these days, man? We're talking about what's happening *now!*" So I
know exactly what you're saying. And I had this all the time. All
the time. And even after the book was published, I was still attacked
by many of the black militants for having spent my time working
on this when I should have been out there fighting cops. And I said,
"listen, at the same time these cops are doing this here in San
Francisco, Bull Connor and his bullies are doing the same thing
down in the South. I can't stop him, but what I'll try to do each day
that I'm here, when I hear that Bull Connor is turning dogs and
hoses on others, I'll go back home and I'm going to write the best
paragraph that I can write that day; I'll make it so good that it'll be
read long after Bull Connor and Hayakawa are dead and the cops are
all gone. That's how I'm going to write this." And that was it. I'm
still being attacked like that. [Yesterday] when the students were
asking me questions, I was a bit apprehensive, since we were at the
Black Student Union [the LSU African American Cultural Cen-
ter]. Usually, when I'm on these campuses, I get this question,
"where were you during that time?" And I say, "well, I was
writing *The Autobiography of Miss Jane Pittman,* or I was writing
In My Father's House—but that's not good enough for many of these
questions. So I can go back to what they are saying about Zora
Neale Hurston. I can understand it because the same thing's been
directed toward me.

JL: You mentioned your admiration for Jean Toomer's *Cane* last
night. When did you first read him?

EG: I discovered *Cane* in the sixties. I thought it was so poetic—
you know, Sherwood Anderson knew about that book, and I'm
almost certain that he mentioned it to Gertrude Stein and Hemingway because of those little things in Hemingway's first collection
of stories, *In Our Time*—he has those little breaks between each
one of those stories, and I wonder if he didn't get that from having
read Toomer's *Cane;* and of course, *Cane* came out much earlier.

JL: I wanted to ask you about this dichotomy of African American writers that seems to be emerging, using Hurston and Wright
as exemplars, as foremother and forefather. This sets her up as
representing the pastoral, vernacular tradition, and Wright as the
embodiment of the literature of protest. Personally, I've always
looked at your work as an ideal synthesis between those two.

EG: I would think so; without ever really having anyone explain it to me like that before. I don't know where Hurston got her influences from, but I feel that Wright sort of followed Dostoyevsky and all down the line, the naturalistic writers. I could read Dostoyevsky, but he's so overpowering—I read *Crime and Punishment, The Brothers Karamazov,* but he had less influence over me than the other writers, definitely less than Turgenev and Tolstoy, or Gogol, whom I used to love reading. Maybe I've always been much more attracted by the—not pastoral, but some of it. Vivian keeps telling Grant that it's so pastoral [on the plantation]; if he stays long enough he'll see the other meanings of it. I think that's what I have in my writing—you have that pastoral, agrarian thing—the fields, and the streams and the trees, and all that sort of thing, but then there's that other thing going on all the time, and you do go to the towns and get involved. But Wright's work is so concentrated on that other thing.

JL: Yes—on revolution and protest—but you have that too, though, and there are very powerful social issues in all your books.

EG: But you read! [laughter] But other people are going to read without seeing I do this. One of the worst criticisms—the one bad thing that was written about *Miss Jane Pittman*—was written by a black woman who reviewed the book for a Chicago paper. At that time I was on everybody's short list—Ellison and me. That being the time of the Baldwins, the Barakas, the Don Lees—we were all supposed to do that. And she said that that book was the most boring book she had read, and the only reason she read it was that she was supposed to review it.

JL: I can't understand how anyone could say your books are boring; in fact, many times you take on the most provocative, explosive issues. For instance, the new book examines violence, the incarceration of black men, and all kinds of brutality and degradation. But I'm a great admirer of *Of Love and Dust,* another provocative book, one that examines inter-racial love. I wonder what challenged you to write that book—it must have taken a lot of courage to include not one, but two such plots.

EG: I had to get a novel out in order to get my stories [*Bloodline*] published. Just as Faulkner said he wrote *Sanctuary* to make some money! Well, I was trying to think of a plot; I had written "Three Men" already, about a guy killing a guy in a fight and being put in prison. And of course the guy, Proctor, wants to get out of that place; but another prisoner, Munford, says "well, you're going to be just like me if you do get out." So anyway, in *Of Love and Dust,* I have him come out, with his name changed from Proctor to Marcus, because Proctor of course [in "Three Men"] stays in there. Marcus, however, says "to hell with this; I'm not going to stay in here." So he comes out and works on this plantation. That's the kind of thing that went on during that time—you could bond prisoners out and they'd be bonded to a plantation for years and years. And I've known it happen to a guy. So I said, if I get this guy out, he's going to cause problems, because he's that kind of guy—who would want to wear silk shirts and brown and white shoes in that corn field, with no hat on his head [laughter]. This guy's going to be a mess! They're going to have a lot of trouble with him. Okay, he's going to do things. And then too, I knew of white overseers who had gone with black women on the plantation—and everyone else knew it too. So I just got those two things together, and it was the easiest book to write. Because I had a character who I found funny. I was thinking about Muhammad Ali when I was writing that book, who talked so much about what he could do—he was in the background. He was called Cassius Clay at the time. But I was also thinking about another friend of mine, who was killed in San Francisco. One of these tough guys—I mean he was tough! And he was sort of Marcus's color, sort of brown skinned, with a mixture of Indian, black and white. He wore the clothes, and had the cars, was a lover boy. And because of Marcus's character, if Marcus looks at this beautiful woman over here and he finds out someone else has got her, he's going to do something; so why not just reverse the thing, and make him do the other thing. And by the way, some lady wrote a good review of *Catherine Carmier;* I got a letter from her after *Of Love and Dust* came out, saying "Mr. Gaines, I'll *never* review another book of yours again!" She didn't mention the race thing, but she mentioned the vulgarity. No, I had no problem in writing that story; I just said, this has happened.

JL: Well, it occurred to me that you might be doing something

like what Faulkner does in a lot of his work—Wright too—
Faulkner takes a stereotype and works with it. *Absalom* could be
said to have been written from the old expression, "but would
you want your sister to marry one?"; and then he makes something
magnificent out of it. I thought maybe you were thinking of some
of those pulp novels like *Mandingo* or *Drum,* and what could be
made out of them.

EG: No, I've never read *Mandingo,* although I've seen it on
television. I don't read that stuff. You see, one thing about Louisiana—it's produced just about everything we can imagine.

JL: We don't need pulp!

EG: Not if you've been around here long enough! You don't need
that other stuff! [laughter]. We have it here, in religion, in race, in
color-consciousness between African Americans and Creoles, we
have Cajuns over here, we have that group over there—and I come
from that kind of background. We had the great landowners, the
sharecroppers, the small towns, uptown, and back of town, the
swamps, the bayous—there's a story behind every tree. Of course
you have the great ghost stories and so on. I read these other
writers like Turgenev to see how to do things, but I know the story
is already there. I hadn't read Eudora Welty when I was in college.
When I read her "A Worn Path," I'm thinking to myself, we've
experienced that. I've grown up in small towns, I've walked with my
mother and step-father on these old long roads, I know what cold is
all about. And I've told her that two or three times, how much
influence "A Worn Path" has had on my writing, especially on
"The Sky is Gray."

JL: Do you think many white writers have written with accuracy
about the black experience, aside from Welty and Faulkner?

EG: I don't know, I've read them more than I have anyone else.
I think Warren aimed at it—I think some of the younger writers
today are trying to do as well as they can to get a better picture
without being too stereotyped. Then there's Reynolds Price—I
think he tries to describe black life accurately—especially with
black women.

JL: I don't want to leave you without discussing what I see as a
central concern in all your books, even in *Miss Jane Pittman,*
namely, the problem of achieving manhood, particularly for black

men, but the way I read it, you're describing the problem in terms of all men.

EG: Absolutely.

JL: Do you think we as Southerners face a special problem in this respect?

EG: I think we think that being a big tough guy, like a football player, or a bully, is being a man. This is the kind of thing that I'm saying all the time, that that isn't what makes a man. This is what Munford is saying to Proctor in that jail—"just because you can go have a child doesn't make you a man; just because you can knock a man down, does not make you a man." This is the responsibility of man; taking responsibility for the whole, all human-ity, is what I think manliness is. It seems that too many of the whites are afraid to take that kind of responsibility, and so many of the blacks have been denied that kind of responsibility, and refuse to accept it because of their long denial. The whites just say, I can be a man just by being a football player, or a sheriff, or a politician. The other thing doesn't seem as absolutely necessary. I hope I'm not only speaking for blacks; you use the tools that you have, and because I am African American, and most of my characters are, I put the situation there. But I could do the same thing with white characters, in different ways of course.

JL: Going back to what we were talking about earlier—whether whites can write about blacks, or vice versa—and I know you've been asked a lot about whether a man can write about a woman, and you've certainly proved you can. My favorite short story, with the possible exception of "The Sky is Gray," is Willa Cather's "Neighbor Rosicky," which is about a man and the way he behaves toward his family and his society. In fact, that story reminds me very much of the men in your work, who realize that being a man is more an outreaching to other people, accepting responsibility, and passing something on. Like Grant, we hope, does; it's certainly what Jefferson *does* do.

EG: And maybe Jim in *Of Love and Dust* will do something too when he leaves that plantation, and will go on to something else. If he learned anything, he learned it by having been around Marcus, or he would have probably have stayed there driving Red Hannah, drinking beer in the side room on Saturday, not caring about anything else, just going along. Maybe he will move on to something else. Maybe even Philip Martin in *In My Father's House* could do something else.

JL: I think it's also remarkable in your work—and of course your remarks about your aunt testify to this—that frequently it's women who teach men how to be men, who teach them the importance of "standing."

EG: She was the greatest influence in my life. I never heard her complain. But I left when I was fifteen. She died five years after that. She crawled on the floor, winter and summer, looked after us, cooked, washed the clothes. They washed on these old washboards; we would bring everything to her. You brought the clothes to her, the water, the bar of soap, the washboard. She sat on a bench and braced herself against the rim of the tub, washing. When she cooked the food, she sat on a little bench by the old wood stove. And we brought her the food, the seasonings. She did all that. We had a garden beside the house. In the afternoons, when it becomes cool, she used to go into the garden; she had a little short-handled hook, and would work with it among the vegetables we had. There was always somebody leaning against the fencepost, talking to her, and they would go on for a couple of hours, until it was time for her to go in and warm the food. But whites and blacks would come—an old Cajun fellow used to come there and sell things, and sit on the steps and talk for a long time. They'd drink coffee, and talk about the weather. He'd never come inside, of course, he just sat on the steps—she used to sit by the door.

JL: Was he an inspiration for Albert Cluveau?

EG: Oh no. In a way, maybe the better side of Albert Cluveau, if there was a good side. He was very close to Miss Jane, and they fished together. But there was such an assassin in False River at that time. I could take you to the grave of the teacher who was killed. That was based on a real incident. I changed things around, because I didn't know what he looked like—of course his name wasn't Albert Cluveau. I was giving a talk at the Rotary Club at False River once, and afterwards an old Cajun fellow came up to the lectern and beckoned to me; I leaned over, and in almost a whisper, he said "I know of whom you speak" [laughter]. But I heard stories when I was a small kid coming up about this man.

JL: I'm interested in how you use people such as Albert Cluveau and other characters who are seemingly ripe in the traditional Southern manner for being treated as grotesques—you never really do that. You never really push them into the category of these strange, twisted characterizations like those of Flannery O'Connor or Carson McCullers, or even some of Faulkner's characters. Your characters always seem to be more fully rounded, no matter how despicable they are.

EG: Someone said that about Luke Will in *A Gathering of Old Men:* they said I may have helped the Klan, because I made Luke Will so human. At the very end, Luke Will knows he cannot bow to Charlie. He tells one of the other guys, "I have to go out there—and if anything happens, look out after my wife and children."

JL: I think especially when you talk about these characters like Sidney Bonbon—he's so moving in many ways, although he has very bad qualities too.

EG: If the world was different, he never would have married Louise, he would have married Pauline. He would have had those little bad mulatto kids running around shooting at each other with bee-bee guns! [laughter].

JL: One of the reasons I love *Of Love and Dust*—and all your work, really—and this partly comes just from Louisiana—it's not just black and white, it's got all kinds of characters from different backgrounds—it certainly makes you multicultural in that sense.

EG: Right, I'm from that kind of background.

JL: Do you think that in that respect your books speak more for America than people suspect?

EG: I think I'm much more American than most people are. I know I have access to things white, and Cajun, and of course African. I can look at all those three bloods at times—I can put them all together, I can look at them individually, and see which one has taken over inside of me on certain days. I know that the blood of all those are in me. My great grandmother on my mother's side was half black and half Native American—I don't know the tribe—it was in South Louisiana. Her husband, my great-grandfather, James—I'm named after him—looked just like Faulkner. In fact

someone saw his picture in my house, and he said "Isn't that Old
Man Jimmy McVay? And I said, no, that's a white Southern writer
named William Faulkner. He said, well, he looks just like Jimmy
McVay." He was a very small man. On the other side, my father's,
my grandmother and my mother were were much darker. But you
can go back four or five generations—it comes down to what is
American? Would someone deny that I am as patriotic or as
American as any other person? It isn't worth my arguing. Or to be
black or white and try to deny these things. Would a black say,
"you're an African"? I have too much mixed in me, and too much
of the culture. I don't know any other culture but American
culture. I don't know any European culture, or any Indian culture
before. Something, somewhere—all of it came into me. And that's
the way I've tried to look at my characters. That's why so many of
my young men refuse to be denied their position—Marcus, and
all the others who say "you're not going to push me around—
because I know who I am." Then of course you get the other type. I
like to start out with the stereotype—I always have them—in every
book there's one of them. I had the minister start out as the
stereotypical old black minister in A Lesson Before Dying, just
doing odd jobs around the place. But at the end he seems stronger
than Grant, in a way. But I have that sort of type, for example in Of
Love and Dust, with Bishop; Marcus treats him like a dog. He
tells the old people that that boy "stuck his foot in a house that's
slavery built."

   JL: He is a stereotype out of the reconstruction plantation novels.

   EG: I like to have a contrast like that. There's contrast in "Three
Men" with Munford, a guy who can love on Saturday night, who
knows he'll be back in jail again. Proctor's a type who'll think and
think. So he lies in his bunk and looks out and tries to find a star
that never cheats.

   JL: A lot of people involved in the multicultural movement are
saying that America is just a construct of different groups, that
there's no point in thinking of ourselves as united, as having an
American identity, because if you do you always fall into the trap of
accepting white America's values and ideas. What do you think
about that? Is there any value in thinking of ourselves as Americans today?

EG: I think of myself as an American. I look at my own family around me, and I'm the oldest. There are twelve of us, and I can not see any two of us who are really alike. My brothers are all different, my sisters are different. We all love each other; we get together for Mother's day, or Christmas or New Year, whatever. Most of my brothers and sisters are in California—the other two live here in Louisiana—they come out to the coast sometimes. I don't think we have to be imitative of whites just because we think of ourselves as Americans. I've heard that we're not a melting pot, we're like salads in a salad bowl, we're all the little pieces that make up the salad.

JL: I like the idea of a kaleidoscope better, because the colors are always shifting and blending together. I've been really struck looking at Zora Neale Hurston's supposedly "white" novel, *Seraph on the Suwanee*. People say, well, she just painted her black characters white—they're really black. But they aren't black characters. I studied their dialect very carefully, because I knew she had, when she worked for the Federal Writers Project, and read all these things about Crackers—and there are differences. But on the other hand, those characters, black and white, do talk alike in the Florida bush. There's a tremendous overlap between black and white speech. When we go to Europe, or Africa, for that matter, we all realize we're Americans.

EG: Yes, they'll let you know that you're American! That you're not French, you're not British, you're not African, you're an American. I remember walking down a hallway in a hotel we were staying in in France—this was in Angers—I can't speak much French— and I said "Bon jour, madame," to one of the maids. She said something in French and I said, "I'm afraid I can't speak French," and she said, "Oh—Américain?" [laughter].

JL: Let me ask you about getting the MacArthur, which is such a signal honor, and an appropriate tribute to your genius. What were your feelings on getting that?

EG: You know what happened—I was in Miami, and they called USL [the University of Southwestern Louisiana]. I have a rule there for them not to give out my telephone number unless there's an emergency. So they called and said to the secretary, this is the MacArthur Committee, I'd like to speak to Mr. Gaines. She told them I was in Florida, and that she couldn't give out my telephone number. The next day they called back and were told the same thing by a second person. They called back a third time and said "we *must* speak to Mr. Gaines." So the Chair of the department said, you give us your number and we'll have him call you back. That's what happened. When my Chair called me in Miami and told me they had called, I thought they were calling me for a recommendation. Finally I spoke to the person, and she said, "Mr. Gaines, we finally got you. Congratulations, you are a MacArthur Fellow." And I thought, "Oh God! That's what you've been calling about?" And the next thing I said was, "How much do I get?" [laughter]. They had a hard time getting in touch with me to give me this money! What my wife and I are doing is putting it in the bank—we didn't buy a yacht! We didn't buy a Rolls Royce, or quit our jobs. And she's still an attorney in Miami, and I'm still teaching at USL.

JL: I want to ask you about that; you've told many stories that involve the law; that's been a big problem for African Americans over the years, because of course we don't really have equal justice under the law in many cases. It's a big issue, particularly in *A Lesson Before Dying*. I wonder if your wife's legal expertise has helped you think about these issues, because I hear she's a very fine attorney.

EG: She is—but we never discuss these issues. I've been very close to policemen in San Francisco—I have brothers who are cops. I have brothers who are probation officers. I've known guards. Back in my hard drinking days back there in the sixties and the seventies I used to drink with policemen in bars in San Francisco—so I've been around lots of cops. Another thing—when I lived on False River, I went to Catholic school for years in New Roads. The people on the plantation—the husband was the sheriff at that time. He picked me up every day. I was on the riverbank, and he would take me to the courthouse and I had to walk from there back of town to my school. So all my life I've been around sheriffs—this was a decent sheriff—and I've known a couple of deputies. But he was a very decent man, a huge man with huge hands and huge feet. He died a few years ago.

JL: So he was a stereotype in appearance, but not in actions.

EG: No—I remember once I wanted to shine his shoes, because he was taking me into New Roads. He told me, in this deep voice, "I don't want you to shine my shoes." He was telling me, I don't want you to have to shine shoes. I used to have a shoe shine box, and would make a few nickels and dimes. I was thinking about that time when I wrote *A Gathering of Old Men*.

JL: I thought there was a real shift in the way we saw Candy in that book. At the beginning she seems really positive, concerned and loving; but as we move through the story we start thinking about her the way we do about the historic "Big Missy" figure. She's very paternalistic in many ways—but it's so subtle and gradual—am I reading that portrayal correctly?

EG: Well, yes. She has a duty—her duty is to continue that old patriarchal tradition. And then you see the kindness of looking after Mathu—she'll drop anything to take somebody to the doctor, or to call—whatever she has to do. But then, she has to have that control too. She will not let go—"you have to obey me."

JL: That was really dramatic in the movie, because Holly Hunter was so with it, in her tight jeans and her mod haircut—but she got stronger and stronger as the movie went forward, and became more of a threat to the integrity of the men.

EG: Of course. I don't know if it was in the movie, but in the book, Mapes tells her, "sooner or later, these guys are going to figure you out, and you're going to be the one they're attacking."

JL: Are you pleased that Holly Hunter won the Academy Award this year?

EG: I haven't seen the film. We had a couple of pictures taken together when we were filming *A Gathering of Old Men*. I talked to her sometimes. Richard Widmark was the hardest guy to talk to. I talked a little to him—more with Woody Strode, Joe Seneca and with Schlondorff.

JL: You've mentioned that you've thought about things you might want to write about now. Could you expand on that?

EG: Well, I have a couple of things in mind—a couple of novellas. One is "The Man Who Whipped Children." It's about—when did this start happening? That we as blacks always whipped our children—is that an African tradition, or not? Is it a Germanic tradition where a certain discipline exists? I knew there was a man on that plantation where I lived, who would, if the father was absent, whip the bad children, if one of them needed to be controlled in order to keep him from going to Angola where he would be killed. That's one of the stories I want to work with—what happened to him when the whole plantation system shifted and broke down, and he remarried and had other children.

I have another one, I think—I want to do something with what I call "The Girl Who Lived Across the Fence." It's about a girl who grows up to be a young woman and eventually commits suicide. She's one of these girls who's nearly white, like *Catherine Carmier,* and has problem after problem. These are things that I may never do—I don't know when I'll get to it, or when I'll start, or if I'll change things around—maybe they'll be stories and not novellas.

JL: You're not thinking of going back to those early efforts to write about the army or your earlier experiences in San Francisco?

EG: I hope not—but I'm saving that material—I have it at the Dupree library at USL. It's all in trunks over there, so someone else can look at it and see why this isn't publishable, because the soul wasn't in it, I suppose.

JL: Can people look at those now?

EG: No, people can only look at the different drafts of the published books.

JL: It sounds as though there's quite a bit in the early manuscripts that would be different from the published works.

EG: Oh yes. In *Miss Jane Pittman* there were some parts that were like a short biography—and *Catherine Carmier* had so many changes!

JL: I think that's quite usual with first novels—O'Connor just about went wild trying to finish *Wise Blood.*

EG: *Of Love and Dust*—there were several different drafts there. Early on, Ed Doctorow [who was Gaines' editor at the time] told me, "I loved the first half and I loved the second half, but they don't have anything to do with each other! [laughter]. So I've saved the drafts. I used to just throw them on the floor, and on the weekends I'd pick them up and toss them in a box. I think at the library they've tried to put the pages together. They're handwritten on yellow paper without lines, so anyone who wants to look at them will really have a job!

Index

329

332   Index

Heath Anthology of American Literature,
   The, 288
Hemingway, Ernest, 10, 11, 13, 18, 26, 27,
   41, 52, 55, 64, 66, 73, 76, 85, 90, 98,
   104, 108, 115, 133, 134, 144, 175, 191,
   196, 197, 201, 207–08, 211, 221, 242,
   243, 244, 246, 254, 266, 290–91, 315;
   "Fifty Grand," 91; *In Our Time,* 134,
   317; *The Old Man and the Sea,* 51; "The
   Undefeated," 51
Hicks, Granville, 109
Hippie movement, 52
History and literature, 38, 102, 189, 314;
   romantic, 69, 229, 303. *See also* Past
Hopkins, Lightnin', 3, 4, 99, 100
Houston, University of, 190
Hughes, Langston, 175
Humor, 184, 202, 212–13, 214–15, 232, 241,
   244, 246, 311. *See also* Jokes
Hunter, Holly, 327
Hurston, Zora Neale, 85, 311, 315, 317,
   325; *Seraph on the Suwanee,* 325

Industrialization of South, 260, 261, 284
Informer, The (O'Flaherty), 227
Interracial cooperation, 250

Jackson Mental Institution, 94
James, Henry, 46, 55, 192
Jefferson, Augusteen (Gaines's aunt),
   16–17, 50–51, 56–57, 82, 99, 101–02,
   120–21, 137, 182, 278, 283, 290, 293,
   298, 322
Jim Crow laws, 258
John Henry, 262
Johnson, Charles, 282
Jokes, 8, 311. *See also* Humor
Jones, Leroi (Amiri Baraka), 78, 318
Jones, Madison, 188, 197; *A Cry of Ab-*
   sence, 188
Joyce, James, 11, 13, 22, 52, 67, 87, 98,
   110, 137, 196, 197, 243, 244, 246, 298;
   Dubliners, 64, 76, 92, 227, 246; *Finne-*
   gan's Wake, 205; "Ivy Day in the Com-
   mittee Room," 76, 205; *A Portrait of the
   Artist as a Young Man,* 265; *Ulysses,*
   11, 64, 144, 208, 301

Karl, Frederick, 178; *American Fictions,*
   178
Keller, Helen, 239
Kennedy, John F., 78, 189

Kennedy, Robert, 189
Kerouac, Jack, 224
Killens, John O., 315
King, B.B., 112, 313
King, Martin Luther, 37, 78, 85, 91, 95,
   129, 131, 140, 152, 164, 186, 189
King, Rodney, 253, 274
Klan, Ku Klux, 168, 323
Knopf, Alfred (publisher), 128, 195, 196

Laney, Ruth, 262, 272, 284
Lardner, Ring, 53
Lay My Burden Down (Botkin), 94, 95, 153
Leadbelly, 209
Lee, Don (Haki Madhubuti), 318
Library of Congress, 193
Life Magazine, 187
Lincoln, Abraham, 95
Lincoln Portrait (Copland), 211
Los Angeles Times, 314
Louis, Joe, 91, 95
Louisiana, as literary subject, 14, 42, 68,
   69, 73, 87, 110–11, 116, 119, 137, 150,
   152, 172, 199, 229, 298; Gaines's ambiva-
   lence toward, 67
Louisiana Public Broadcasting, 284
Louisiana State Library, 94
Louisiana State University, 94, 153, 154,
   234
Louisiana State University African Ameri-
   can Cultural Center, 317
Louisianans as audience, 46
Long, Huey, 94, 95, 153–54, 233–34; *Every
   Man a King,* 234
Lowe, Willa G., 289
Lynching, 250, 263

MacArthur Award, 277, 280, 288, 291, 293;
   story of Gaines's hearing of it, 325–26
Magnolia Mound Plantation, 284
Mailer, Norman, 195
Malcolm X, 19, 129; *The Autobiography of
   Malcolm X,* 84
Male characters, 225–26, 227. *See also*
   Male-female relationships; Manhood as
   theme; Fathers and fatherhood as theme
Male-female relationships, 226–27, 228
Mandingo (Onstott), 320
Manhood as theme, 30–31, 34, 40–41, 114,
   157–58, 167, 170, 227, 239, 240, 241–42,
   245, 269, 271, 305, 320–22; defined, 321;
   peculiarities of Southern manhood
   model, 321